DIAMONDS
Are a Girl's Best
Friend

DIAMONDS
Are a Girl's Best Friend

◇

Women Writers on Baseball

◇

EDITED BY

Elinor Nauen

Faber and Faber

BOSTON • LONDON

Published in the United States in 1994 by Faber and Faber, Inc., 50 Cross Street, Winchester, MA 01890.
Introduction, Collection, and Notes copyright © 1993 by Elinor Nauen
The acknowledgments on pp. 291–295 constitute an extension of this copyright notice.

Library of Congress Cataloguing-in-Publication Data

Diamonds are a girl's best friend: women writers on baseball / edited by Elinor Nauen.
    p. cm.
    ISBN 0–571–19819–8
    1. Baseball–Literary collections. 2. American literature–Women authors.
    I. Nauen, Elinor.
    PS509.B37D45 1994
    810.8'0355–dc20   93–10897
                                                                                CIP

Jacket design by Mary Maurer
Printed in the United States of America

*For my brother Charlie, who took me to the
World Series
For my twin B. Varda, "it's like laughing into
a mirror"
And for Johnny, thank you thank you love you*

We shall find peace. We shall hear the angels, we shall see the sky sparkling with diamonds.
—Chekhov, *Uncle Vanya*

Contents

Section II: Why We Love It

Section III: Analysis of Baseball

Introduction

◊

*A*h, *baseball* . . . pointless and circular and beautiful. Nothing better than an afternoon at the ballpark–that most perfect of diamonds–where life's as simple as a slow roll foul down the first base line, where anyone can be the star, the chosen, the hard-breathing champ.

Including women? It's fashionable to say that baseball rejects and excludes us. By this is generally meant that we don't play professionally. True, but neither do 250,000,000 out of 250,010,000 in this country, women *and* men.

The truth is, women have always been part of the world of baseball, at least as fans and writers. The first mention of "base ball" in literature, according to the *Oxford English Dictionary,* is from Jane Austen's 1815 *Northanger Abbey*:

> It was not very wonderful that Catherine, who had nothing heroic
> about her, should prefer cricket, base ball, riding on horseback,
> and running about the country at the age of fourteen, to books.

If that seems a bit skimpy, jump a hundred years ahead to the United States. Women writers were busy spewing out religious tracts and moralistic stories for young people with baseball settings, while more worldly actresses and divas provided commentary for *Baseball* magazine.

Then for a long time it seemed all or nothing–if a woman was a fan at all she had to be like Myrt Power, who in 1955 won $32,000 on "The $64,000 Question" for coming up with such arcane facts as the seven players with more than 3,000 lifetime hits and the five future Hall of Famers struck out by Carl Hubbell in the 1934 All-Star Game.

And not long ago my keeping score made a lot of men nervous. They would quiz me–"How many lifetime homers did Mel Ott hit?" and that sort of thing–as if I couldn't be a fan at all if I didn't know everything. That's changed. These days, in the same way that women can be in the workforce with mid-level ambition, we can like baseball with haphazard interest. Out at Yankee Stadium a couple of summers ago, I looked down the row and noticed that all the women were keeping score and none of the men were.

No one mentioned it; no one seemed to notice. Where women *are* noticed
is at the movies; check out Susan Sarandon as an intelligent groupie in *Bull
Durham*; and Geena Davis in *A League of Their Own,* based on the true story
of the All-American Girls Professional Baseball League, set up in 1943 because the boys were off fighting World War II.

These days women account for nearly half of all paid admissions to the
ballpark—and for a substantial chunk of good baseball writing. *Diamonds
Are a Girl's Best Friend* brings together poems, essays, and fiction that tell
of women's experiences in and around baseball, from consuming longing
to distaste, from a lifetime as sister, daughter, or wife to short stops at a
ballpark.

Women and men start their baseball lives differently, to be sure. Men
fans usually played as kids, while women usually didn't. It wasn't feminine,
and anyway, organized ball—Little League—was closed to girls until twenty
years ago. Even today, not many girls grow up with baseball moves burned
in their muscles. But the otherworldly grace of the athlete is given to few;
while women do indulge in dreams of diamond glory, not many expect
them to come true. It's discouraging and unfair that women aren't pushed
toward sports, but in a way it's freeing. We can like baseball without feeling
like secret failures for never pitching in the World Series. We can have
baseball however we want—our own urgencies or odd, one-person teams,
our own way of enjoying a summer day over the green and under the blue.
We may feel relieved at baseball's gentleness—no one tackles or punches
or fouls anyone. Women may, in fact, have *more* than men, who mostly
aren't interested in ogling. "I watch baseball for the butts," a friend said.
"What do men look at?"

In an essay called "American Fiction," the English writer Virginia Woolf
described Ring Lardner as writing "the best prose that has come our way.
. . . That this should be true of *You Know Me, Al,* a story about baseball,
a game which is not played in England, a story written often in a language
which is not English, gives us pause. To what does he owe his success? . . .
We gaze into the depths of a society which goes its ways intent on its own
concerns. Games give [Lardner] what society gives his English brother—a
clue, a centre, a meeting place for the divers activities of people whom a
vast continent isolates, whom no tradition controls."

Woolf has touched on one aspect of baseball's appeal, the way in which
it can give us a tradition that unites us into Americans. How else does it
inspire writers, in particular women? First, there are all the reasons any
writer chooses baseball as a subject: It's beautiful, absorbing, a soap opera
that gets more interesting the more attention you pay. Second, a baseball
work can be about baseball and "about" anything else. The leisurely pace
of a game allows writers the space to deal with any issue, big or small: birth

or death or politics. Third, and probably most relevant to *Diamonds*, base-ball is played on the fields of the imagination as much as on the diamond, and these fields don't require physical strength or grace. Anyone who pays attention may write brilliantly or accurately, may have a terrific insight or theory.

At first as I researched *Diamonds* I worried that I'd have to use every little scrap I could lay my hands on; I was delighted and surprised at how much material there turned out to be. While I tried to be inclusive and various, if I liked a piece it went in, if I didn't it didn't. As with any anthology, what the editor liked is what the reader gets. Interestingly, with a few exceptions, the writers included here have produced only a single poem or story about baseball. Even Marianne Moore, famous for being a fan, has only two poems about the sport.

Look for pieces that extol everything from the great icons ("Jackie Robin-son" by Hilma Wolitzer, "Red Barber" by Barbara Grizzuti Harrison) to a catcher's legs (Bernadette Mayer's "Carlton Fisk Is My Ideal") to one of the stranger teams of all time (Mary Leary's "Poor Is Poor, Broke Is Broke"). Don't miss Patricia Highsmith's disturbing "The Barbarians," Josephine Jacobsen's delicate "Deaf-Mutes at the Ballgame," Anna Quindlen's charm-ing and honest "A Baseball Wimp" or Eve Babitz's sexy "Dodger Stadium." See what women were saying back in the first decade of the 20th century, with three selections from *Baseball* magazine ("Petticoats and the Press Box," "The Lady Fan," and "On Just Being a Fan"). *Diamonds* has oddballs and elegies and humor, all the rough fences and startling plays and amazing throat-catching moments of baseball itself.

New York City
May 1993

SECTION I

◇

Coming to the Plate

MARIANNE MOORE

◊

Baseball and Writing

Suggested by post-game broadcasts.

Fanaticism? No. Writing is exciting
and baseball is like writing.
  You can never tell with either
    how it will go
    or what you will do;
  generating excitement—
  a fever in the victim
  pitcher, catcher, fielder, batter.
    Victim in what category?
*Owl*man watching from the press box?
    To whom does it apply?
    Who is excited? Might it be I?

It's a pitcher's battle all the way—a duel—
a catcher's, as, with cruel
  puma paw, Elston Howard lumbers lightly
    back to plate, (His spring
    de-winged a bat swing.)
  They have that killer instinct;
  yet Elston—whose catching
  arm has hurt them all with the bat—
    when questioned, says, unenviously,
"I'm very satisfied. We won."
    Shorn of the batting crown, says, "We";
    robbed by a technicality.

When three players on a side play three positions
and modify conditions,

the massive run need not be everything.
  "Going, going . . . " Is
  it? Roger Maris
has it, running fast. You will
never see a finer catch. Well . . .
"Mickey, leaping like the devil"—why
    gild it, although deer sounds better—
snares what was speeding towards its treetop nest,
      one-handing the souvenir-to-be
      meant to be caught by you or me.

Assign Yogi Berra to Cape Canaveral;
he could handle any missile.
  He is no feather. "Strike! . . . Strike *two!*"
  Fouled back. A blur.
  It's gone. You would infer
  that the bat had eyes.
  He put the wood to that one.
Praised, Skowron says, "Thanks, Mel.
  I think I helped a *little* bit."
    All business, each, and modesty.
    Blanchard, Richardson, Kubek, Boyer.
      In that galaxy of nine, say which
      won the pennant? *Each.* It was he.

Those two magnificent saves from the knee—throws
by Boyer, finesses in twos—
  like Whitey's three kinds of pitch and pre-
    diagnosis
  with pick-off psychosis.
  Pitching is a large subject.
  Your arm, too true at first, can learn to
  catch the corners—even trouble
    Mickey Mantle. ("Grazed a Yankee!
My baby pitcher, Montejo!"
    With some pedagogy,
    you'll be tough, premature prodigy.)

They crowd him and curve him and aim for the knees. Trying
indeed! The secret implying:
  "I can stand here, bat held steady."
    One may suit him;

none has hit him.
Imponderables smite him.
Muscle kinks, infections, spike wounds
require food, rest, respite from ruffians. (Drat it!
　　Celebrity costs privacy!)
Cow's milk, "tiger's milk," soy milk, carrot juice,
　　brewer's yeast (high-potency)—
　　concentrates presage victory

sped by Luis Arroyo, Hector Lopez—
deadly in a pinch. And "Yes,
　it's work; I want you to bear down,
　　but enjoy it
　　while you're doing it."
　Mr. Houk and Mr. Sain,
　if you have a rummage sale,
　don't sell Roland Sheldon or Tom Tresh
　　Studded with stars in belt and crown,
the Stadium is an adastrium.
　　O flashing Orion,
　　your stars are muscled like the lion.

LESLEY HAZLETON

◇

First Game

It was a sunny, dry September Sunday—the kind of day that can convince an unsuspecting stranger that New York is a wonderful place to spend the summer. I was fresh off the plane from Israel. It was only my second day in the United States, but my friends here had made the shocked discovery that I had never even seen a baseball diamond. So they took me out to the ball game. Thurman Munson had been killed in a plane crash a few weeks before, and the Yankees weren't going to be in any World Series that year. But this particular Sunday had been declared Catfish Hunter day. Ole Catfish was retiring, and New York had turned out for him.

Maybe it was in comparison with the parched browns of Israel at summer's end. Maybe it was the combined smell of hot dogs and marijuana drifting over the stands. Maybe it was the light. All I know for sure is that when I emerged from the tunnel and stood there in the first tier, looking out over home base, I gasped at the perfect greenness of it. So this was a diamond.

What happened then was everything I expected from America. A brass band, heavy on the epaulets and the drums. High-stepping marching girls in white rubber bootees and pompons, throwing silver plywood rifles twisting into the air. A whole ceremony right on the field, including Catfish's mother, wife and two young boys, and of course Catfish himself—the archetype of the huntin'-shootin'-fishin' man. Speeches were made and messages read out from presidents of various organizations, including one President called Jimmy Carter. Gifts were hauled, driven and led onto the field (television sets, Toyota cars and a live elephant, respectively). And then came a hush as Catfish approached the microphone.

"There's three men shoulda been here today," he said. "One's my pa"—riotous applause—"one's the scout that signed me"—more riotous applause—"and the third one"—pause—"is Thurman Munson." Riot. Fifty thousand people up on their feet and roaring, including my friends. The fifty thousand and first—myself—looked on in bewilderment. I missed Catfish's next sentence, but I'll never forget the last one of that brief speech. "Thank you, God," he said, "for giving me strength, and making me a ball-player."

And suddenly I too was up on my feet and cheering. It was the perfect American day, the perfect American place, the perfect American sentence. That combination of faith and morality, sincerity and naiveté, was everything my Old-World preconceptions had led me to expect, and as I watched Catfish walk off the field into the sunset of the Baseball Hall of Fame, leading his little boy with one hand and the elephant with the other, I felt that I had had my first glimpse of a mythical place called America.

Three hot dogs, two bags of peanuts, three glasses of beer and nine innings later, I was amazed to find out how much I already knew about baseball. In fact I'd played a simpler form of it as a schoolgirl in England, where it was called rounders and was played exclusively by rather upperclass young ladies in the best public schools, which in England of course means the best private schools. Yet though we played on asphalt and used hard cricket balls, and played with all the savagery that enforced good breeding can create, we never dreamed of such refinements as I saw that afternoon. The exhilaration of sliding into base! That giant paw of the glove! The whole principle of hustle! A world awaits the well-bred young Englishwoman in the ballpark. But for me the most splendid of these splendors was to watch the American language being acted out.

Though I knew no Americans when I lived in England—those were the years when America was still considered a brash black sheep of the family, so to speak, and was not mentioned in polite society—I came to know many in the years I lived in Israel. And since they were the only people with whom I spoke English, I picked up their language. I could touch base, give a ballpark figure, strike out and reach first base long before I ever realized that these were baseball terms. I could be out of the ball game, let alone out of the ballpark. I could play ball—even hardball when I had to. There were times when I climbed the walls, and accused others of being off the wall. And it seemed I had a talent for throwing the occasional curve ball in an argument. . . .

That September Sunday in Yankee Stadium, the American language loaded the bases and gave me a grand slam home run. It came alive for me, and with it, American culture. Baseball was suddenly my code to understanding this culture, the key to the continent. And I knew that I'd really arrived in America one rainy afternoon a couple of years later, the kind of afternoon that lends itself to sitting at your desk, staring out the window and daydreaming. Slowly, I realized that I had just emerged smiling from the classic 10-year-old-boy's all-American fantasy: seventh game of the World Series, three runs down, bases loaded, two out, and I'm up at bat. I take a strike on the first pitch. The crowd is roaring. Another strike on the second pitch. The crowd roars even louder. And then comes the third pitch, right where I want it. . . .

NANCY LEMANN

◇

from *Sportsman's Paradise*

Orient Point, Long Island.

The guests are arriving, across the lawn. It is Friday afternoon. The men are coming in on the late train in the parlour car, and others have come on the ferry boat steaming in on the blue sea at dusk with gay lights.

My old flame, Hobby Fox, is sitting on a deck chair in the night alone. He is the nephew of Constant Fox, the heart throb. Possibly Hobby is too gruff and crusty to be an exact heart throb. But he is one anyway. "His eyes are so blue it just makes you want to go jump in the river," as Margaret commented.

Usually he sits obliviously on the porch reading the stock pages or the sports pages, listening to the baseball games on the radio in a low masculine drone, and smoking a cigar, with his slightly burnt-out air. He has a certain burnt-out air. Distracted by his memories, perhaps.

Friday evenings after work the young men go to the baseball games in their suits and ties and sunglasses, having plain American fun. It touches my heart, because they don't have plain American fun where I come from, it is too exotic and remote for that, it is the dark side. They don't have baseball in New Orleans. It's not normal enough to have baseball.

In New York I learned quite a bit about baseball, as to many a Northerner it is his great love. But what interested me about it was not perhaps the same thing that interested them. I like how all the ball players have marital problems and personality problems and need sports psychiatrists, and especially in baseball, where you don't have to be that athletic, or it's not as strenuous in a way the players are all dissipated wrecks with drug problems, chain-smoking. That would maybe work in New Orleans. Baseball would maybe work in New Orleans because all the players are dissipated wrecks with troubled relationships with their fathers, chain-smoking. But they are tough guys. Except for when they retire, then they cry. The whole thing is an emotional roller coaster, at least for me, trying to keep up with their problems. That's what I like about it.

I saw a baseball player hold a press conference to announce his retirement. Big, burly guy with a mustache. Six feet tall, extremely manly, big rough tough guy. "I had a dream," he said. "Ten years ago I was a kid with two bad knees who wanted to be a baseball player." He stopped and looked down at his speech. He bit his upper lip. Time passed. He was silent. Finally you realized that he was stopping because he was trying to compose himself. Still he remained silent. You got the picture, he was struggling. But then finally he said, "And I'm just glad that dream came true"—sobbing, screaming, crying, literally falling completely to pieces. Then he just walked away from the whole podium and cried. See what I mean?

I like how they have so many emotions even though they are crusty sports figures. Actually I know one ex-baseball player who is a crusty figure without having so many emotions—Hobby Fox. At Carolina, Chapel Hill, he was drafted by the Major Leagues and spent a season with the Atlanta Braves. He was a pitcher. Then he decided to go to law school. It seems he had a motley career.

Currently world editor of the New York Examiner, he was an athlete, a man's man, an old pro, who had been around the block a million times at age thirty-six. Among the young couples he is an outsider, but then so am I. The young couples ceaselessly pursue their innocent amusements— boating, dinner parties, bridge, etc. Their innocence bemuses me. I have more in common with the misanthrope.

He wears sweat pants emblazoned with the legend, Duck Hunting Club of New Orleans, an old-fashioned sleeveless ribbed undershirt, and tennis shoes. He has a sort of crusty gruff demeanor, which for some reason has inspired the children with idolatry in his behalf. Although he is a misanthrope he often finds himself with the responsibility of the children, who follow him around, and with whom he is quite gruff, but tender, if the truth be told.

It is his peculiar blend of tenderness and disinterest, I think, that has inspired their confidence.

Hobby always has the radio tuned in to the baseball games in a low masculine drone, redolent of Yankeefied spring and summer afternoons. Mr. Underwood too has a love of baseball and also keeps the games on in the office at night if he works late. Due to these influences I find that I myself am developing a growing obsession with baseball and the need to chronicle the progress of the New York team that I follow. Hobby taught me a lot about it. He doesn't follow his old team in Atlanta. He follows the New York team while here. His father loved the St. Louis Cardinals, because in his day they were the team of the South. They were an all-black team, all extremely cultivated, and they had the most beloved manager in baseball. The manager of the New York team is completely listless. The personality of the New York team mystifies me. They have a certain elegance, I think, because they are so stoic. If they get a home run or something good they try not to smile or act excited. If someone gets a home run, he comes out of the dug-out and gives a curtain call, tipping his hat to the crowd, seeming rather quaint or courtly—and they only do this in New York, I'm told—but maintaining a gruff though courtly exterior. Equally, if they lose or get slaughtered they betray no emotion other than seeming mildly dejected. It results in a certain elegance because the other teams are more volatile and make obnoxious displays at every sign of advancement.

Also the New York team is riddled with problems. If you like problems, you've come to the right place, with the New York team. Each player has a dazzling array of problems: drug problems, drug rehabilitation, alcohol de-tox, injuries, marital problems, personality problems, nervous break-downs and psychological problems, also confidence problems.

Yet at the same time as they are afflicted with a ceaseless array of problems, it is the National Pastime, plain American fun, heartwarming, wholesome, one thing that draws everyone together, the very young and the very old, and has an innocence, a certain basic innocence, good for the children, a chance to go forth with the heroes, a good thing for the boys.

The other thing I like about the New York team is that they are underdogs. I love that. I would never root for the favorite. I like how they are always struggling, getting slaughtered twice in one night in double-headers, being exhausted by rain delays or playing extra innings until two in the morning, losing. Adversity becomes them, as adversity can be becoming if its object has character. There is a poignance in their struggle. Plus, then if they suddenly win, it is all the more affecting. The New York team always loses and is stoic, elegant, dejected. But to the stars through adversity.

Then if they suddenly win I am suffused with a sense of well-being, and if they lose I feel doleful and listless. I have a ceaseless constant need to listen to every single game and keep up with everyone's problems. But my love for baseball is inexplicable—never before did I take the slightest interest in sports. Never was there one subject so boring to me as sports.

Now I even listen to the sports talkshows in the middle of the afternoon on the radio hosted by falling New York lunatics who remind me of Mr. Underwood, who sound off in deep Bronx and Queens accents about what burns them up. "I've had it," they passionately avow, referring to sports figures who irritate them or contracts negotiated that are too expensive. Often they slip into dreamy recollections of ball players from the 30s on the Yankees or Brooklyn Dodgers, distracted by their memories, exhibiting a marked preference for the older teams of the American League, and if someone calls them up to ask a question about upstarts in the National League they say, "I've had it." Sometimes they go berserk on the show and start insulting the callers and have complete breakdowns ending up screaming out to the caller, "Shut up! Shut up! Shut up!" and then disconnect the phone line in a fury. "You're a schmuck. You're crazy. You're giving me a nervous breakdown. Shut up!" Once I heard a nut call up who was equally as much of a lunatic as the announcer. The nut launched into a rambling unconnected story about a glamour girl who kissed him at a baseball game. Then he started swearing. "Do not take the name of the Lord in vain," said the announcer solemnly to the nut. "That is where I draw the line." It's a funny place to suddenly draw the line, considering that he spends the rest of the time raving like some kind of insane maniac. Then the nut started sounding off about what burned him up in sports and the announcer lost his cool again and started screaming. "You need a brain transplant. You're driving me crazy. Shut up!" And these nuts go at it forty-eight hours a day. They spend forty-eight hours a day analyzing these subjects on the radio. Sports, baseball, contracts, they analyze it for forty-eight hours a day. I turn on the radio at two in the morning and there they are, talking in strange voices like they're mentally unbalanced, analyzing everything. "New York did not play Philadelphia tonight," the announcer will be saying in a ghostly strangled voice, "Tidewater played Philadelphia tonight. A minor league team played Philadelphia tonight. Schmucks!" he screams, in his New York parlance. This analysis had to do with one night when a lot of people on the New York team had injuries and they had to call up a lot of rookies from the farm team. I know about these things now. Suddenly I'm a sports fanatic, listening to sports talk shows twenty-four hours a day.

"Cincinnati is not going to make it. Cincinnati is through. Finished. It's over for Cincinnati!" Screaming. Long silences. Tortured strangled voices. Here they were referring to the pennant race and who would be in the World Series.

In New York they had a romance with failure—uncharacteristic of the North. It began in the old days, at the Polo Grounds, with a series of eccentrics as managers and a ball club that could never win.

Everyone was in tortures over it. That's what kills me about baseball, how everyone is in tortures over it as if it were the most serious thing that could ever be. Like the nuts who call up the sports channel on the radio all day to analyze everything. In the articles in the Tribune the commissioner of baseball would always have all these tortured quotes about integrity and self-delusions in long tortured ponderings, when it's only about baseball. I mean, you'd think they were talking about World War II. Like the most grave subject. The baseball commissioner agonizing over principles, integrity, abstractions as if he were Aristotle, not the baseball commissioner.

What I prefer is the team that had the romance with failure. They used to be arrogant and cocky and make obnoxious displays at every sign of advancement, just like everyone else, and everyone hated them for it, because they were so arrogant and cocky. Then the manager told them not to gloat or make such displays, so now they all act like laconic Southern gentlemen. I personally like them better that way. But of course it's not a New York type of attitude, and the New Yorkers hate them that way. They have articles in the newspapers interviewing the players about how they feel about this and their resultant tortured ponderings—like the baseball commissioner agonizing over sporting matters—as they ponder their broken dreams or fond hopes or failures, in sports.

Mr. Underwood had a box at the baseball games with other big cheeses, the Governor, millionaire race track owners, retired bandleaders, etc. Actually the retired bandleader in his entourage was a poignant figure, somehow out of place, being Southern. He could care less about baseball. He was used to seedy dives on Bourbon Street. Baseball just wasn't his thing. It was written on his face, in his countenance, everything about him, did not say Baseball. Being from Bourbon St., I can certainly understand why the Southern bandleader did not feel an affinity for baseball, as I never did before either until I realized how it has its dark side, or generally from spending five years in New York, but certainly on Bourbon Street the idea of baseball is but a remote image of a boy in the 1920s with a baseball cap in the sweet afternoon sun or sterling Northern twilight in some halcyon idea of America from which New Orleans is indescribably remote. But Mr. Underwood loved it all—retired sports figures, troubled prize fighters, washed-up Southern bandleaders—in his box of big cheeses at the game.

Hobby had a more ambivalent attitude, having played in the Major Leagues himself, and there were times when I got the feeling that he had left his heart there. Being thirty-five and out of practice I doubt he could go back. Though I hear of players who are forty-two and forty-three, such as relief pitchers. I guess he did not play long enough or make enough of an impression to come back to a career in baseball as a coach or manager. He listened to the games but did not often speak of his past in baseball. Also he had been a newspaperman now for too many years to think of much else. But once I saw in his room in Orient the Louisville Slugger that he used in Atlanta for it was inscribed with the team and had his name burned on to it. He kept it with him, then. Some reminder of an innocence, which baseball surely represents, though it certainly has its dark side, so it seems to me at least. Every time I ask him about one of the players, he launches into a long story about how the fellow was a drug addict, or on trial, or just got out of alcohol detox or jail. I had no idea that baseball had such a dark side, or was so riddled with problems, but of course, that's what I like about it.

He was telling me about a pitcher who thought it was his day off and took LSD. He happened to hear on the radio that his team was playing that night in Chicago—which he had forgotten. So he hopped on a plane to Chicago tripping on LSD and pitched a no-hitter.

Later he was on trial and told the judge that when you're on LSD in a ball game, it makes the ball look like a grapefruit when it's coming at you, so it's easier to hit.

Also Hobby told me that on his team in Atlanta it was one of the first years that they had a sports psychiatrist for the ball club. He went crazy at the end of the season.

The TV announcers discuss these problems during their ceaseless banter at the game even though they are so All-American it seems they wouldn't want to admit them, and were all players themselves before they became announcers. The other night New York was playing Philadelphia and the announcers were discussing the pitcher for Philadelphia before the game. One of the announcers is a kindly old man who seems at times virtually senile and can't seem to keep track of what is going on. You'd think that maybe baseball in his day had less problems to it, at least in terms of psychiatry. But they were talking about the pitcher and he said, "Frank is back on the mound right now but it seems last year he had some psychological problems," looking out at ten trillion viewers on TV. Then he chuckled fondly, after saying the word "psychological problems," shaking his head in bemusement, but at the same time with concern, and then got a sort of rueful, whimsical smile, looking at the other announcer to elaborate.

"I was talking to him and he explained, 'I was giving myself a nervous breakdown.' Ha ha. He went to Harvard but he just got out of alcohol detox. He's a great pitcher, Bob. The only question is, can he keep out of the hootch."

Keep out of the hootch—I'm not sure whether that means stay out of the looney bin or stay off the sauce.

Harvard, alcohol detox, baseball and psychological problems—you have to admit that's a pretty weird mixup.

There was a rain delay, and they called in a sort of sports weather man. He was a cornball. The announcers are always sentimental and enthusiastic.

"What about the weather, Jim? Do you think we'll play?"

"I know we will, Bob. In about forty-five minutes, you'll see this storm clear up and they will start the ball game."

"How can you be so sure?"

"This is my life, Bob. I'm obsessed with the weather. I love it. It's my life."

Then the announcers chuckle and shake their heads fondly in bemusement.

On certain Fridays since this April, Hobby had been taking me to the baseball games—whenever he could get away from the office.

Friday night we went to a double-header. The stadium announcer keeps droning on throughout the game on a loudspeaker in a cheerful voice, "Alcoholic beverages . . . Anti-social behavior . . . People drinking . . . Taking drugs . . . " Admonishing potential abusers of these vices. There are a lot of Police. Sometimes horrifying brawls break out in the stands. "Here comes trouble," said a fan when a weirdo with a menacing expression came up to take his seat and the weirdo heard him and got mad. "Shut up! Who are you calling trouble, schmuck, shut up. Shut up!" As everyone knows, the attitude of the New York fans is "What have you done for me lately?" Meaning if the team is losing the fans are filled with loathing and disgust—this is why they call the radio talk shows at two in the morning to ceaselessly analyze all the problems and complain about how disgusted they are and go berserk etc. The New York stadium is like a latent catastrophe waiting to happen. But it never really does, in baseball. An innocence is inexorably attached to the game no matter how many people go crazy or how many drug problems or etc. arise.

Hobby and I had left the office late, to go out that night to the ball park, which had been named, oddly enough, for a pitcher from Louisiana, Sportsman's Paradise. It was a glamorous night in New York. The temperature was ninety degrees. I take a perverse satisfaction in the heat because the Northerners can't stand it, they're not used to it, whereas the Southerners are. Also it was humid and the sky was a thick cobalt blue as night fell.

We left the office at 7 P.M., in the midst of the usual gigantic summer traffic jam to Long Island. With everyone leaving all at once for the same place, Long Island, at exactly the same time. It does seem kind of ridiculous. That route out of New York, it's a dying-looking sort of place, but it's gutty, as they say in baseball. And that's why I find it glamorous, because it is gutty. The ball park is the most glamorous place in New York to me, because it is the most gutty. When I was young the East Coast was beauteous and promising; now it is gutty. There's one benefit of growing older, for I like it better gutty.

We were listening to the radio announcers call the game on the way out, as we were late due to the traffic. The radio droned on, describing as usual a demoralizing loss, but a certain rugged masculinity emanated from the sporting world, as the game droned on.

While passing that gutty landscape to Queens, Hobby was telling me about his father, one's parents' love. Though in his parents' case it was something less than love, which made him misanthropic, I think. Then we came into the ball park in a hot summer twilight. The stadium was a swirling vortex of chaos, as usual. It remained hot throughout the night.

It had been a fair day at the office for Hobby. The President of Burma quit, causing some flurries in the international section.

"Now it will be a swirling madhouse of unled people," I said. "Do you think you'll have to go there?" I asked him.

"No. But I am going to call Dolores." Dolores was his new secretary.

"How do you like Dolores?"

"She's a swirling vortex of human secretarial potential," he said, to kid me.

He was having some problems with his secretary. It was a measure of his character. He always answered his own phone, for instance, which I find that no one in a reasonably high position in New York would generally ever do. And he was a true big cheese. The reason why he always answered his own phone was because his secretary, formerly a woman of a certain age named Mary Louise, was such an antiquated person, that as she perambulated slowly from office to lunch to the fulfillment of her personal errands, her official duties often fell behind . . . and Hobby was too courtly to ask for a different secretary. Finally Mary Louise retired. Then came Dolores.

I felt that Hobby seemed to seclude himself. "You go to work, you go to Long Island, but you seclude yourself," I said to him.

"I go to work, often I have to work in Orient too. This doesn't leave much time for square dancing," he said. "But I am not totally secluded. I know you, don't I?" He looked at me sideways, askance, with those dazzling blue eyes.

It was a hot July night, and we lost very badly twice, a double-header. But there is something dashing and brave about the huge cavernous stadium with its excessive quality, I mean its excess, too many people, claustrophobic, swirling madhouse of chaos. The stadium is a vortex of true and complete chaos. I mean it's not exactly bucolic, being as it is in New York City, though outside of Manhattan, in Queens, it is unpretentious, gutty. Of course I like it that way. Stan's Sports World and Stan's Sports Bar populated the area. Pulsating with madness. What I like best is when the young men come straight from work, in their suits and ties and sunglasses, emanating a certain gentility or plain American history. They come in pairs or threes. Brave of them to withstand the heat and the chaos, for the sake of their innocent sport, and dashing of them in their cavernous, unlovely stadium, in the bad conditions, losing. The gallantry of their broken dreams and shining hopes in each situation, such as the double-header Friday night.

One thing about baseball that used to hurt my feelings, though of course my understanding is limited, was when they made trades. They kept making huge dramatic trades at deadlines in the middle of the night. They traded the handsomest player. They traded the one who had been there the longest. They made so many trades of sentimental favorites that the only possible consolation I could find for them was that the game itself is the only constant.

I found it to be poignant. But then again, I find a lot of things to be poignant.

So on certain Fridays since this April, Hobby started taking me to the baseball games. Our entire relationship revolves around baseball. As he is an athlete and ex-jock, and now I am a sports fan even though I used to hate sports, like many a woman, I don't doubt. But now it's like I'm glued to the radio—"Don't bother me, the football game is on." Football. Not only baseball but every other sport in existence. Though of course baseball is the most elegant, has the most grace, is the most quaint.

The baseball game last night was truly a metaphor for the human condition. They had two rain delays, one half-an-hour and, shortly thereafter, an hour. It was raining lightly even when they played. It was a night game and unseasonably cold. In short, the conditions for the fans were terrible or could not have been worse, and yet a lot of people stayed in the stadium until two in the morning. It was like a small dinner party, as the announcer said. It was the die-hards. They were like feisty old-timers who just wouldn't quit. They were a metaphor for the human condition. They were in it for the long haul, not only in perseverance, but enjoying it. You have to love the attempt, even if the attempt is a failure. Anyway they were sitting there with umbrellas in the stands at two in the morning like maniacs.

I tried to talk to Hobby about our feelings, and he was receptive, but the only problem is my talk was excessively lame. Feelings, I murmured, I have feelings too, I'm a human being—I mean, Jeez, for pity's sake, what am I talking about?

"What do you think is going to happen?" I said finally.

"I think you're going to drive me crazy," he said, and looked at me sideways, askance, with those dazzling blue eyes.

So we're just two jocks sitting in the stands at two in the morning watching a baseball game. Plus in New York, up North, how strange.

Why is it that I cannot reconcile myself with the past.

It reminds me of Gary Cooper and Marlene Dietrich eyeballing each other world-wearily in Morocco. Why is it I am pursued by my memories, with my heart broken by them.

As often in baseball, there were some late heroics. Someone saved the day at the last minute, "eking out a last minute victory," as the announcer says. How can they always eke out these last minute victories? Maybe it could be the same for us. Maybe it is not too late for us.

Some people think baseball is slow. But not only do I disagree with that, I like it when they have rain delays, extra innings, and any other thing that can stretch it out even more, to be as long and slow as possible.

My whole life revolves around sports now. As time wore on Hobby also introduced me to the basketball season as exemplified by Madison Square Garden, which is like a smoldering Babylonian prison. I mean you'd think it would be plain American fun. But Madison Square Garden is more squalid than the baseball stadium. Taking the subway, you go through Pennsylvania Station where many lunatics convene. Each person is alone and yet each person is engaged in a loud conversation with himself, making an insane cacophony that reverberates throughout the place. One thing about New York: in the subway or on any street corner, any man feels free to just start spouting his philosophy. A woman spoke in tongues on the 34th Street platform; nearby was a Jamaican evangelist. Everything is shrouded in smoldering iniquity and teeming squalor. New York, the Grunewald, the sporting news.

But it is actually plain American fun. Because I have found that when you are in a theater watching a movie, say, I find that you still think about your worries, while watching the movie. You can't get away from your worries, even while watching a movie. If you are depressed you will be even more sad in the theater. Whereas if you are watching a baseball game, or listening to the sporting news on the radio in the ceaseless low masculine drone, or at a basketball game in Madison Square Garden, it is truly relaxing to the mind, and for that time you forget your worries. You're all in it together—lunatics, screaming sports fans chewing cigars, scuzzy men in checkered jackets with hacking coughs—you are all in it together, in something innocent.

ELISAVIETTA RITCHIE

◇

I've Never Written a Baseball Poem

I didn't even make
the seventh grade
girls' third team

substitute.
Still can't
throw straight.

Last Easter, scrub game
with the kids,
I hit

a foul right through
Captain Kelly's French doors,
had to pay.

Still, these sultry
country nights
I watch

the dark ballet
of players sliding
into base,

and shout "Safe!
He's safe! He's home!"
and so am I.

LYNN RIGNEY SCHOTT

◊

Spring Training

The last of the birds has returned—
the bluebird, shy and flashy.
The bees carry fat baskets of pollen
from the alders around the pond.
The wasps in the attic venture downstairs,
where they congregate on warm windowpanes.
Every few days it rains.

This is my thirty-fifth spring;
still I am a novice at my work,
confused and frightened and angry.
Unlike me, the buds do not hesitate,
the hills are confident they will be
perfectly reflected
in the glass of the river.

I oiled my glove yesterday.
Half the season is over.
When will I be ready?

On my desk sits a black-and-white postcard picture
of my father—skinny, determined,
in a New York Giants uniform—
ears protruding, eyes riveted.
Handsome, single-minded, *he* looks ready.

Thirty-five years of warmups.
Like glancing down at the scorecard

in your lap for half a second
and when you look up it's done—
a long fly ball, moonlike,
into the night
over the fence,
way out of reach.

GAIL MAZUR

◊

The Idea of Florida
during a Winter Thaw

Late February and the air's so balmy
snowdrops and crocuses may be fooled
into early blooming. Then, the inevitable blizzard
will come, blighting our harbingers of spring,
and the glum yards will go back undercover.
Odd to think that in Florida it's strawberry
season—shortcake, waffles, berries and cream
will soon be pencilled on the coffeeshop menus.

In Winter Haven, the ballplayers are stretching
and preening, dancing on the basepaths,
giddy as good kids playing hookey. Now,
for a few weeks, statistics won't seem
to matter, for the flushed boys are muscular
and chaste, lovely as lakes to the retired men
watching calisthenics from the grandstands.
Escapees from the cold work of living,

the old men burnish stories of Yaz and the Babe
and the Splendid Splinter. For a few dreamy dollars,
they sit with their wives all day in the sun,
on their own little seat cushions, wearing soft caps
with visors. Their brave recreational vehicles
grow hot in the parking lot, though they're
shaded by liveoaks and bottlebrush trees
whose soft bristles graze the top-racks.

At four, the spectators leave in pairs, off
to restaurants for Early Bird Specials.
A salamander scuttles across the quiet
visitors' dugout. The osprey whose nest is atop
the foul pole relaxes. She's raged all afternoon
at balls hit again and again toward her offspring.
Although December's frost killed the winter crop,
there's a pulpy orange-y smell from juice factories. . . .

Down the road, at Cypress Gardens, a woman
trainer flips young alligators over on their backs,
demonstrating their talent for comedy—stroke
their bellies and they're out cold, instantaneously
snoozing. A schoolgirl on vacation gapes,
wonder if she'd ever be brave enough
to try that, to hold a terrifying beast
and turn it into something cartoon-funny.

She stretches a hand toward the toothy sleeper
then takes a step back, to be safe as she reaches.

ROCHELLE NAMEROFF

◇

Backyard

for Larry

"There are two theories on hitting the knuckleball.
Unfortunately, neither of them works."

It was all so serious
as he taught me,
digging the knees together:

a deliberate hunkering,
the back & forth wiggle
shifting the weight.

It screws yr behind in the ground he said.
Protection I guess
or the secrecy of boys.

He called it
The Stan Musial Crouch,
& man how I practiced

getting it right to unwind
breathless exquisite & deadly.
The permission to love

without going crazy.
& o big brother,
how much I remember.

LETTY COTTIN POGREBIN

◇

from *Deborah, Golda and Me*

My baseball mentor was my cousin Danny, who was six years older than I and lived next door. Danny kept track of the Dodgers in bulging scrapbooks he fashioned out of black composition notebooks with spidery white designs on the cover, the kind I filled with arithmetic problems and geography homework. It was my job to paste in newspaper stories about Jackie Robinson, Pee Wee Reese, Billy Herman, and Dixie Walker; that's how I knew their names and positions. As we listened to the play-by-play on the radio (neither of us had a television in those days), Danny explained the rules of the game and taught me how to record the action on an official scorecard. He let me hang around when he and his friends played stickball in the street—and when the planets were in perfect alignment, I even had a turn at bat. To this day, I have Danny to thank for the excitement I feel when I first enter a baseball stadium.

DORIS KEARNS GOODWIN

◊

From Father, with Love

The game of baseball has always been linked in my mind with the mystic texture of childhood, with the sounds and smells of summer nights and with the memories of my father.

My love for baseball was born on the first day my father took me to Ebbets Field in Brooklyn. Riding in the trolley car, he seemed as excited as I was, and he never stopped talking; now describing for me the street in Brooklyn where he had grown up, now recalling the first game he had been taken to by his own father, now recapturing for me his favorite memories from the Dodgers of his youth – the Dodgers of Casey Stengel, Zack Wheat, and Jimmy Johnston.

In the evenings, when my dad came home from work, we would sit together on our porch and relive the events of that afternoon's game which I had so carefully preserved in the large, red scorebook I'd been given for my seventh birthday. I can still remember how proud I was to have mastered all those strange and wonderful symbols that permitted me to recapture, in miniature form, the every movement of Jackie Robinson and Pee Wee Reese, Duke Snider and Gil Hodges. But the real power of that scorebook lay in the responsibility it entailed. For all through my childhood, my father kept from me the knowledge that the daily papers printed daily box scores, allowing me to believe that without my personal renderings of all those games he missed while he was at work, he would be unable to follow our team in the only proper way a team should be followed, day by day, inning by inning. In other words, without me, his love for baseball would be forever incomplete.

To be sure, there were risks involved in making a commitment as boundless as mine. For me, as for all too many Brooklyn fans, the presiding memory of "the boys of summer" was the memory of the final playoff game in 1951 against the Giants. Going into the ninth, the Dodgers held a 4–1 lead.

Then came two singles and a double, placing the winning run at the plate with Bobby Thomson at bat. As Dressen replaced Erskine with Branca, my older sister, with maddening foresight, predicted the forever famous Thomson homer–a prediction that left me so angry with her, imagining that with her words she had somehow brought it about, that I would not speak to her for days.

So the seasons of my childhood passed until that miserable summer when the Dodgers were taken away to Los Angeles by the unforgivable O'Malley, leaving all our rash hopes and dreams of glory behind. And then came a summer of still deeper sadness when my father died. Suddenly my feelings for baseball seemed an aspect of my departing youth, along with my childhood freckles and my favorite childhood haunts, to be left behind when I went away to college and never came back.

Then one September day, having settled into teaching at Harvard, I agreed, half reluctantly, to go to Fenway Park. There it was again: the cozy ballfield scaled to human dimensions so that every word of encouragement and every scornful yell could be heard on the field; the fervent crowd that could, with equal passion, curse a player for today's failures after cheering his heroics the day before; the team that always seemed to break your heart in the last week of the season. It took only a matter of minutes before I found myself directing all my old intensities toward my new team–the Boston Red Sox.

I am often teased by my women friends about my obsession, but just as often, in the most unexpected places–in academic conferences, in literary discussions, at the most elegant dinner parties–I find other women just as crazily committed to baseball as I am, and the discovery creates an instant bond between us. All at once we are deep in conversation, mingling together the past and the present, as if the history of the Red Sox had been our history too.

There we stand, one moment recollecting the unparalleled performance of Yaz in '67, the next sharing ideas on how the present lineup should be changed; one moment recapturing the splendid career of "the Splendid Splinter," the next complaining about the manager's decision to pull the pitcher the night before. And then, invariably, comes the most vivid memory of all, the frozen image of Carlton Fisk as he rounded first in the sixth game of the '75 World Series, an image as intense in its evocation of triumph as the image of Ralph Branca weeping in the dugout is in its portrayal of heartache.

There is another, more personal memory associated with Carlton Fisk, for he was, after all the years I had followed baseball, the first player I actually met in person. Apparently, he had read the biography I had written on Lyndon Johnson and wanted to meet me. Yet when the meeting took place,

I found myself reduced to the shyness of childhood. There I was, a professor at Harvard, accustomed to speaking with presidents of the United States, and yet, standing beside this young man in a baseball uniform, I was speechless.

Finally Fisk said that it must have been an awesome experience to work with a man of such immense power as President Johnson – and with that, I was at last able to stammer out, with a laugh, "Not as awesome as the thought that I am really standing here talking with you."

Perhaps I have circled back to my childhood, but if this is so, I am certain that my journey through time is connected in some fundamental way to the fact that I am now a parent myself, anxious to share with my three sons the same ritual I once shared with my father.

For in this linkage between the generations rests the magic of baseball, a game that has defied the ravages of modern life, a game that is still played today by the same basic rules and at the same pace as it was played one hundred years ago. There is something deeply satisfying in the knowledge of this continuity.

And there is something else as well which I have experienced sitting in Fenway Park with my small boys on a warm summer's day. If I close my eyes against the sun, all at once I am back at Ebbets Field, a young girl once more in the presence of my father, watching the players of my youth on the grassy field below. There is magic in this moment, for when I open my eyes and see my sons in the place where my father once sat, I feel an invisible bond between our three generations, an anchor of loyalty linking my sons to the grandfather whose face they never saw but whose person they have already come to know through this most timeless of all sports, the game of baseball.

MOLLY O'NEILL

◊

Coming to the Plate

*W*hen *Paul O'Neill* steps to the plate for the Cincinnati Reds tonight, he will embody the hopes of most of the 52,000 fans at Riverfront Stadium and, for at least one pitch, he will be the focal point of over 50 million televisions across America. He will also be at the center of our family's field of dreams. Since 1928, when our father, a former minor league pitcher, began throwing screwballs on his family's farm, the Series has been our manifest destiny. Baseball kept our father alive.

Tonight will be Paul's first official World Series appearance. But it isn't his first World Series experience. He has been playing baseball as if his life depended on it since he was two years old. He had to. His four older brothers would have used him as a base if he hadn't learned how to swing a bat. In addition, our father had quite a lot on his mind–a baseball career that ended in a World War II paratrooping accident, a dicey ditch-digging business, six children and an achieving wife–and he never seemed to remember any of his sons' names until he heard them announced over the public address system at the Little League park.

For ten years, my mother said, her sons seemed like an endless progression of different-colored flannel uniforms that needed to be washed. My brothers were all baseball stars. It was the roll of some very large cosmic dice that kept Paul playing the game. Two others were scouted and chose early retirement over the major leagues. One became a poet; another grew his hair long and became an entrepreneur. We all knew the consequences of these acts. "I could end up T. S. Eliot and Michael could be Donald Trump," my brother Robert said last week. "For Dad, it wouldn't come close to what Paul's doing."

We grew up in Columbus, Ohio. In a neighborhood where most children grew up Lutheran or Methodist, we grew up Baseball. It is a way of life that is as whimsical and superstitious as any other religion. Our neighbors, who

were primarily academics from Ohio State University, weren't always toler-
ant of our rituals. The ecstasy of winning a round of home run derby by
slamming a tennis ball over the fence that divided our dusty backyard from
the manicured lawn next door completely escaped Mr. Walter, the owner
of the manicured lawn.

His complaints ignited a slow-seething battle between my parents. To my
mother, who was loath to offend, the solution was obvious: stop hitting
balls. "Children can read," she would proclaim. "Children can take music
lessons or ballet lessons." This irreverence astounded my father, who also
didn't understand why parking his backhoe in the driveway embarrassed my
mother. While they battled, a steady stream of balls continued to sail over
the fence.

Mr. Walter, a soft-spoken widower, decided that we were incorrigible
and spent the afternoons huddled on his back porch holding a rosary. When
the ball hit the plywood backstop, he would pass a bead. When it smacked
off the bat, he prayed harder. When a ball passed over the fence, he
dropped his rosary, retrieved the offending sphere and retired it to his
house. He thought that we possessed an inexhaustible supply of balls. He
was wrong. On a given afternoon, we might run out of tennis balls but there
were soft balls, hard balls, whiffle balls, soccer balls, Nerf balls, kick
balls . . .

We moved away from that neighborhood when Paul was six years old.
On moving day, Mr. Walter delivered hundreds of different balls, all neatly
packaged in oversized cardboard storage boxes. It was his offering: his
prayers had been answered. I was 15, had retired from softball three years
before, and it seemed like providence that I would have my own bedroom
where I could scribble deep and meaningful poetry in my diary and listen
to top 40 music. My brothers were jubilant because the new house was set
in the middle of four acres of potential baseball diamond.

By that time, they were a team. They had begun a ten-year reign over
Central-Ohio Little League. Cincinnati had the Big Red Machine; Columbus
had the O'Neill Boys. My oldest brother, Michael, was 13 and had an 80-
mile-an-hour fastball. My brother Pat, who was 11, had a mean curveball.
Kevin was a catcher. Robert was a pitcher. My father was the Little League
coach. Paul wanted to play but he was too young for anything more than
the backyard games.

The backyard games had become very serious. My brothers weren't just
a team, they were a franchise. They built a baseball diamond and worked
as the grounds crew to keep the infield grass groomed. They acted as park
security and cleared the clubhouse, which in off-game times doubled as a
shed for our pony, Tonka. As players, they only appeared in full equipment.

They looked like miniature major leaguers, so many sawed-off chess pieces in a game that began before any of us were born.

We all knew that some day we would play the game for real. It just took a couple of decades to figure out the positions we would play.

A lot of the figuring occurred intra-brother. There was brutal competition for the mound. Winning mattered most, so the position usually belonged to Michael. Kevin, who was four years younger, was the catcher, and because Michael pitched as wild as he did fast, Kevin had a strong attachment to his face guard, chest guard, shin guards and helmet. It didn't surprise any of us when, at 13 years old, Kevin retired from baseball and started playing football. He liked the equipment.

Games of "hot box" – one player on first, another on second and a runner in between – proved that Pat, who loved the game more than any other brother, possessed the least physical gift. He is built a little too low to the ground. Robert, although five years younger, was Mike's singular competition for the mound. He pitched smart and steady. Paul was stuck with leftovers. He was just a little boy when the rest of my brothers entered adolescence, en masse. He started facing Michael when he was eight years old. The others were sick of being hit by pitches. Paul took any pitches he could get.

His earliest training as a competitor was as a sort of pillow for his older brothers' Gestalt therapy. In the years when Robert fought to unseat Michael on the pitcher's mound, he relaxed by challenging Paul to 25-point games of one-on-one basketball. Coolly, Robert would allow a 23-point lead. And then, with the same dramatic effortlessness every afternoon, Robert would take the next 25 points from Paul.

The game never changed, and neither did Paul's reaction. "You cheater," he would shriek, hurling the basketball and storming into the house to call our mother at the hospital where she worked. "Mom," he would sob into the phone, after our mother had been paged from a death bed or an emergency room, "Robert cheated."

Paul had a sense of injustice early on. He criminalized his individual tormentors. If an older brother was in the process of winning, he was "lucky." If he won, he had "cheated," and Paul would follow the sinner around with challenges for rematches phrased in a sportsmanlike manner: "What's the matter, cheater? Afraid you won't get lucky again?" My father interceded occasionally. "Quit torturing the darned baby, will ya?" he'd say.

Although usually, a game was a game in our house, a winner was a winner and only losers needed umpires. During his early childhood, the injustice for Paul was birth order: In the end, it may have been a lucky break. He was two years old when the older boys began to dominate Plain City.

Cincinnati had Crosley Field; Ohio Little League had Plain City. It was a Little League–scale replica of a major league park in an Amish community 25 miles northwest of Columbus. Plain City had a grass infield, dugouts and uniformed umpires. It had a scoreboard, a concessions stand and stadium-style stands. The Plain City games were our World Series. My father, the coach, would sit on the bench chewing like Don Zimmer. My brothers would play out their Catfish Hunter fantasies.

My mother and I would sit in the stands with Paul. He wore little sun-suits and I remember the way his blond curls smelled, the way the mosquitoes buzzed around us on those muggy Midwestern summer evenings. My attendance was mandatory, I was furious and bored and carried books like Sylvia Plath's *Bell Jar* to read during the game. But Paul, from whom I was inseparable for the first eight years of his life, kept me connected to the game.

There was a dirt race track surrounding the Plain City ball park and one night, an Amish man steered his horse and buggy around the track during the bottom of the sixth and final inning. In his Abraham Lincoln hat and top coat, the buggy driver looked like something out of a 19th century museum. Michael was playing right field in that game. His team was one run up, with a runner on base and two out, when a routine fly ball landed at his feet. He was watching the horse and buggy. "He missed the ball, Ollee," Paul said, his earliest and enduring pronunciation of my name recalling the boxer Muhammed Ali. "Tell him to get it," he screamed.

He was too old to sit on my lap when Robert began pitching. If he had persevered, I suppose Robert would have been a reliever. He'd do anything to prevent a batter getting ahead of him. If they did, he collapsed. In one tied game at Plain City, with the bases loaded on walks and a full count, he began sobbing into the mitt on his left hand and consoling himself with his right hand, which was slipped down the front of his flannel green and white pinstriped pants. "My god," whispered our horrified mother.

Maybe Paul learned from his older brothers' mistakes; he certainly learned the symmetry between baseball and life. Like the rest of us, he wasn't surprised when Robert, who was already being looked at by major league scouts, retired from baseball at age 15 and took up poetry and tennis. Even more than batters getting ahead of him, Robert loathed fielders who blew the play on a perfect groundball pitch.

He is the only brother who believes that he might have made a mistake about baseball. When Paul negotiates his contract, Robert, who is now 30 years old and weighs 220 pounds, is quick to point out that he, not Paul, was the m.v.p. of Plain City. "It's on the records," he says. "M.v.p. 1972. Paul only got most valuable pitcher and that was in 1974."

In a reversal of their one-on-one games, Robert calls Paul "lucky." "He's the only one who could go to the Ohio State Fair and blow the balloon off the clown's mouth and come home with all the prizes," he says.

Paul's luck went as unnoticed as his performance on the Little League field did. A few years later, when he broke his ankle sliding into second base in Plain City, nobody thought it was a big deal that he played right field in a cast and led the team in batting. That's what O'Neill Boys do.

Besides, the world had started to change. As an all-city high school player, Michael was engaged in a haircut battle. Today, he says that it was symptomatic of his "uncoachableness." Then, he said, "What difference does it make how long my hair is if I am blowing away the batters?" Scouts still watched him, but he realized that his career potential was limited during his first year of college. "During a game after a particularly rough fraternity party," he told me yesterday, "I saw three balls coming at me instead of one."

Something similar happened to Pat in his senior year of high school. He quit baseball so that he could work in a grocery store and buy a car.

Paul was too young to drive a car or suffer the long-reaching ripples of Woodstock nation that washed over the rest of our adolescence. He kept playing baseball. My father, his top four prospects benched for life, focused exclusively on Paul. He called his youngest son "Mike, Pat, Kev or Rob, no, Paul." By the time he was in high school, Paul was the only one living at home. The rest of us were being socially relevant in places like Haight Ashbury and Provincetown.

Paul was at home when our parents began to look older. He called our father Little Buddy, and Old Timer. In 1980, when the telephone rang in our parents' kitchen with the news that Paul was Cincinnati's fourth-round draft pick, the Old Timer cried.

Nobody else was surprised. Nevertheless, the process of Paul's career pulled us back together, back into the story of our childhood, complete with the unresolved challenges and the echoes of "Cheater!" and "Luck!"

As Paul moved between single, double and triple A baseball, our other brothers drifted between careers. I suppose they tended some demons and doubt. Nobody talked about it. Everybody rooted for Paul. But since we grew up in the church of Baseball, we know why our father has outlived four of his brothers, we know what kept him alive during emergency bypass surgery the year that Paul moved up to the majors, we know about teams, we know for what we cheer.

None of it surprises us. Last week, sitting in a Broadway theater, in the middle of the second act of *Lettice and Lovage*, I had an irrepressible urge to put on my Walkman, which was tuned to WFAN. Paul had called me from the locker room before the game; I just had this feeling. I tuned in to an announcer yelling, "It's over the right field fence! A home run for O'Neill." My companion was amazed. I wasn't surprised.

Several nights later, I was watching the game on television when the Reds clinched the pennant. A few minutes passed before my brother Robert called. He was watching the post-game shows at his home in Cincinnati. "I haven't seen Paul on the screen," he said. "I have this feeling he's standing by his locker, waiting for somebody to come and tell him he's the m.v.p." We listened to each other breathe and listened as our separate televisions announced that two relief pitchers had been named joint m.v.p.'s.

"Oh, man," said Robert, "OK, look. I have this big pumpkin, OK? It's going to say 'REDS' in big victorious letters and I am going to put a candle in it and I'm going to take it over and put it on Paul's front porch before he gets home. He'll spend the whole night trying to figure out who did it. It might give him a laugh. He might think it's lucky."

After a pause, my brother Robert continued his declaration of full adulthood. "Look I gotta go, OK?" he said. "See you at the game on Tuesday. Wear red."

JANE LEAVY

◊

from *Squeeze Play*

April 5 *My grandmother,* Delia Bloom Berkowitz, lived one block from Yankee Stadium in a building called the Yankee Arms. In all the time I knew her, she never set foot in the Stadium whose shadow crossed her parlor at five o'clock on summer afternoons. I told my friends you could see the out-field wall from her front window, which was a lie, and that you could hear the crack of the bat in her living room before you could hear Mel Allen's voice on the radio, which may or may not have been true. Exaggeration was a way of life for me then.

Delia Berkowitz was a small woman with large breasts and lots of rose sachet in her dresser drawers. I am her size and Mom says I have her shape. When she died the only thing I asked for was the porcelain heart in which she kept her rose sachet. I keep paperclips in it now.

Sometimes when I think about how I ended up here, standing in a locker room full of naked men I do not know talking about good skull, which is what the Washington Senators call a blow job, I think about her. I think probably she'd laugh but only in private, the way she did when I was three and told an old maiden aunt to buzz off or I'd shoot my airplane up her vagina. I can still see Grandma peering through the glass french doors try-ing not to laugh, or at least I think I can.

I think somebody gives you permission for the things you do, permission to put paperclips where once there was rose sachet. Somebody gave me per-mission to do this and that somebody was her.

When I was four, she put on her open-toed shoes and I put on my Mary Janes and we took the CC train downtown to Saks Fifth Avenue to buy me a baseball glove. A few of the trains still had those old straw seats then, and the bristles caught in my tights and we almost missed the stop while trying to get me untangled. I always got tangled up when I tried to be a girl.

We bought a glove, the only one they had, a Sam Esposito model, and though no one including me had ever heard of him, I told Grandma he was a Yankee. Many years later, I looked him up in the Baseball Encyclopedia and found he retired the year we bought the glove that bore his name. What did Saks know?

Sammy was my first hero. He played ten years in the majors, all but eighteen games for the Chicago White Sox, and retired in 1963, with a career batting average of .207, disappearing into the fine print of the Baseball Encyclopedia, where everyone is created equal even if they only hit eight home runs lifetime.

I took Sammy with me everywhere, including to Temple on the High Holy Days. Services were held in the ballroom of the Concourse Plaza Hotel at the corner of 161st Street and the Grand Concourse up the hill from the Stadium, where visiting teams stayed in Babe Ruth's day. Delia Berkowitz was a religious woman, but she loved her grandchildren more than she loved God. And so she hid me and Sammy and my transistor radio inside her mink coat until we got past the old men downstairs in their prayer shawls and yarmulkes. I told everyone she got the coat two sizes too big because she wanted to make room for Sam and me. My mother says she got it two sizes too big because it was on sale. Maybe. But that isn't why she wore it to Temple on warm fall afternoons.

The drapes in the ballroom were thick burgundy velvet with gold-braided ties. Any self-respecting five-year-old could get lost in the folds of those drapes, which I did, watching a fraction of the 1964 World Series from the ballroom window while my grandmother prayed and sang for my future. I heard the shofar in one ear and Mel Allen in the other.

The hotel sat just high enough upon the hill that a forty-inch person standing on tippy-toes in her best Mary Janes could see over Joyce Kilmer Park, where black men still called Negroes sold towers of undulating balloons to white children, past Addie Vallin's ice cream parlor, where Grandma ate one too many ice cream sodas and consigned herself to an adulthood of diabetes, to the concrete and copper of the outfield wall, which parted just enough to allow a glimpse of centerfield and a flanneled figure running hard after an unseen ball. This was how I saw things then. This was my reality—a swath of vision cut through a gap in the outfield wall.

By the time I was nine I knew I was going to grow up to be Joey Proud, the Yankees centerfielder. My parents, who had other faults, never bothered to tell me this might be a problem. Every afternoon I practiced against the garage door of their home at 5234 Eldridge Court in New Rochelle, New York. Bending, scooping, making the throw; one knee to the gravel, hands caressing the ball in the pocket of my Sam Esposito glove, making the peg from deep centerfield to an X chalked on the middle of the garage door. It was the only house in the neighborhood painted pink.

Every day when the sun went down, the whole damn thing vibrated. I couldn't believe they had done this to me. My father was sympathetic but all he said was, "Your mother is bored."

Every night I stood in front of the television watching the game and practicing my swing. I always swung for the seats. I even practiced fouling the ball off my foot. Mom would come in the den and find me limping around the rug, walking off the pain. I never said a word and neither did she. By the time I was nine I knew you gotta play hurt.

Joey came up in 1968, the summer of Bobby Kennedy and the riots. Everybody said he was the next Mickey Mantle, which of course was the kiss of death. Like the Mick, Joey was a white boy who could run black. And like the Mick, Joey didn't stay whole very long. Mantle was a hick with a blond cowlick and unspeakable dreams. Joey was a city kid with curly black hair who grew up playing sewer ball in Sheepshead Bay and running for the BMT. "So much for country hardball," he used to say.

Guys who knew him when talk about the time he hit one twelve sewers. The legend prospered, and by the time he showed up at St. John's his freshman year, it was commonly accepted fact that he had decimated a pink Spaldeen one June afternoon with a swat that left half the ball on Avenue X and the other half on Avenue Y. They called him the Sultan of Spaldeen.

His looks were as prodigious as his stroke. He was Cupid in flannels: with smiling green eyes, the longest lashes you've ever seen, and brows that met above his nose and made him look more serious than he ever was. He was a kid from the nabe; a hang-out kind of guy. "*Che si dice,*" he always said. What's happening? What do you say? "*Che si dice?*" the writers asked after every game.

He was born Joey Provenzano, the only son of Anthony and Juliana, who made the best pizza crust in the borough and wanted something better for their son. Joey promised to get a good education. And he did. His first week at St. John's, the athletic director changed Joey's name to Proud. "Marketing," he explained.

Joey's mom, who never learned to speak English, went to mass and prayed for forgiveness. Joey knelt beside her and muttered in Italian that it would be okay. Years later, long after baseball made it easy for him to stop going to Sunday mass, Joey crossed himself every time he stepped into the batter's box. Needless to say, so did I.

St. John's also tried to make Joey a switch-hitter so he would be even more like Mickey Mantle. Joey was a pure left-handed hitter; a natural for the Stadium's short rightfield porch. He told the coaches: "*A-fan-culo.*" Joey never told anyone to get fucked in English.

Everybody thought he was just being proud. But that wasn't it at all. Mickey was Joey's hero just as Joey was mine. Unlike me, Joey didn't try to imitate Mickey's every gesture. Joey refused to presume he was going to be as good as the Mick.

He signed with the Yankees the day his freshman season ended and received an unprecedented bonus worth almost as much as Mantle made that year, his last in the majors. Joey also initiated a special clause in his contract allowing him to wear his own tailor-made flannel uniform. Joey was the real thing, all right. He was also allergic to polyester.

On his first major league at bat, he hit a home run, a soaring, titanic shot that seemed to foreshadow the arc of his ambitions. The stadium went crazy. All those Yankee haters from Brooklyn cuckolded by Walter O'Malley purged their pain with a whoop of delight for one of their own. Joey rounded the bases and found his hero, the Mick, waiting for him at home plate. He went 3 for 4 that day with 3 RBIs and was deep into a postgame oration when Pete Sheehy, the clubhouse man, came and whispered in his ear that his father was dead of a heart attack, at age forty-five. Dropped dead in the stands as Joey rounded the bases in the bottom of the first.

Joey went home to Brooklyn that night, buried his father a day later, and was in the starting lineup when the Yankees started a three-game set against the Red Sox the day after that. "You gotta play hurt," Joey said.

From then on, he played every day as if his heart might break. Sportswriters are very big on heart. If a guy doesn't choke on a 3–2 pitch in the bottom of the ninth, they say he's got heart. Joey Proud made "heart" a cliché. He said he had never seen things so clearly; had never seen the ball so well. He had an eternity to decide what to do with every pitch. After three months in the majors, he was hitting .391, with 17 home runs and 51 RBIs. He was zoned with the angels.

In those days, my grandparents spent their summers playing bingo on the boardwalk in Long Beach. They wanted no part of the heat of the Bronx or the pennant race. So it was late September before I got to see Joey for myself at the Stadium. We had box seats along the third base line. It was a cold, raw night. By the end of the fifth, dew was embracing the outfield grass. I clenched my teeth so they wouldn't chatter. By the bottom of the ninth, the stands were almost empty and my mother was agitating to leave. Chocolate cake was waiting at Grandma's. Joey Proud was waiting on deck.

The game meant nothing except on its own terms. Win or lose, the Yankees were still going to finish fifth. Joey was still going to be Rookie of the Year.

I can close my eyes and see that uppercut swing as he pointed the bat again and again at the pitcher. He had a habit, between swings, of curling his fingers around the bat, one finger at a time, the way you play an arpeggio on a piano. It was as if he couldn't quite get a grip on something; as if he knew everything was one swing from flying out of his grasp.

He lunged at the ball, which was low and away, and turned instinctively toward first. A slow roller, they call it, a slow roller to short. It had infield hit written all over it. In moments like this, baseball forces you to make a choice. You can watch the shortstop charging, or the path of the ball, or the runner racing down the baseline against the geometry of aerodynamic flight. You cannot watch it all.

Joey was maybe a yard from the bag, straining to beat out the inevitable, when his leg caved in. The violence of the injury was oddly beautiful to see. He was a dancer in mid-leap, his legs extended beyond reach or reason. He hung there for an instant, or so it seemed, before the force of gravity sucked him to the ground, splayed in the basepath, covered with chalk. His fingers kept feeling for the bag.

"*Cretino*," he said, "*cretino*."

They carried him off the field on a stretcher and into the hospital, where surgeons cut off his tailor-made flannel uniform and tried to reconfigure his shredded Achilles tendon. He promised he'd be back. And he was. But he was never really the same.

Two years later, they moved him from center to first, and then finally to designated hitter. Joey said they cut off his balls the day they told him to put away his glove. My father said Willie was better anyway and maybe even Mickey, which was supposed to make me feel better, but it didn't. Joey was my guy. One time, Grandma and I stood outside the Stadium waiting for an autograph for an hour. Joey farted as he walked by.

I read his bio, *Proud of the Yankees*, and committed his stats to memory. I knew his wedding date and the birth weight of his two daughters and his only son, Joey Jr., who was born two months early and frail. But it was the unknowns that consumed me. What if Joey hadn't tried to beat out the throw on a meaningless bouncer to short on a raw September night?

They say that every great slugger has a hole in his swing, a vulnerable place in the arc of presumed contact. Joey had a hole in his leg and another in his heart. He was a real-life hero with a real-life Achilles heel. I couldn't have known it then, but I think maybe that's what I liked so much about him, that prodigious what-if.

In the spring of 1972, Dad was transferred to Richmond. I couldn't get the Yankee games on the radio anymore, which was probably just as well considering I was entering puberty surrounded by magnolia trees and blossoming Southern belles. Then Mom left, and Grandma died a year later, without ever having set foot in the Stadium, without ever regretting it, without teaching me how to be a girl. I dialed her number every night and listened to the ring, waiting for someone to answer. Finally someone did and I stopped calling.

That fall they tore down the House That Ruth Built, demolishing the green copper frieze that cast a shadow over my childhood. In his last at bat before the wreckers came, Joey hit a ball out of Yankee Stadium. The Yankees were playing the Orioles that night, so I was listening with the transistor under my pillow. I remember the silence before the pitch. "Proud steps in. McNally rocks and deals. The pitch is swung on and . . . it's going. It's going. It's *still* going! Holy cow! It's gone *out* of Yankee Stadium!"

Joey had done what no one, not Ruth, not Gehrig, not Mantle, had ever done before. And all it did was rekindle all those what-ifs. A kid found the ball later on 158th Street, half a block from Grandma's window.

The season ended. The Bombers finished fourth and I got my period. My career as a Yankee was over.

BETTE BAO LORD

◊

from *In the Year of the Boar and Jackie Robinson*

Shirley had reached the top of the stairs when suddenly from nowhere Mabel appeared. "Hey, you wanna play stickball?"

Shirley turned to see whom the girl was asking. No one else was around. "Me?"

"Yeah, you. How about it?"

Shaking her head, Shirley smiled and started down the steps. Mabel, riding on the handrail, whizzed by and blocked her progress on the first landing. "Why not?"

"Dumb hands. No can catch." Shirley slipped past and continued on, only to find the way blocked again on the second landing.

"Nothing to it. I'll show ya."

Shirley shook her head again.

"Come on, it's fun."

"Yes, fun. But nobody take me on team."

"Leave that to me."

Shirley still hesitated. But Mabel was hardly the patient sort and pulled her by the sleeves into the school yard. When the others saw her coming, they groaned.

"What ya want to bring the midget for?"

"Oh no, ya don't. Not on my team."

"Are you kidding me?"

"Yeah. She'd bow first and then ask permission to cop a fly."

"Send her back to the laundry."

"The only way she can get in this game is to lie down and be the plate."

Shirley was ready to leave quietly, but Mabel hissed through her teeth, "Who says my friend Shirley here can't play?"

Advancing with mighty shoves, she pushed each objector aside.

"You, Spaghetti Snot?

"You, Kosher Creep?

"You, Damp Drawers?

"You, Brown Blubber?

"You, Dog Breath?

"You, Puerto Rican Coconut?"

Mabel was most persuasive, for everyone named now twitched a shoulder to signal okay. "That's what I thought. And as captain, I get first pick and Shirley's it."

When the sides were chosen, Mabel pointed to a spot by the iron fence. "Shirley, you play right field. If a ball comes your way, catch it and throw it to me. I'll take care of the rest."

"Where you be?"

"I'm the pitcher."

"Picture?"

"Ah, forget it. Look for me, I'll be around."

Resisting the temptation to bow, Shirley headed for her spot.

Mabel's picture was something to see. First, hiding the ball, she gave the stick the evil eye. Then, twisting her torso and jiggling a leg, she whirled her arm around in a most impressive fashion, probably a ritual to shoo away any unfriendly spirits, before speeding the ball furiously into the hands of squatting Joseph.

Once in a great while, the stick got a lucky hit, but the Goddess Kwan Yin was again merciful and sent the ball nowhere near the fence.

After the change of sides, Mabel stood Shirley in place and told her she would be first to hit. Shirley would have preferred to study the problem some more, but was afraid to protest and lose face for her captain. Standing tall, with her feet together, stick on her shoulder, she waited bravely. Dog Breath had a ritual of his own to perform, but then, suddenly, the ball was coming her way. Her eyes squeezed shut.

"Ball one!" shouted the umpire.

"Good eye!" shouted Mabel.

Shirley sighed and started to leave, but was told to stay put.

Again the ball came. Again her eyes shut.

"Ball two!"

"Good eye!" shouted the team. "Two more of those and you're on."

Shirley grinned. How easy it was!

Sure enough, every time she shut her eyes, the ball went astray.

"Take your base," said the umpire.

Mabel came running over. "Stand on that red bookbag until someone hits the ball, then run like mad to touch the blue one. Got it?"

"I got."

Mabel then picked up the stick and with one try sent the ball flying. In no time, Shirley, despite her pigeon toes, had dashed to the blue bookbag. But something was wrong. Mabel was chasing her. "Go. Get going. Run."

Shirley, puzzled over which bookbag to run took next to a chance and sped off. But Mabel was still chasing her. "Go home! Go home!"

Oh no! She had done the wrong thing. Now even her new friend was angry. "Go home," her teammates shouted. "Go home."

She was starting off the field when she saw Joseph waving. "Here! Over here!" And off she went for the green one. Just before she reached it, she stumbled, knocking over the opponent who stood in her way. He dropped the ball, and Shirley fell on top of the bag like a piece of ripe bean curd.

Her teammates shouted with happiness. Some helped her up. Others patted her back. Then they took up Mabel's chant.

> "Hey, hey, you're just great
> Jackie Robinson crossed the plate.
> Hey, hey, you're a dream
> Jackie Robinson's on our team."

Mabel's team won. The score was 10 to 2, and though the Chinese rookie never got on base again or caught even one ball, Shirley was confident that the next time . . . next time, she could. And yes, of course, naturally, stickball was now her favorite game.

"Who is dodgers?" Shirley asked.

That question, like a wayward torch in a roomful of firecrackers, sparked answers from everyone.

"De Bums!"

"The best in the history of baseball!"

"Kings of Ebbets Field!"

"They'll kill the Giants!"

"They'll murder the Yankees!"

"The swellest guys in the world!"

"America's favorites!"

"Winners!"

Mrs. Rappaport clapped her hands for order. The girls quieted down first, followed reluctantly by the boys. "That's better. Participation is welcome, but one at a time. Let's do talk about baseball!"

"Yay!" shouted the class.

"And let's combine it with civics too!"

The class did not welcome this proposal as eagerly, but Mrs. Rappaport went ahead anyway.

"Mabel, tell us why baseball is America's favorite pasttime."

Pursing her lips in disgust at so ridiculous a question, Mabel answered. " 'Cause it's a great game. Everybody plays it, loves it and follows the games on the radio and nabs every chance to go and see it."

"True," said Mrs. Rappaport, nodding. "But what is it about baseball that is ideally suited to Americans?"

Mabel turned around, looking for an answer from someone else, but to no avail. There was nothing to do but throw the question back. "Whatta ya mean by 'suits'?"

"I mean, is there something special about baseball that fits the special kind of people we are and the special kind of country America is?" Mrs. Rappaport tilted her head to one side, inviting a response. When none came, she sighed a sigh so fraught with disappointment that it sounded as if her heart were breaking.

No one wished to be a party to such a sad event, so everybody found some urgent business to attend to like scratching, slumping, sniffing, scribbling, squinting, sucking teeth or removing dirt from underneath a fingernail. Joseph cracked his knuckles.

The ticking of the big clock became so loud that President Washington and President Lincoln, who occupied the wall space to either side of it, exchanged a look of shared displeasure.

But within the frail, birdlike body of Mrs. Rappaport was the spirit of a dragon capable of tackling the heavens and earth. With a quick toss of her red hair, she proceeded to answer her own question with such feeling that no one who heard could be so unkind as to ever forget. Least of all Shirley.

"Baseball is not just another sport. America is not just another country. . . . "

If Shirley did not understand every word, she took its meaning to heart. Unlike Grandfather's stories which quieted the warring spirits within her with the softness of moonlight or the lyric timbre of a lone flute, Mrs. Rappaport's speech thrilled her like sunlight and trumpets.

"In our national pastime, each player is a member of a team, but when he comes to bat, he stands alone. One man. Many opportunities. For no matter how far behind, how late in the game, he, by himself, can make a difference. He can change what has been. He can make it a new ball game.

"In the life of our nation, each man is a citizen of the United States, but he has the right to pursue his own happiness. For no matter what his race, religion or creed, be he pauper or president, he has the right to speak his mind, to live as he wishes within the law, to elect our officials and stand for office, to excel. To make a difference. To change what has been. To make a better America.

"And so can you! And so must you!"

Shirley felt as if the walls of the classroom had vanished. In their stead was a frontier of doors to which she held the keys.

"This year, Jackie Robinson is at bat. He stands for himself, for Americans of every hue, for an America that honors fair play.

"Jackie Robinson is the grandson of a slave, the son of a sharecropper, raised in poverty by a lone mother who took in ironing and washing. But a woman determined to achieve a better life for her son. And she did. For despite hostility and injustice, Jackie Robinson went to college, excelled in all sports, served his country in war. And now, Jackie Robinson is at bat in the big leagues. Jackie Robinson is making a difference. Jackie Robinson has changed what has been. And Jackie Robinson is making a better America.

"And so can you! And so must you!"

Suddenly Shirley understood why her father had brought her ten thousand miles to live among strangers. Here, she did not have to wait for gray hairs to be considered wise. Here, she could speak up, question even the conduct of the President. Here, Shirley Temple Wong was somebody. She felt as if she had the power of ten tigers, as if she had grown as tall as the Statue of Liberty.

Before long, Shirley was infected by a most severe case of Dodger fever. Not even strawberry ice cream could lure her away from the radio when Red Barber was broadcasting the latest adventure of de Bums. Truly nothing else mattered. Not the heat that glued her skin to the plastic chair, not an outing to the beach, not even a movie followed by a beef pot pie at the Automat. Every time Number 42 came to bat, she imagined herself in Jackie Robinson's shoes. Every time the pigeon-toed runner got a base, she was ready to help him steal home. And when Jackie's sixteen-game hitting streak ended, Shirley blamed herself. On that day, she had had to accompany her parents to greet Mr. Lee from Chungking. Obviously, it was her absence from the radio that had made all the difference.

Neither Mother nor Father shared her enthusiasm. In fact, they welcomed the mayhem that emanated from the talking box as if it were a plague of locusts at harvest time. But none of their usual parental tricks succeeded in undoing the spell. What could possibly compete with the goose bumps Shirley sprouted each time Gladys Gooding and her organ led the crowd at Ebbets Field in the singing of "The Star Spangled Banner"?

REBECCA STOWE

◇

Willie Horton

Tiger Stadium, 1972: I'm sitting in the left-field seats with my husband and some friends. It's my first game at Tiger Stadium in ten years—I'd been too busy being a Beatlemaniac during high school to pay much attention to baseball. But I'm older now, more mature, a college student, practically a *matron*. The opposing team is up and the batter hits a fly ball to left field. Willie lumbers after it, but he's not in time; it drops in, base hit, the crowd boos. I'm furious—how *dare* they? A group of drunks behind us starts chanting, "Trade 'im." "Booooo," hisses my husband, a mere *hockey* fan. "Don't listen to them," I shout to poor Willie, who's practically slumping inside himself he's so hurt and upset. "You just go up there and hit a home run. You'll show them!" And next at bat, he does—he sends one flying and the crowd roars. And cheers. And screams. And Willie, God love him, comes running around the bases, beaming and happy and forgiving as a child. That does it; I'm hooked. Back in love with baseball. Willie was "my" Tiger.

I grew up in a home where the radio was permanently set on WJR; I thought George-Kell-and-Ernie-Harwell was one word. I'd fall asleep listening to my parents discussing the merits and flaws of various Detroit players, and by the time I was twelve I wanted one of my own, a Tiger, my very own player to root for and adore. In 1962, my goals in life were to be the first woman governor of Michigan and to marry Rocky Colavito. I was crazy about him, in love the way only a twelve-year-old who knows nothing about it can be. It was my love for him, rather than baseball, that led me to my first game at Tiger Stadium—that 22-inning, 7-hour marathon with the Yankees, which the Tigers lost despite Rocky's heroic 7 hits in 10 at-bats: more than Maris, Mantle, and Berra combined. Seven hours was a long time for a preteen whose only interest in baseball was Rocky Colavito, but was I weary? Never. During the "boring parts" (i.e., when the Yankees were at bat), I sat happily carving ROCKY in the chest of a stuffed Tiger my father bought me to keep me quiet.

Seasons passed. Rocky went back to Cleveland and the Beatles replaced baseball as my passion, even though my mother tried valiantly to keep my interest alive. "You need a new Tiger," she'd say hopefully. "What about Al Kaline?" Oh, pul-*eeeze*. *Every*body loved Al Kaline. *She* loved Al Kaline. I wouldn't be caught *dead* loving the same Tiger my *mother* loved! My mangy old stuffed Tiger got tossed in the closet with the rest of my childhood. I still followed the Tigers and rooted for them faithfully, but it was mostly out of regional loyalty, during a time when practically the whole country was happily Detroit-bashing, calling it the Murder Capital of the U.S. and making other snide remarks. I secretly adored Al, and of course, I liked Stormin' Norman Cash . . . and I was kind of interested in this new Tiger, this local kid everybody kept comparing to some "Campy" guy. Willie Horton; Willie the Wonder. I thought it was great he hit so many home runs, but what was a "ribby"?

It wasn't love yet, it was more like a flirtation. I liked him because he was a ghetto kid, the son of a coal miner and the youngest of nineteen children. He was so poor when he was growing up he almost had to drop out of school because he didn't have shoes. When he signed with the Tigers, the first thing he did was buy a house for his parents. The guy had class.

Being sentimental, I liked that before his first All-Star Game, he ran around the field collecting his heroes' autographs. I also took note that he gave cookouts for the Tigers' grounds crew. I thought it was amusing when he showed up at spring training overweight and said, "I only eat two meals a day. I just like snacks." When he took off twenty-two pounds and Tiger manager Charlie Dressen presented him with a twenty-two-pound ham and told him not to eat it all at once, I could identify. It was the sixties, and while I was no radical, my consciousness was getting raised. So I liked that he donated time to work with ghetto kids, "kids who don't know what middle class means." Right on, Willie. And besides, he swung a mean bat.

I went off to college and got married, but not to Rocky. All anyone could talk about was Denny McLain and his damn organ. Willie the Wonder, meanwhile, was falling out of favor with the press and the fickle, fickle fans. The first time they booed him he got so upset he didn't show up the next day. Everyone was outraged, but I just grew more fond of him. The more they dumped on Willie, the more I liked him—how, I asked, can you not like someone who has two sons with the same first name?

Just about then, I went to that fateful game. When we got home, I called my mother with the good news that I'd found my Tiger. "Who?" she asked. "Willie!" I said joyfully. "Oh," she said after a pause. "That big baby?"

Yes, that big baby. Because of him I fell back in love with baseball. In learning about Willie, I learned about the game, something he, being an inveterate fan, would appreciate. I also learned a kind of pidgin baseballese. "His stats are solid," I'd say. "He's horribly underrated as a fielder." "Have you forgotten that game in '69 when he tied the AL record for outfielders with eleven putouts?" "And what about that perfect throw in game five of the '68 World Series when he nipped Lou Brock at the plate?"

No one quarreled with Willie's power. In the five seasons he played more than 140 games for the Tigers, he hit between 25 and 36 homers. Pitchers were terrified of him. Third basemen backed up. He was known as both a power hitter and a power squeezer. "My ribs still hurt," New York manager Ralph Houk complained after Willie grabbed him during a Yankee-Tiger brawl, to which Willie replied, "He was lucky I just squeezed him." Willie was a one-man gang in brawls. After watching him in action, umpire Marty Springstead contended, "Willie is the strongest man in the league. Willie is the strongest man in *any* league."

It was true that he was injury-prone and rarely made it through an entire season. He invariable began the year leading in something—home runs or runs batted in (so *that's* a "ribby"!)—but he would pull a hamstring or tear a ligament or get hit in the head. Detractors squawked "Hypochondriac!" but how do you fake knee surgery? If he could play, he'd play—this is the man who got *hit by a car* while chasing the team bus and got up, grabbed a cab, went out to the stadium, and played!

But did the fans appreciate him? NO! On opening day in '73, forty-some-odd thousand fans cheered the Tigers as they were introduced—all except Willie, who got some jeers. Detractors called him moody, but how would *they* feel if they went into their offices and found forty-some-odd thousand hissing former fans stuffed into their cubicles?

He was human, but I liked those feet of clay. Every year at spring training, he'd arrive early and fat, using the "I just like snacks" routine, and when that didn't work, he'd say he couldn't help it, he had heavy muscles. (He did; he was going to be a boxer until his father saw him get beat up on TV and nixed that career.) He'd get upset when he didn't get to play and skulk off to the clubhouse, but he'd always get over it and end up back on the bench, cheering more heartily than the most vehement fan. Yes, he tended to sulk, but he'd always bounce right back and with boundless enthusiasm, come to the park five hours before anyone else, to work out with weights and practice his swing with a broom handle. (As a rookie, he'd show up for the team bus an hour and a half early to make sure it wouldn't leave without him.) When he became a DH in 1975, he'd spend his bench time pretending he was out in left field, thinking about how he'd field the ball. "I just want to play," he said. "I don't care if I have to play in the street."

The man loved baseball.

"The Tigers are my family," he said over and over, and even when they traded him in 1977, after all those years of loyal service, he still proclaimed, "I'll always be a Tiger." Yes, he was sentimental, but what's wrong with that? He had cried when the Tigers traded Mickey Lolich, but so did a lot of other people I knew.

I kept an eye on Willie after he got traded, and I was very proud when the *Sporting News* named him the American League's Comeback Player of the Year in 1979. As the DH in all 162 games for the Seattle Mariners, he hit 29 homers and had 106 RBIs, showing exactly what he could do if he played every day.

He went back down to the minors after another season in Seattle, his eighteen-year major league career over, and I didn't hear anything about him again until 1985, when I was out at Yankee Stadium cheering my newest Tiger, Chet Lemon. "Horton?" I asked while glancing at the Yankee roster. "Could that be Horton as in *Willie*?" Sure enough; Billy Martin, the man who, when managing the Tigers, had challenged Willie to a fistfight, had brought him to the Yanks as something called a "tranquillity coach."

Tranquillity and Willie didn't go together. I did remember his once saying, "I just judge everybody as a human being—even umpires," but that hardly qualified him for Buddhahood. Unless the TC was just a euphemism for the guy who sits on the players when they get out of line, it made no sense at all. Unless it was a joke, it wasn't funny.

Willie was a Tiger, not a Yankee. Willie was tempestuous, not serene. It was his perturbability that made Willie so wonderful—he was human and real, not a baseball card. If Willie wasn't Willie, who was I? I longed to see him come charging out of the dugout to toss a few umpires around, or at least to pout and stomp, but nothing happened. Even Billy Martin was restrained.

The Tigers won and Chet got a hit, but I found myself pouting and stomping and wishing *I* could toss a few umpires around. Somebody had to be disappointed and petulant. Somebody had to be Willie.

ANN HOOD

◇

Memoir

Baseball is in my blood. Like the light hair and eyes I inherited from my father, and the hot Italian temper I got from my mother, a love of baseball runs through my veins. Until recently, I was not sure where my passion for the sport came from. Sometimes I thought it began long ago, on summer trips to Fenway Park, when my family would drive in our oversized Chevy to Boston, park in a garage near Government Center, and take the T out to the ballpark.

As I grew older and more accustomed to our routine, my father's neatly arranged exact subway fare used to annoy me. In his pocket, I knew, he carried small bills to pay for hot dogs and beer and a souvenir program. In his wallet he had the exact amount needed to retrieve the car at day's end. What about the unknown? I used to think. But for us, that lay in the game itself. The great catch by Carlton Fisk. The Yaz home run. The pitching of Luis Tiant and Bill Lee.

It was around that same time, when my father's proclivity for careful planning bothered me, that I fell in love with the Red Sox third baseman. He was blond and blue-eyed, Number 8. I used to watch, awestruck, as he ran for balls. Once I saw him race into the dugout and emerge, arm raised high, fist clutching the baseball for an out. On our way home from games, as my father drove exactly 55, I lounged in the back seat and recalled Butch Hobson at bat, or running the bases.

In college, I dragged friends to shopping malls when he made appearances. There I would stand, in a crowd of ten-year-old boys, at Lincoln Mall, waiting for a closer look at Butch and an 8 by 10 signed photo. That photo still sits in my parents' garage, pressed into a scrapbook, surrounded by movie ticket stubs and matchbook covers and dried corsages from boys now forgotten. Sometimes I even gave Butch Hobson credit for my love of baseball.

I moved to New York City on an early summer day in 1983. It was, I remember, a perfect day for baseball. I like to think I went right then out to a ballpark, but I know this is not true. My first trip was a few days later, out to Yankee Stadium, where I was yelled at for rooting against the home team. But how could a girl from Rhode Island, a loyal Red Sox fan, become a Yankees fan? Impossible.

Like my need for a good book beside my bed, and coffee in the morning, I need baseball. So the next time the need to see a game struck me that first summer here, I boarded the number 7 train for Shea Stadium, where a young Mets team was just being formed. Butch Hobson had long ago left Boston; my heart was free. I developed a crush on the Mets' catcher, Gary Carter. I had a new apartment in a new city, a boyfriend who, in a certain light, even resembled Carter, and a baseball stadium just a subway ride away. I had found my home away from home.

Last year I won a bet. A man at a wedding I attended bet me I couldn't name the entire 1976 Red Sox team. It was a foolish bet. I had already won three margaritas from him on Mets stats.

"I know baseball," I warned him.

"Sure," he said. "Sure, you do. *Anybody* can know about the Mets. All you have to do is read the paper. But the Red Sox? 1976? Forget it."

I took a breath and began. "Yaz played first that year," I told him.

He narrowed his eyes.

I continued. The names sounded almost magical. As I recited them, I remembered those trips to Fenway Park, when a ride on the T from Government Center seemed brave and exciting. "Dwight Evans," I said, like a special incantation. "Jim Rice. Fred Lynn."

The man cleared his throat. He looked at his friend. "I've never seen a girl who knows baseball like this," he said. Then he looked at me. "Third base," he said.

I smiled. "Third base," I repeated, and imagined a long ago summer when my heart soared as I watched Number 8 leap into the dugout and emerge victorious. "Third base was Butch Hobson," I said, and collected my win.

"How did you get to be such a baseball fan?" the man said, shaking his head.

Even then I did not know that it was genetic, inherited from a woman I never got to know. That day I just shrugged and said, "I love the game. That's all."

Last year I found Butch Hobson again. My father called and told me he was managing the Pawtucket Red Sox. "Remember what a crush you had on him?" He sent me clippings from the sports pages of the *Journal*, inky arrows pointing to Butch.

When he was named the new manager of the Red Sox, my father called to tell me. "Maybe you'll come back where you belong," he said. "A Red Sox fan again."

That's when I asked him, Did he remember when my love of baseball began?

He didn't. Instead, he told me this: "My mother," he said, "loved the Cincinnati Reds. Listened to every game on the radio. The saddest day in our house was when the catcher blew the World Series, went back to his hotel room, and killed himself. I'll never forget that. I was just a kid. It was the early thirties and my mother cried when she heard the news."

I never knew my father's mother. In old faded photographs she looks back at me like a stranger. Now I know she isn't. It is because of her that baseball is in my blood. Like most things, it was passed on to me, the way these days, when I leave my apartment to catch the number 7 train to Shea Stadium, I have in my pocket exactly enough change for two subway tokens, one to get me to the game, and the other to take me back home.

ANNIE DILLARD

◊

from *An American Childhood*

Not only that, but the Pirates were in the cellar again. They lived in the cellar, like trolls. They hadn't won a pennant since 1927. Nobody could even remember when they won ball games, the bums. They had some hitters, but no pitchers.

On the yellow back wall of our Richland Lane garage, I drew a target in red crayon. The target was a batter's strike zone. The old garage was dark inside; I turned on the bare bulb. Then I walked that famously lonely walk out to the mound, our graveled driveway, and pitched.

I squinted at the strike zone, ignoring the jeers of the batter—oddly, Ralph Kiner. I received no impressions save those inside the long aerial corridor that led to the target. I threw a red-and-blue rubber ball, one of those with a central yellow band. I wound up; I drew back. The target held my eyes. The target set me spinning as the sun from a distance winds the helpless spheres. Entranced and drawn, I swung through the moves and woke up with the ball gone. It felt as if I'd gathered my own body, pointed it carefully, and thrown it down a tunnel bored by my eyes.

I pitched in a blind fever of concentration. I pitched, as I did most things, in order to concentrate. Why do elephants drink? To forget. I loved living at my own edge, as an explorer on a ship presses to the ocean's rim; mind and skin were one joined force curved out and alert, prow and telescope. I pitched, as I did most things, in a rapture.

Now here's the pitch. I followed the ball as if it had been my own head, and watched it hit the painted plastered wall. High and outside; ball one. While I stood still stupefied by the effort of the pitch, while I stood agog, unbreathing, mystical, and unaware, here came the doggone rubber ball again, bouncing out of the garage. And I had to hustle up some snappy fielding, or lose the ball in a downhill thicket next door.

The red, blue, and yellow ball came spinning out to the driveway, and sprang awry on the gravel; if I nabbed it, it was apt to bounce out of my mitt. Sometimes I threw the fielded grounder to first—sidearm—back to the crayon target, which had become the first baseman. Fine, but the moronic first baseman spat it back out again at once, out of the dark garage and bouncing crazed on the gravel; I bolted after it, panting. The pace of this game was always out of control.

So I held the ball now, and waited, and breathed, and fixed on the target till it mesmerized me into motion. In there, strike one. Low, ball two.

Four balls, and they had a man on. Three strikeouts, and you had retired the side. Happily, the opposing batters, apparently paralyzed by admiration, never swung at a good pitch. Unfortunately, though, you had to keep facing them; the retired side resurrected immediately from its ashes, fresh and vigorous, while you grew delirious—nutsy, that is, from fielding a bouncing ball every other second and then stilling your heart and blinking the blood from your eyes so you could concentrate on the pitch.

Amy's friend Tibby had an older brother, named Ricky; he was younger than I was, but available. We had no laughing friendship, such as I enjoyed with Pin Ford, but instead a working relationship: we played a two-handed baseball game. Tibby and Ricky's family lived secluded at the high dead end of Richland Lane. Their backyard comprised several kempt and gardened acres. It was here in the sweet mown grass, here between the fruit trees and the rhubarb patch, that we passed long, hot afternoons pitching a baseball. Ricky was a sober, good-looking boy, very dark; his father was a surgeon.

We each pitched nine innings. The other caught, hunkered down, and called each pitch a ball or a strike. That was the essence of it: Catcher called it. Four walks scored a side. Three outs retired a side, and the catcher's side came on to pitch.

This was practically the majors. You had a team to root for, a team that both received pitches and dished them out. You kept score. The pitched ball came back right to you—after a proper, rhythmical interval. You had a real squatting catcher. Best, you had a baseball.

The game required the accuracy I was always working on. It also required honor. If when you were catching you made some iffy calls, you would be sorry when it was your turn to pitch. Ricky and I were, in this primitive sense, honorable. The tag ends of summer—before or after camp, before or after Lake Erie—had thrown us together for this one activity, this chance to do some pitching. We shared a catcher's mitt every inning; we pitched at the catcher's mitt. I threw as always by imagining my whole body hurled into the target; the rest followed naturally. I had one pitch, a fast ball. I couldn't control the curve. When the game was over, we often played another. Then we thanked each other formally, drank some hot water from a garden hose, and parted—like, perhaps, boys.

On Tuesday summer evenings I rode my bike a mile down Braddock Avenue to a park where I watched Little League teams play ball. Little League teams did not accept girls, a ruling I looked into for several years in succession. I parked my bike and hung outside the chain-link fence and watched and rooted and got mad and hollered, "Idiot, catch the ball!" "Play's at first!" Maybe some coach would say, "Okay, sweetheart, if you know it all, you go in there." I thought of disguising myself. None of this was funny. I simply wanted to play the game earnestly, on a diamond, until it was over, with eighteen players who knew what they were doing, and an umpire. My parents were sympathetic, if amused, and not eager to make an issue of it.

At school we played softball. No bunting, no stealing. I had settled on second base, a spot Bill Mazeroski would later sanctify: lots of action, lots of talk, and especially a chance to turn the double play. Dumb softball: so much better than no ball at all, I reluctantly grew to love it. As I got older, and the prospect of having anything to do with young Ricky up the street became out of the question, I had to remind myself, with all loyalty and nostalgia, how a baseball, a real baseball, felt.

A baseball weighted your hand just so, and fit it. Its red stitches, its good leather and hardness like skin over bone, seemed to call forth a skill both easy and precise. On the catch—the grounder, the fly, the line drive—you could snag a baseball in your mitt, where it stayed, snap, like a mouse locked in its trap, not like some pumpkin of a softball you merely halted, with a terrible sound like a splat. You could curl your fingers around a baseball, and throw it in a straight line. When you hit it with a bat it cracked—and your heart cracked, too, at the sound. It took a grass stain nicely, stayed round, smelled good, and lived lashed in your mitt all winter, hibernating.

There was no call for overhand pitches in softball; all my training was useless. I was playing with twenty-five girls, some of whom did not, on the face of it, care overly about the game at hand. I waited out by second and hoped for a play to the plate.

SHIRLEY JACKSON

◊

from *Raising Demons*

Before the children were able to start counting days till school was out, and before Laurie had learned to play more than a simple scale on the trumpet, and even before my husband's portable radio had gone in for its annual checkup so it could broadcast the Brooklyn games all summer, we found ourselves deeply involved in the Little League. The Little League was new in our town that year. One day all the kids were playing baseball in vacant lots and without any noticeable good sportsmanship, and the next day, almost, we were standing around the grocery and the post office wondering what kind of manager young Johnny Cole was going to make, and whether the Weaver boy—the one with the long arm—was going to be twelve this August, or only eleven as his mother said, and Bill Cummings had donated his bulldozer to level off the top of Sugar Hill, where the kids used to go sledding, and we were all sporting stickers on our cars reading "We have contributed" and the fundraising campaign was over the top in forty-eight hours. There are a thousand people in our town, and it turned out, astonishingly, that about sixty of them were boys of Little League age. Laurie thought he'd try out for pitcher and his friend Billy went out for catcher. Dinnertime all over town got shifted to eight-thirty in the evening, when nightly baseball practice was over. By the time our family had become accustomed to the fact that no single problem in our house could be allowed to interfere in any way with the tempering of Laurie's right arm, the uniforms had been ordered, and four teams had been chosen and named, and Laurie and Billy were together on the Little League Braves. My friend Dot, Billy's mother, was learning to keep a box score. I announced in family assembly that there would be no more oiling of baseball gloves in the kitchen sink.

We lived only a block or so from the baseball field, and it became the amiable custom of the ballplayers to drop in for a snack on their way to the practice sessions. There was to be a double-header on Memorial Day, to open the season. The Braves would play the Giants; the Red Sox would play the Dodgers. After one silent, apoplectic moment my husband agreed, gasping, to come to the ball games and root against the Dodgers. A rumor got around town that the Red Sox were the team to watch, with Butch Weaver's strong arm, and several mothers believed absolutely that the various managers were putting their own sons into all the best positions, although everyone told everyone else that it didn't matter, really, *what* position the boys held so long as they got a chance to play ball, and show they were good sports about it. As a matter of fact, the night before the double-header which was to open the Little League, I distinctly recall that I told Laurie it was only a game. "It's only a game, fella," I said. "Don't *try* to go to sleep; read or something if you're nervous. Would you like an aspirin?"

"I forgot to tell you," Laurie said, yawning. "He's pitching Georgie tomorrow. Not me."

"*What?*" I thought, and then said heartily, "I mean, he's the manager, after all. I know you'll play your best in *any* position."

"I could go to sleep now if you'd just turn out the light," Laurie said patiently. "I'm really quite tired."

I called Dot later, about twelve o'clock, because I was pretty sure she'd still be awake, and of course she was, although Billy had gone right off about nine o'clock. She said she wasn't the least bit nervous, because of course it didn't really matter except for the kids' sake, and she hoped the best team would win. I said that that was just what I had been telling my husband, and she said *her* husband had suggested that perhaps she had better not go to the game at all because if the Braves lost she ought to be home with a hot bath ready for Billy and perhaps a steak dinner or something. I said that even if Laurie wasn't pitching I was sure the Braves would win, and of course I wasn't one of those people who always wanted their own children right out in the center of things all the time but if the Braves lost it would be my opinion that their lineup ought to be revised and Georgie put back into right field where he belonged. She said *she* thought Laurie was a better pitcher, and I suggested that she and her husband and Billy come over for lunch and we could all go to the game together.

I spent all morning taking movies of the Memorial Day parade, particularly the Starlight 4-H Club, because Jannie was marching with them, and I used up almost a whole film magazine on Sally and Barry, standing at the curb, wide-eyed and rapt, waving flags. Laurie missed the parade because he slept until nearly twelve, and then came downstairs and made himself an enormous platter of bacon and eggs and toast, which he took out to the hammock and ate lying down.

"How do you feel?" I asked him, coming out to feel his forehead. "Did you sleep all right? How's your arm?"

"Sure," he said.

We cooked lunch outdoors, and Laurie finished his breakfast in time to eat three hamburgers. Dot had only a cup of coffee, and I took a little salad. Every now and then she would ask Billy if he wanted to lie down for a little while before the game, and I would ask Laurie how he felt. The game was not until two o'clock, so there was time for Jannie and Sally and Barry to roast marshmallows. Laurie and Billy went to the barn to warm up with a game of ping-pong, and Billy's father remarked that the boys certainly took this Little League setup seriously, and my husband said that it was the best thing in the world for the kids. When the boys came out of the barn after playing three games of ping-pong I asked Billy if he was feeling all right and Dot said she thought Laurie ought to lie down for a while before the game. The boys said no, they had to meet the other guys at the school at one-thirty and they were going to get into their uniforms now. I said please to be careful, and Dot said if they needed any help dressing just call down and we would come up, and both boys turned and looked at us curiously for a minute before they went indoors.

"My goodness," I said to Dot, "I hope they're not nervous."

"Well, they take it so seriously," she said.

I sent the younger children in to wash the marshmallow off their faces, and while our husbands settled down to read over the Little League rule book, Dot and I cleared away the paper plates and gave the leftover hamburgers to the dog. Suddenly Dot said, "Oh," in a weak voice and I turned around and Laurie and Billy were coming through the door in their uniforms. "They look so—so—*tall*," Dot said, and I said, "Laurie?" uncertainly. The boys laughed, and looked at each other.

"Pretty neat," Laurie said, looking at Billy.

"Some get-up," Billy said, regarding Laurie.

Both fathers came over and began turning the boys around and around, and Jannie and Sally came out onto the porch and stared worshipfully. Barry, to whom Laurie and his friends have always seemed incredibly tall and efficient, gave them a critical glance and observed that this was truly a baseball.

It turned out that there was a good deal of advice the fathers still needed to give the ballplayers, so they elected to walk over to the school with Billy and Laurie and then on to the ball park, where they would find Dot and me later. We watched them walk down the street; not far away they were joined by another boy in uniform and then a couple more. After that, for about half an hour, there were boys in uniform wandering by twos and threes toward the baseball field and the school, all alike in a kind of unexpected dignity and new tallness, all walking with self-conscious pride. Jannie and Sally stood on the front porch watching, careful to greet by name all the ballplayers going by.

A few minutes before two, Dot and I put the younger children in her car and drove over to the field. Assuming that perhaps seventy-five of the people in our town were actively engaged in the baseball game, there should have been about nine hundred and twenty-five people in the audience, but there seemed to be more than that already; Dot and I both remarked that it was the first town affair we had ever attended where there were more strange faces than familiar ones.

Although the field itself was completely finished, there was only one set of bleachers up, and that was filled, so Dot and I took the car robe and settled ourselves on top of the little hill over the third-base line, where we had a splendid view of the whole field. We talked about how it was at the top of this hill the kids used to start their sleds, coasting right down past third base and on into the center field, where the ground flattened out and the sleds would stop. From the little hill we could see the roofs of the houses in the town below, half hidden in the trees, and far on to the hills in the distance. We both remarked that there was still snow on the high mountain.

Barry stayed near us, deeply engaged with a little dump truck. Jannie and Sally accepted twenty-five cents each, and melted into the crowd in the general direction of the refreshment stand. Dot got out her pencil and box score, and I put a new magazine of film in the movie camera. We could see our husbands standing around in back of the Braves' dugout, along with the fathers of all the other Braves players. They were all in a group, chatting with great humorous informality with the manager and the two coaches of the Braves. The fathers of the boys on the Giant team were down by the Giant dugout, standing around the manager and the coaches of the Giants.

Marian, a friend of Dot's and mine whose boy Artie was first baseman for the Giants, came hurrying past looking for a seat, and we offered her part of our car robe. She sat down, breathless, and said she had mislaid her husband and her younger son, so we showed her where her husband was down by the Giant dugout with the other fathers, and her younger son turned up almost at once to say that Sally had a popsicle and so could he have one, too, and a hot dog and maybe some popcorn?

Suddenly, from far down the block, we could hear the high-school band playing "The Stars and Stripes Forever," and coming closer. Everyone stood up to watch and then the band turned the corner and came through the archway with the official Little League insignia and up to the entrance of the field. All the ballplayers were marching behind the band. I thought foolishly of Laurie when he was Barry's age, and something of the sort must have crossed Dot's mind, because she reached out and put her hand on Barry's head. "There's Laurie and Billy," Barry said softly. The boys ran out onto the field and lined up along the base lines, and then I discovered that we were all cheering, with Barry jumping up and down and shouting, "Baseball! Baseball!"

"If you cry I'll tell Laurie," Dot said to me out of the corner of her mouth.

"Same to you," I said, blinking.

The sky was blue and the sun was bright and the boys stood lined up soberly in their clean new uniforms holding their caps while the band played "The Star Spangled Banner" and the flag was raised. From Laurie and Billy, who were among the tallest, down to the littlest boys in uniform, there was a straight row of still, expectant faces.

I said, inadequately, "It must be hot out there."

"They're all chewing gum," Dot said.

Then the straight lines broke and the Red Sox, who had red caps, and the Dodgers, who had blue caps, went off into the bleachers and the Giants, who had green caps, went into their dugout, and at last the Braves, who had black caps, trotted out onto the field. It was announced over the public-address system that the Braves were the home team, and when it was announced that Georgie was going to pitch for the Braves I told Marian that I was positively relieved, since Laurie had been so nervous anyway over the game that I was sure pitching would have been a harrowing experience for him, and she said that Artie had been perfectly willing to sit out the game as a substitute, or a pinch hitter, or something, but that his manager had insisted upon putting him at first base because he was so reliable.

"You know," she added with a little laugh, "*I* don't know one position from another, but of course Artie is glad to play anywhere."

"I'm sure he'll do very nicely," I said, trying to put some enthusiasm into my voice.

Laurie was on second base for the Braves, and Billy at first. Marian leaned past me to tell Dot that first base was a *very* responsible position, and Dot said oh, was it? Because of course Billy just wanted to do the best he could for the team, and on the *Braves* it was the *manager* who assigned the positions. Marian smiled in what I thought was a nasty kind of way and said she hoped the best team would win. Dot and I both smiled back and said we hoped so, too.

When the umpire shouted, "Play Ball!" people all over the park began to call out to the players, and I raised my voice slightly and said, "Hurray for the Braves." That encouraged Dot and *she* called out, "Hurray for the Braves," but Marian, of course, had to say, "Hurray for the Giants."

The first Giant batter hit a triple, although, as my husband explained later, it would actually have been an infield fly if the shortstop had been looking and an easy out if he had thrown it anywhere near Billy at first. By the time Billy got the ball back into the infield the batter—Jimmie Hill, who had once borrowed Laurie's bike and brought it back with a flat tire—was on third. I could see Laurie out on second base banging his hands together and he looked so pale I was worried. Marian leaned around me and said to Dot, "That was a nice try Billy made. I don't think even *Artie* could have caught that ball."

"He looks *furious*," Dot said to me. "He just *hates* doing things wrong."

"They're all terribly nervous," I assured her. "They'll settle down as soon as they really get playing." I raised my voice a little. "Hurray for the Braves," I said.

The Giants made six runs in the first inning, and each time a run came in Marian looked sympathetic and told us that really, the boys were being quite good sports about it, weren't they? When Laurie bobbled an easy fly right at second and missed the out, she said to me that Artie had told her that Laurie was really quite a good little ballplayer and I mustn't blame him for an occasional error.

By the time little Jerry Hart finally struck out to retire the Giants, Dot and I were sitting listening with polite smiles. I had stopped saying "Hurray for the Braves." Marian had told everyone sitting near us that it was her boy who had slid home for the sixth run, and she had explained with great kindness that Dot and I had sons on the other team, one of them the first baseman who missed that long throw and the other one the second baseman who dropped the fly ball. The Giants took the field and Marian pointed out Artie standing on first base slapping his glove and showing off.

Then little Ernie Harrow, who was the Braves' right fielder and lunched frequently at our house, hit the first pitched ball for a fast grounder which went right through the legs of the Giant center fielder, and when Ernie came dancing onto second Dot leaned around to remark to Marian that if Artie had been playing closer to first the way Billy did he might have been ready for the throw if the Giant center fielder had managed to stop the ball. Billy came up and smashed a long fly over the left fielder's head and I put a hand on Marian's shoulder to hoist myself up. Dot and I stood there howling, "Run run run," Billy came home, and two runs were in. Little Andy placed a surprise bunt down the first-base line, Artie never even saw it, and I leaned over to tell Marian that clearly Artie did not understand all the refinements of playing first base. Then Laurie got a nice hit and slid into second. The Giants took out their pitcher and put in Buddy Williams, whom Laurie once beat up on the way to school. The score was tied with two out and Dot and I were both yelling. Then little Ernie Harrow came up for the second time and hit a home run, right over the fence where they put the sign advertising his father's sand and gravel. We were leading eight to six when the inning ended.

Little League games are six innnings, so we had five more innings to go. Dot went down to the refreshment stand to get some hot dogs and soda; she offered very politely to bring something for Marian, but Marian said thank you, no; she would get her own. The second inning tightened up considerably as the boys began to get over their stage fright and play baseball the way they did in the vacant lots. By the middle of the fifth inning the Braves were leading nine to eight, and then in the bottom of the fifth Artie missed a throw at first base and the Braves scored another run. Neither Dot nor I said a single word, but Marian got up in a disagreeable manner, excused herself, and went to sit on the other side of the field.

"Marian looks very poorly these days," I remarked to Dot as we watched her go.

"She's at *least* five years older then *I* am," Dot said.

"More than that," I said. "She's gotten very touchy, don't you think?"

"Poor little Artie," Dot said. "You remember when he used to have temper tantrums in nursery school?"

In the top of the sixth the Braves were winning ten to eight, but then Georgie, who had been pitching accurately and well, began to tire, and he walked the first two batters. The third boy hit a little fly which fell in short center field, and one run came in to make it ten to nine. Then Georgie, who was by now visibly rattled, walked the next batter and filled the bases.

"Three more outs and the Braves can win it," some man in the crowd behind us said. "I don't *think*," and he laughed.

"Oh, *lord*," Dot said, and I stood up and began to wail, "No, no." The manager was gesturing at Laurie and Billy. "No, no," I said to Dot, and Dot said, "He can't do it, don't let him." "It's too much to ask of the children," I said. "What a terrible thing to do to such little kids," Dot said.

"New pitcher," the man in the crowd said. "He better be good," and he laughed.

While Laurie was warming up and Billy was getting into his catcher's equipment, I suddenly heard my husband's voice for the first time. This was the only baseball game my husband had ever attended outside of Ebbets field. "Put it in his ear, Laurie," my husband was yelling, "put it in his ear."

Laurie was chewing gum and throwing slowly and carefully. Barry took a minute off from the little truck he was placidly filling with sand and emptying again to ask me if the big boys were still playing baseball. I stood there, feeling Dot's shoulder shaking against mine, and I tried to get my camera open to check the magazine of film but my fingers kept slipping and jumping against the little knob. I said to Dot that I guessed I would just enjoy the game for a while and not take pictures, and she said earnestly that Billy had had a little touch of fever that morning and the manager was taking his life into his hands putting Billy up there in all that catcher's equipment in that hot shade. I wondered if Laurie could see that I was nervous.

"*He* doesn't look very nervous," I said to Dot, but then my voice failed, and I finished, "does he?" in a sort of gasp.

The batter was Jimmie Hill, who had already had three hits that afternoon. Laurie's first pitch hit the dust at Billy's feet and Billy sprawled full length to stop it. The man in the crowd behind us laughed. The boy on third hesitated, unsure whether Billy had the ball; he started for home and then, with his mother just outside the third-base line yelling, "Go back, go back," he retreated to third again.

Laurie's second pitch sent Billy rocking backward and he fell; "Only way he can stop it is fall on it," the man said, and laughed.

Dot stiffened, and then she turned around slowly. For a minute she stared and then she said, in the evilest voice I've ever heard her use, "Sir, that catcher is my son."

"I beg your pardon, ma'am, I'm sure," the man said.

"Picking on little boys," Dot said.

The umpire called Laurie's next pitch ball three, although it was clearly a strike, and I was yelling, "You're blind, you're blind." I could hear my husband shouting to throw the bum out.

"Going to see a new pitcher pretty soon," said the man in the crowd, and I clenched my fist, and turned around and said in a voice that made Dot's sound cordial, "Sir, that pitcher is *my* son. If you have any more personal remarks to make about any member of my family–"

"Or mine," Dot added.

"I will immediately call Mr. Tillotson, our local constable, and see personally that you are put out of this ball park. People who go around attacking ladies and innocent children–"

"Strike," the umpire said.

I turned around once more and shook my fist at the man in the crowd, and he announced quietly and with some humility that he hoped both teams would win, and subsided into absolute silence.

Laurie then pitched two more strikes, his nice fast ball, and I thought suddenly of how at lunch he and Billy had been tossing hamburger rolls and Dot and I had made them stop. At about this point, Dot and I abandoned our spot up on the hill and got down against the fence with our faces pressed against the wire. "Come on, Billy boy," Dot was saying over and over, "come on Billy boy," and I found that I was telling Laurie, "Come on now, only two more outs to go, only two more, come on, Laurie, come on. . . . " I could see my husband now but there was too much noise to hear him; he was pounding his hands against the fence. Dot's husband had *his* hands over his face and his back turned to the ball field. "He can't hit it, Laurie," Dot yelled, "this guy can't hit," which I thought with dismay was not true; the batter was Butch Weaver and he was standing there swinging his bat and sneering. "Laurie, Laurie, Laurie," screeched a small voice; I looked down and it was Sally, bouncing happily beside me. "Can I have another nickel?" she asked. "Laurie, Laurie."

"Strike," the umpire said and I leaned my forehead against the cool wire and said in a voice that suddenly had no power at all, "Just two strikes, Laurie, just two more strikes."

Laurie looked at Billy, shook his head, and looked again. He grinned and when I glanced down at Billy I could see that behind the mask he was grinning too. Laurie pitched, and the batter swung wildly. "Laurie, Laurie," Sally shrieked. "Strike two," the umpire said. Dot and I grabbed at each other's hands and Laurie threw the good fast ball for strike three.

One out to go, and Laurie, Billy, and the shortstop stood together on the mound for a minute. They talked very soberly, but Billy was grinning again as he came back to the plate. Since I was incapable of making any sound, I hung onto the wire and promised myself that if Laurie struck out this last batter I would never never say another word to him about the mess in his room, I would not make him paint the lawn chairs, I would not even mention clipping the hedge. . . . "Ball one," the umpire said, and I found that I had my voice back. "Crook," I yelled, "blind crook."

Laurie pitched, the batter swung, and hit a high foul ball back of the plate; Billy threw off his mask and tottered, staring up. The batter, the boys on the field, and the umpire, waited, and Dot suddenly spoke.

"William," she said imperatively, "*you catch that ball.*"

Then everyone was shouting wildly; I looked at Dot and said, "Golly." Laurie and Billy were slapping and hugging each other, and then the rest of the team came around them and the manager was there. I distinctly saw my husband, who is not a lively man, vault the fence to run into the wild group and slap Laurie on the shoulder with one hand and Billy with the other. The Giants gathered around their manager and gave a cheer for the Braves, and the Braves gathered around *their* manager and gave a cheer for the Giants, and Laurie and Billy came pacing together toward the dugout, past Dot and me. I said, "Laurie?" and Dot said, "Billy?" They stared at us, without recognition for a minute, both of them lost in another world, and then they smiled and Billy said, "Hi, Ma," and Laurie said, "You see the game?"

I realized that my hair was over my eyes and I had broken two fingernails. Dot had a smudge on her nose and had torn a button off her sweater. We helped each other up the hill again and found that Barry was asleep on the car robe. Without speaking any more than was absolutely necessary,

Dot and I decided that we could not stay for the second game of the double-header. I carried Barry asleep and Dot brought his dump truck and the car robe and my camera and the box score which she had not kept past the first Giant run, and we headed wearily for the car.

We passed Artie in his green Giants cap and we said it had been a fine game, he had played wonderfully well, and he laughed and said tolerantly, "Can't win 'em all, you know." When we got back to our house I put Barry into his bed while Dot put on the kettle for a nice cup of tea. We washed our faces and took off our shoes and finally Dot said hesitantly that she certainly hoped that Marian wasn't really offended with us.

"Well, of course she takes this kind of thing terribly hard," I said.

"I was just thinking," Dot said after a minute, "we ought to plan a kind of victory party for the Braves at the end of the season."

"A hot-dog roast, maybe?" I suggested.

"Well," Dot said, "I *did* hear the boys talking one day. They said they were going to take some time this summer and clean out your barn, and set up a record player in there and put in a stock of records and have some dances."

"You mean . . . " I faltered. "With *girls?*"

Dot nodded.

"Oh," I said.

When our husbands came home two hours later we were talking about old high school dances and the time we went out with those boys from Princeton. Our husbands reported that the Red Sox had beaten the Dodgers in the second game and were tied for first place with the Braves. Jannie and Sally came idling home, and finally Laurie and Billy stopped in, briefly, to change their clothes. There was a pickup game down on Murphy's lot, they explained, and they were going to play some baseball.

ELINOR NAUEN

◇

How Hans Became an American

I've been sitting at my desk a lot
staring at my father.
It's a picture taken in summer
a few months before he died.
He's looking at me
with a wry and knowing
—did he know?—
expression. He looks like a man
who needs a private joke
to get a proper snapshot.
He's looking straight at me, even as I sit
in a cold May, a little too tired,
the Yanks getting beat 4–1 in the 5th
by Oakland out on the coast,
a lackluster they'll-never-catch-up game
Rasmussen not getting shellacked
just doesn't have anything
and neither do the hitters.
Gone native in his Arizona retirement
Dad is wearing a bola tie and looks shrunken, frail.
I liked to kiss him on the top of his bony head
in the desert mornings.

He took all of us to a game only once, my first, I was ten,
Charlie was eight, Lindsay was twelve
and the baby was left home.
We drove all the way from South Dakota
up to Minneapolis

to see the Twins play the Yankees
(my team).
Daddy was a refugee from Nazi Germany
and Mom was English.
They were grownups
who'd never seen a game either. They went
because he was the father of Americans
and I was a little baseball fanatic.

Mom sat quietly for about twenty minutes
fanning herself with a straw sunhat and beaming
then asked, when does the game begin?
Look down there, we said.
It was already the second inning
but I still don't think she spotted it.
I think she was waiting for the play by play.
The familiar radio sounds
so different in the ballpark.

Daddy wore plaid shorts over his white skinny legs
and puffed a cigar.
He began to like baseball
when he found someone
who knew less about it than he did.
He explained it all to Mom
mostly according to his own logic—
He had an accountant's sense of symmetry
and the diamond pleased him—
the implication of infinity.
The profusion of numbers and their richness
impressed him . . .
and it was a damn nice summer day.
I think now of those bleachers
old Metropolitan stadium full of stolid Scandinavians
who never corrected him—
that would have spoiled their fun.
Mom would ask: Where's that chap running off to now?
And Dad would explain:
He goes home because he has nowhere else to go . . .

My brother and I spent most of the time under the stands
scrapping with baby Twinkies—

Twins fans who didn't take to our rooting for the enemy.
Charlie thinks he remembers a game-winning
Bobby Richardson grand slam.
I only recall the Yanks winning in the 10th
and the incredibly intense luxury of that lagniappe inning.

Daddy stuck with baseball too.
Like the voting
that made him proudest as a naturalized citizen
he quietly exulted
at being able to talk to his kids
about what they liked to talk about
which was sports. What pleasure
it gave him
to be able to call
   (those Sunday calls!—this is later
   after we'd all left home)
and say, "So, Mattingly's still leading the league"
or "I see where the Yankees aren't doing too well." . . .

But tonight there's an amazing comeback
another 10th-inning heroic to call home about
   ("I see where the Yankees are going great guns")
though it's a few second basemen later
and the serene and splendid Willie Randolph
who pulls it out for the team.

JUDY KATZ-LEVINE

◇

Calling

Falling asleep in the afternoon,
I forget that my father has died.
I anticipate him calling me up,
asking me how my writing is going,
and am I thinking about having children.
Making a joke or two. "Don't worry,
Mom and I will never be lonely."
Then I fall into deeper sleep, he
loses me, traveling in his car, the green
chevrolet, to old baseball fields
which are sweet with rye grass
and lush stadiums, his pals throwing
him the ball—"Give me some pepper, Al."

LINDA KITTELL

◇

What Baseball Tells Us About Love

—for Sherman

1

On the scorecard you gave me, I find
the difficult scratchings, the notes and stats
you ask me to read looking
for something about success
or failure:
Twenty-three times, Lou Gehrig
came to bat for the Yankees
with the bases loaded
and twenty-three times, Lou Gehrig
hit a grand slam.
Then I see you've added: *Shouldn't love*
be that way? Shouldn't love be
a grand slam every time?

2

Lou Gehrig played baseball
for seventeen years and everyone knows
he played in most every game. Everyone knows
he played only for the Yankees.
But up in the stands, maybe—like you—studying a program,
sat his wife, sat Eleanor
who watched Gehrig carefully enough
to see when his step
began to falter, to notice how
ground balls hit
him in the chest and his long-armed swing
barely dribbled out

a single. Eleanor Gehrig watched
the Iron Horse dwindle
to ninety pounds and never stopped to say:
"You're not the man
you used to be," never told him she saw
the end of the game.
I imagine she only held him
closer at night
and went on.

3

Joe DiMaggio reached the Show
two years before Lou Gehrig
left, two years before the Iron Horse began
to fade. And what you and I remember first
about Joe was his once
ridiculous coffee ad, or maybe his once
failed marriage to Marilyn Monroe. Just like
we never saw Gehrig play, we never saw
DiMaggio, every day of your life
and more, send roses to a grave, or imagined
her fingers dialing his number, her voice calling
Joe, Joe into the dead air. *Joe,*
she told him once, *you've never heard
such cheering! Yes, I have,* he said to her quietly.
Yes, I have.

4

My husband Ron was born in 1951 and 1951
was the last year DiMaggio played. By seventeen,
Ron was the best player in Idaho, the fastest
in the outfield, most solid at first base, and sometimes
wild but always hard
when he took the mound. But our life, it seems,
has turned far from glamorous. We take
our turns, Ron and I, in the stands. I watch him
with you, throwing rocks across a brook and know
the next day his arm
will throb from trying. He watches me
try to toss a good metaphor, one that will zing
and flash at your center. I say:
look deeper into the game, friend. I say:

look deeper into a life, a love.
To make anything last, there's got to be more
than a grand slam.
There has to be a good coach
to draw the line-up and good men
already on base. There have to be players
in the minors and wives
in the stands. There has to be someone
to say that love
ain't always perfect, that love
doesn't always win the game, that love
might not be lots of cheering or a neatly blackened square
on a scorecard.
No, Sherman, love
might be quiet—a fire crackling, birds reappearing
on the edge of lawn, the center of you knowing
that once you slip it on and oil it up,
that old worn glove will feel
even better
than when it was new.

MABEL HITE

◇

On Just Being a Fan

I used to think that the baseball men had the queerest jargon in the world. I still think so.

Once I remember, after I had met Mr. Donlin, and after I had come to take some interest in the sporting extras, I was skipping through an inning play when I came across a sentence that almost made my heart stand still. The sentence read: "Donlin got tired of life and suicided at the plate." It flashed through my mind that he had failed to hit the ball and then in a fit of disgust had killed himself. After I convinced myself that it was not so bad as that, I looked further down in the column and found where he had come smilingly up again. Really, a person who has a particular friend playing the game ought not read the sporting page, as he will find where the friend died at second, or had his head chopped off by the pitcher, or had any number of heartless things done to him.

There is nothing I delight in more than sitting in the grandstand and playing the game with my husband. It is almost as exciting as being out on the diamond; for the most part I believe I get more stirred up in the grandstand than Mr. Donlin does on the diamond. Sometimes I get happy enough to dance while at a game, and sometimes at the remarks the men around me make, I want to rise right up and say something mean. Just the other day in one inning I heard Mr. Donlin called a "pill" and an "angel." It is truly wonderful how a player can run the gamut of creation, from a chimpanzee to a seraphim, all in one game; if he hits a three-bagger he has a seat among the heavenly elect while if he misses he is on easy terms with Milton's hosts.

Of all the misunderstood, unfortunate people in the world, the umpire has the biggest place in my pity. I would not be an umpire at any salary. I dislike any scene over the decision of the umpire. I believe that there ought to be a rule against a player making any stand against the umpire, under penalty of removal from the game. If the captain can kick, why not the manager, or the president of the club! I often wonder why Kipling doesn't write a poem vindicating the lowly umpire.

Some people think that all there is to the game is for one man to throw the ball, another to hit and a third to catch it. But the more I come to know about the game, the less I find I know. It is the greatest of the sciences. I might almost say that a baseball player is born, not made. But after one is born, he has to go through an endless amount of tiring humdrum. Behind every good player is about 18 years of hard practice. A player must go to the field every day of the season, rain or storm, heat or cold. There is no getting around it.

This present season has been the greatest one that baseball has ever known. But a year from now this cannot be said. For each year the game will continue to grow, to become fairer and more interesting.

JEAN HASTINGS ARDELL

◇

A Miracle Year

[Isabel's] father marked her new-born enthusiasm
for the national game with approval. He felt himself
drawn closer to her. An understanding, as pleasant
as it was new and strange, began to spring up between parent and child. . . . Side by side they
would sit at the Polo Grounds.
> P. G. Wodehouse
> "The Pitcher and the Plutocrat"
> *Collier's*
> 1910

Last season's furor over the San Francisco Giants' proposed move to Tampa
Bay affected me. The news hit harder than you'd expect for someone who
has never set foot inside Candlestick Park. But then, the Giants and I go
back a long way.

My father loved the New York Giants. My mother had no interest in the
game; I was an only child. By default, I became my father's baseball companion at Sunday afternoon doubleheaders. Racketing alongside him on the
subway bound for the Polo Grounds—those sublime days when there still
was a Polo Grounds, still a Giants team in New York City—is one of my
earliest memories.

My father took his baseball seriously. He showed me how to keep score
and how to follow the rhythm of the game. Through our trips to the Polo
Grounds, I also came to know my father. At the ball park, he liked to reminisce about the Giants' glory days under John McGraw during the early
1920s. With persistence, I could usually elicit a story about his adventures
as a young man-about-Manhattan.

"Tell me again about the McGraw times," I'd plead, and he would. It was
different at home. My father was a quiet man from the Midwest and did
not much care for small talk. But baseball transformed him. During a game,

he relaxed and joked easily. At the Polo Grounds my father became emotional.

Once this even happened in our living room. The Giants had made a stunning comeback to tie the Dodgers for the 1951 pennant. On the last day of the season, as the galvanic news of Bobby Thomson's home run crackled over our radio, my father leapt from his easy chair, fully alive with excitement. The Giants had stolen the pennant from the hated Dodgers in the bottom of the ninth. It didn't matter that the Yankees won the subsequent World Series for the third straight year—Red Smith's morning-after column in the *New York Herald-Tribune* immortalized that season as "The Miracle of Coogan's Bluff." Ever after, for my father, 1951 would always be "the miracle year." Those were the good times.

By 1957, things had changed. My father had lost his job. Mostly, he chain-smoked and read the papers. I watched the lines in his face deepen. I knew from overhearing my parents' arguments that the current crisis was the latest in his history of failed business ventures. Money was a problem. (Many years passed before my mother found a way to explain the truth of that time. "Your father suffered from Pete Rose disease," she told me. "He loved to gamble.")

I was changing, too. Two years earlier, my parents had insisted that I attend an academically competitive girls' school in Manhattan. At age fourteen, I began to rebel. I spent that spring cutting classes to see (and see again) the new Elvis Presley movie. Instead of going home after school, I'd ride the subway with my girlfriends. We traveled into the Bronx and far out into Brooklyn, where we practiced looking tough.

I had also become indifferent toward baseball. Even Don Larsen's perfect game in the 1956 World Series only briefly revived my interest. Apart from baseball, it seemed my father and I could find little to say to one another. Our conversations usually went like this:

"How was school?"

"Fine."

"Where are you going?"

"Out."

When the Brooklyn Dodgers announced their move to Los Angeles, I barely flinched. That team had no hold on us. My father had always refused to take me to see the Dodgers play. "Ebbets Field is too rowdy," was all he'd say on the matter. But one day in August, my father slammed down his *Herald-Tribune* and said, "Well, it's true. The Giants are leaving, too." Then he went for a walk. I tended to cry easily that summer and I cried then. I suspect that my father wept, too. I do remember that the thought of my father walking the streets, in tears, frightened me.

The following season, the city seemed a colder place to me. New York's crosstown baseball rivalries had given the city a sense of intimacy. Now that was gone. Whatever intimacy our family had enjoyed was also eroding. To my parents' disappointment, I had transferred to the local high school the previous September. Our arguments about my low grades continued; I had a boyfriend and was seldom home. Shortly after the season opened in April, my father and I went up to Yankee Stadium. I wore a thin turquoise corduroy jacket and shivered in the wind. Somehow, it just wasn't the same as those golden summer afternoons at the Polo Grounds. That was our last ball game together.

Five years after the Giants left New York, my father died suddenly. By then, I had dropped out of college and moved across the country. I had a husband and a new baby. I had a new life.

But baseball wasn't through with me. As my sons grew up, they began to play the game. I remember twilight box suppers in the community bleachers and my van filled with boys who smelled like damp puppies after the games. Together, we traveled the freeways to Anaheim Stadium and Dodger Stadium. On vacations, we visited old Comiskey Park and Shea Stadium. We visited Cooperstown's Hall of Fame, where the dusty history of John McGraw's New York Giants can still be found. I told them the stories of my childhood trips to the Polo Grounds.

◇ ◇ ◇

Divorce damages your faith in happy endings. Two divorces can wreck it. When it happened to me, I retreated. For the first time since the age of fourteen, there was no man in my life. I planned to keep it that way. Then friends intervened and introduced me to a former Angel. A California Angel. He hadn't played ball in fifteen years but oh! he had stories to tell. I listened. I took one more chance. We courted at Anaheim Stadium and at our children's Little League games. We married during a break in Summer League.

I would like to report that baseball has redeemed my life, and my family, but this is not entirely true. It's only a game; you win, you lose. Yet I find enough hope within those nine innings to say this: This game is one of the threads that has held my life together. It connects my husband and sons with my father, whom they never met. Some of my happiest memories involve baseball. These links are slightly magical: For example, why is it that I began a book about baseball in the very year the Giants announced they were moving again? I find it odd, too, that twice in my life, I arrived on the same coast as "McGraw's boys." Does this forecast a move to Florida if the Giants change their mind? After twelve years of marriage, I am still amazed to awaken next to a man whose continuing nightmare is one of racing for first base and never quite getting there. This I know: The patterns of our green diamonds work their ways into our lives in marvelous ways. It takes a lifetime to fathom them.

◇   ◇   ◇

The Giants' desire to leave San Francisco last autumn triggered these reflections. Now I understand what happened in 1957 – that confused summer of change – when the Giants announced they were leaving New York. It was a case of rotten timing for my father and me. We lost an essential connection which time and events prevented us from reclaiming. I don't think I'll ever recover from that loss, not really.

Now the Giants have agreed to remain in San Francisco – and I keep wondering. I bet there are plenty of Bay Area fathers and daughters who recall trips to Candlestick Park but who don't talk together much any more. As in 1957, many dads are out of work and short on money. Fourteen-year-old girls are still prone to rebellion. So I'm glad the Giants are staying. I hope those fathers and daughters go out to one more ball game, then another and another – until their talk comes easily again. I hope they learn that such connections are as resilient as – well, the national pastime. I'm hoping for another miracle year.

ROBERTA ISRAELOFF

◇

City Ball

*M*oony, *who's named* for all the obvious reasons—his belly's roughly spherical, as if he'd once swallowed a barrel of baseballs—usually sits right there, in his vinyl recliner to the left of the TV, hands clasped behind his head. Each year, as he shrinks a fraction of an inch, his feet rise slightly off the floor, but it's like the continental drift—you can't see it. He calls everyone on my favorite team a bum and advises managers against any pitching change whatsoever at any time. And this Saturday, which should be no different than any other and hasn't been up to this very minute—in the car we had the same conversations; around exit three of the Cross Bronx Expressway, Webster Avenue, my mother said, That's where Neila Thorpman used to live, and two exits later, as we swung off the highway onto the Grand Concourse she said, I won't even park, we'll just stay a minute, and I said, We'll park, and she does, but first she lets me off and I run upstairs (the door is always open) and into the living room, and there's Moony sitting in his chair—is suddenly special, Moony isn't there.

"What do you mean, not here?" I asked my grandmother, Cassie, who sits with her knees spread as wide apart as the Lincoln Memorial, her skirt and apron making a lap the size of many tables. In it rest her crocheting, two handkerchiefs, three hair combs, an apple, a nougat candy and her change purse. "Where is he?" Where could he possibly be? I tried to remember if I'd seen him walk anywhere recently, especially on a weekend. We used to go out to dinner once a month to City Island, but around the second course he'd say he had to go to the toilet and end up in the kitchen catching the game with the waiters, his food getting cold and Cassie getting mad.

Cassie indicated the window, which looks out over the Armory. I crossed the jungle, her tangle of plants with dust-free leaves, and peered out. There he was, I saw him, Moony and "the kid from downstairs," the Russian kid, the dark-haired, serious Ivan who's three years older than me and wears old clothes. He and Moony were looking toward Kingsbridge Road. Moony had his arm on the boy's shoulder. I knew what he was saying, too: Signals. Signals are the heart of baseball. No one else knows that, except for me and every major league manager, that's all. And then Moony told him some signals. Lick your middle finger and touch the side of your nose, hitch up your pants. And if you don't believe him he'll ask you what you think the manager is doing standing there on the dugout steps anyway? Why do you think he takes long drinks of water and spits three, clean times? It's all signals. Baseball is a game in code, a game of signs between manager, coach, catcher, pitcher, batter. It's not a lonely game. Unwritten letters, entire encyclopedias of baseball knowledge flutter across the field every minute.

That's not how Moony would say it, that was me. Some fans are more poetic than others.

"I can't believe it," I said, and I couldn't.

"Did you ever ask Moony to teach you to play?" Cassie asked. She was looking into thin air, not at me or the television or what she was doing. If she stopped patrolling for as much as a second, who knew what could happen? A particle of dust could fall, a leaf could drop, a smell could come out of nowhere and embarrass her. No, she was always working.

I had never asked him, but that wasn't the point. I never cared about the physical aspect of the game. Not that I wasn't athletic. I made sure I learned how to throw like a boy when I was young, before any of the boys on my block learned. But baseball's subtler side is what hooked me, and for all the years I can remember sprawled on the floor next to the vinyl recliner, listening to Moony digest baseball, I had been hounding him to take me to a game at Yankee Stadium. Cassie and my mother would tell me to lay off, that he was tired, old, fat, too newly into retirement to want to stir. Leave him alone, give him a break, they said. And now he's downstairs with a strange kid.

"I thought we had nothing to do with those Russians," I said. Only last week we were treated to a half hour's harangue on how only poor people cook smelly like the Russians do—this from a woman who doesn't like to use salt—how the husband works two shifts, how their windows face the street, with no shades, how the children are hooligans, murder incorporated, big trouble.

"The girl is wild. His sister, Lana. But the boy is very nice. He comes to visit us some afternoons."

"Oh really." I felt like crying but didn't. It seemed ridiculous to be jealous of my grandfather. When I looked again, I saw Lana, the wild sister, ride her bike toward the field. She jerked the handlebars so it bucked the curb, then gave it a last pedal and levitated off it, abandoned it in midair. The bike, a rusty, clanging racer, ran for a few seconds without her, upright, before crashing into a tree. She ran to the pathetic pile of baseball equipment her brother managed to collect over the months – a broom stick, two tennis balls, two of their father's gloves stuffed one inside the other, fingers sewn together. Then they huddled, all three of them, a conference on the mound. She turned and took 45 paces, turned and threw a pitch. Too high. Not so high, I heard Moony saying. She tried again. Too low. Moony tossed the ball back to her. His arm looked like a tree branch. She scooped the ball out of the dirt. Tried again. This time it came in waist level. Ivan, who'd been waiting with the stick, made a sudden, spastic movement at the last possible second. He twisted his body, his toes came through his sneakers and his shoulder blades sliced through his tee shirt. He smashed the ball, busted its seams, so that as it sailed over the Armory tower it looked like an exploded bird.

Moony wouldn't be saying anything now. He doesn't believe in undue praise.

That's when my mother came up, puffing faintly; she needed to lose some weight. "Where's Moony?" she asked too, first thing.

Cassie indicated the window. "And what's with you," my mother asked, as I moved out of the jungle, steaming, so she could move in and catch a glimpse of her father acting a quarter of his age. I walked to the vinyl chair, looked at it, studied the huge indentation made by Moony, and fell into it. No one expected this. I put my hands behind my head, and moved the seat back so my feet were slightly off the floor. It was the third inning. It always was when we got here. During the commercials I turned to my mother and said, "How's business?"

"Don't be fresh," said Cassie. My mother didn't know whether to laugh or cry. Sometimes she blamed the breakup of her marriage on this one question, asked every week of a surgeon, her husband, who never understood why he should have to apologize to his wife's parents for not having the kind of business Moony meant when he asked, every Saturday at this time, How's business? Business, to Moony, meant sitting on a crate on 8th Avenue and 18th Street, watching lumber supply trucks jockey into driveways, watching Lillie's hands grow arthritic as she works the cash register, watching plumbing hardware go up and down the open elevator, watching couriers with mob connections, watching the cops. The kind of business that gets into the folds of the skin of your hands and under your fingernails. The kind you have to change clothes for. Well, my father used to change clothes too, but into cleaner ones than he stepped out of.

Now it's the bottom of the third, that all important inning, says Moony, when the wild pitcher settles down, when the tired pitcher falters. Moony claims you can predict which games will be no hitters in the third. He did just that with Larsen's game, 1956. So he says.

"You shouldn't make fun of your grandfather," said Cassie, out of nowhere.

"How come you're nicer to Moony when he's not here than when he is?" I asked.

"Someday you'll understand." She sat up suddenly, as if she said something impossibly funny, and reached for her daughter's hand. Cassie's always making jokes no one else gets. Mom, meanwhile, dug around in her pockets for the surprise of the afternoon—these big orange, plastic ears she got at the five and ten which have earplugs inside. When she put them on she looked like something from outer space. "What's the idea?" asked Cassie.

"I can't stand the baseball announcers, Mother," she said. "You know that."

"So turn off the sound, I don't care."

"Don't touch it," I roared, just like Moony, and they turned around to stare at me. I could imitate him to a tee. When Cassie asked if I wanted fruit, I brushed her away with the back of my hand. When she asked How's school, I said "Oke." No one should get in the habit of talking when the baseball game's on.

Only then we heard crazy footsteps out in the hall and a wild knocking, then a slower, heavier step that had to be Moony. Lana burst in—that girl always looked as if centrifugal force tore her apart each night and she had to shake herself down like a cat to get her limbs on straight—yelling, "I didn't mean it. Please. We were practicing curves."

Moony stumbled in next, a purple bruise over his right eye. Ivan was right behind him, as if the boy would have been of any use had Moony fallen backward. Cassie got up in a flutter but remembered to hold her apron out so that her things wouldn't fall. She looked like those statues in rich people's fountains, and she started making those noises which mean I'm not as concerned as I sound.

"Out of my way, Lady," he said. "I'm fine, just fine. Got brushed back, that's all." He sank into his chair which I'd kept warm for him. The cushions gave their familiar whistle at this weight, and the wood creaked too. "I'm fine," he said again. "What's the matter with you? See a crowd?"

Lana ran out, but Ivan stayed, trying to explain exactly what happened. He had his mitt with him. Cassie didn't waste a moment. "You had no business playing ball at all," she scolded her husband. "No business at all."

He gave her the brush. "What's the score here, Donna?"

So that's what I was good for. The score. "Fourth, Top. Two out."

"Yeah? Who's up? Who's ahead?"

"Kaline." Couldn't he tell? I thought that was the point—study the shadows on the field, the way the umpire makes his calls, who's hanging around near the water fountain in the dugout, who's on deck—that's your job, as a fan. Wasn't that what he'd been training me to do? Wasn't that why he never answered me, completely?

"Yanks ahead by one. Three and two on Kaline."

"Thank you," he said. "What's eating her?"

"Think about it," I said. "You'll figure it out."

"I'm calling the doctor, Moony? You hear me?" That was Cassie, who else.

He ignored her. She put down the receiver without dialing, and noticed Ivan standing in the foyer, near the cedar chest, which houses Moony's woolen navy jerseys. The boy was still apologizing. In a moment Cassie would ask him if he needed any nice, warm clothing. Then she'd remove all eight objects from the top of the chest, including the dust cover, explaining how she made it herself with fabric from Russia, how lovely it is to have a cedar chest, ask if his mother has one. Then she'd shake out a jersey, make Ivan slip it on, and cluck sorrowfully when it's way too big, too moth-ball smelly.

When that was over, she brought out a folding chair from the bedroom for Ivan to sit on. "Would anyone like some nice fruit?" she asked.

"Quiet, please," Moony said. "The bum is up."

"Lovely language," Cassie sang. She muttered something in Yiddish and got up to get the apples no one wanted, the same ones she brought out last week. I leaned over and said to Moony, "Do you understand her when she speaks Yiddish?" He brushed me away with the back of his hand—no.

"He's lying," Cassie shouted. Her voice was scratchy when she yelled, but she had the best pair of seventy-five-year-old ears I'd ever seen.

"Now here's an interesting situation," Moony said. I wasn't sure if he was talking to me or Ivan, We both moved closer, dutifully. "Two men aboard, one and two, one out. Good bunter up. Would you have him sacrifice? Or take?"

"Swing away," said Ivan.

"Sharp kid," said Moony.

"Let him take," said Cassie. The man swings and misses. Moony shrugs.

Now there's a conference on the mound. The one question I always wanted to ask Moony was this: what do they really say during these meetings. I didn't think anyone bothered to mention the pitcher's stuff. Whether the pitcher has his stuff is obvious, anyone can see that, even my mother could. No, I thought they call these conferences because first of all the manager wants to take a stroll, he's getting chilly, and the catcher needs to get up, stretch, flip that mask up over his head, you can go crazy looking through bars all day. And the pitcher wants attention. He's been out there struggling all alone. So the other guys come on out and they have a little conversation that goes like this. How's the wife, kids? Fine, fine, couldn't be better. They here today? Nah, kids had a dentist appointment. Too bad. Yeah. Hey, you about ready for that cold beer? You bet! Then the pitcher steps back, rubs his eyes with his fists like a baby, and spits.

"Do that again," Mom said. "I love it when they spit."

"No, not me, I don't like that part," said Cassie. "I like when they give each other love pats on their behinds."

"Lady, we're trying to watch a baseball game here," Moony said.

I had plenty of questions. Like suppose this next guy strikes out. Will the other players talk to him in the clubhouse? Say you go four for four, five RBIs, but your team loses. Are you allowed to be happy later, in the clubhouse? If your team is behind, bases loaded, two out in the bottom of the ninth and you're on deck, do you pray that the guy ahead of you will end it, any way he can, just so you won't have to deal with the pressure? That's how I'd be. That's why you're not a ballplayer, Moony would say. But those are the kinds of questions I'd like to ask, if I weren't in the habit of only asking those questions I already know the answers to.

"You know, Ivan," Cassie said, crocheting again, "my family originally came from a town near Odessa. That's where you're from?"

"Yep," he said. "It is."

"I used to remember a lot about the village," she went on. "When I was a young girl and couldn't sleep, my grandmother knew it was because I had a big memory. And when my parents decided that we'd go to America, the elders of the village walked me around for days. They'd point to things, and I'd remember them. We walked everywhere, they'd point and say, 'That. And that.' And I put everything into my head, each in its own compartment, until I had to cry, 'Enough! I can't fit any more in.'"

Moony got up, reached the set in a single stride, leaned over like a see-saw, and raised the volume.

"You don't need the sound," Cassie said, "you know all the answers. Anyway my mother and I left soon after that, on a boat for America. It was for twenty days. And I had to keep my head tilted so, because I didn't want anything to slip out. I was afraid to yawn, or sneeze, afraid that something would fly out, like where was Mitya's chicken coop, or the color of the school. I kept my eyes closed until America, when we settled in with cousins on the Lower East Side. And then, no paper, no pencil, no peace and quiet."

She stopped. From my mother's expression I knew she had never heard this story before either. Mickey Mantle was at bat. He had a full count, three and two. No one would ask Cassie what happened next so I did.

"I stole a paper bag from the butcher," she said, "and I found a pencil in the gutter and I sharpened it with my teeth. I tore the bag in half and wrote in the tiniest script you can imagine. I wrote for days, two days and two nights straight, in the little corner next to the kitchen."

Mickey Mantle struck out. Roger Maris was at bat. He was the cleanup hitter. Once I thought the term cleanup referred only to Mick. He was the cleanest looking player I'd ever seen. It looked as if he scrubbed his hair with scouring brushes. His Oklahoman blondness was as exotic as anything from Odessa.

"You wrote it all down?" asked Ivan. "You wrote about your entire village?"

"Yes, I did, and then I had no place to put the pages for safekeeping, so I rolled them into a tube and wrapped my hair around them and fastened them with a hair clip. And when I finished, the second night, I went for a walk to the East River, alone, and that's where I first met Moony."

Moony was squirming in his chair. Maris hit a home run and the Yankees went ahead by five. Moony said, "I told you he'd hit one out of here."

But no one was listening to him. "I walked along the river," Cassie said, "feeling as if a fever had lifted. And there, on a field under a streetlight, a field littered with glass, I saw some boys playing a game that reminded me of a game we played at home, called brennball."

"Brennball, I play that game," Ivan said. He was tremendously excited. "I was brennball champion in my town."

"Only this wasn't brennball," Cassie said, "it was American baseball. And I watched a skinny, red-haired man in the field, who used an old leather glove and scrambled to his left, his right. I watched them play the whole night. When it got light and the streetlights went off, the others left. The red head walked toward his bicycle; that's where I was standing. He gave me a ride home on the handlebars."

"Shortstop?" I asked. "You played shortstop?"

"I don't know what she's talking about," Moony said. His hands were gripping the arm rests of the recliner.

"What happened next," Cassie said, "is that I took very sick, very ill, and my mother blamed it on my being out all night. But it wasn't. It was from going into that trance to write out everything that I remembered. She took me to the doctor, who didn't believe me, and they pulled my hair out and all my teeth out, that's what they did in those days, and I came home crying that no one would want to marry me, ever. But Moony did. We called him Moony, then, you know, because his eyes had a far away look, like he was looking for the moon."

"Are you finished?" Moony asked. His eyes didn't look far away now, they looked close, tiny, narrow. He started to get up. He'd never left a game before it was all over. Usually he kept the set on till the game was long over, past the presentation of the Schick player of the day and the Old Spice player of the week, he outlasted all the announcers, the scoreboard, the wrap-up, the theme song—Moony had an affair with televised baseball, usually. He never even got up to go to the bathroom. But now he was on his feet.

"Where're you going, Dad?" My mother sounded concerned. She kept her eyes on him as Cassie started talking again.

"You know how funny it is to think about when we were young. He used to be skinny then. Skinnier than me. Until he got sick and had to stop smoking. That's when he put on all the weight. You know this story, don't you? Oh god, he was so skinny and his hands were always so dirty I never wanted him to come near me. I was afraid I'd hurt him, you see, and I wanted his hands to be clean. Not for years after we were married could I stand him touching me. It sounds funny to say but it's true."

"You talk too much, lady," Moony said, reappearing with his hat, his jacket.

"Where are you going, Moony?" she cried, "Moony, wait."

He slammed the door shut. "I'm his biggest fan," Cassie said.

"Go after him," my mother said. "Go, follow him."

"He doesn't want me," I said.

"Go," said Cassie, standing up. This time everything rolled out of her lap onto the floor. "Go, of course he wants you. What are you waiting for, a silver invitation with your name engraved? He doesn't want anyone else to go after him but you. Go."

So I went. I ran after him. I wouldn't have been surprised if Cassie had engineered the whole afternoon so that she could throw me and Moony together like this. She knew that was what I wanted more than anything.

I was a good half a block behind him, walking toward the bus stop, but he walked slowly and we got on the same bus. I ended up sitting behind him. We didn't acknowledge each other. I wasn't sure where we were going but I had a good idea. We rode under the el tracks. And after about ten minutes I saw it, the beige and blue towers of Yankee Stadium, the giant heart, arising out of nowhere like a modern day castle.

Moony took a few minutes to get his bearings once we were on the street. Then he took off for the ticket windows, all closed now. In fact, people were leaving. I'd lost track of the game, forgot who was winning, couldn't calculate the inning. We kept walking and walking, nearly all around the stadium, until we came to a door marked No Admittance. There Moony stopped and knocked. A man in a cap, with a big stomach, same vintage as Moony, answered, saw Moony, hugged him. They spoke for a few moments, laughed—the man opened the door for Moony and

Moony called me. "This is where the players' wives go in," Moony said. "Jake's an old friend of mine."

We walked through a narrow concrete corridor. We passed arrows pointing to the clubhouse, one to the tunnel. "That's it," Moony said. "Want to go?" It was the tunnel I'd always wanted to explore, the one through which pitchers walked from dugout to bullpen and back. It was the best place to get autographs.

"Nope," I said. "I'll go with you." He kept walking in what seemed like circles, but then just ahead I saw some light, and heard noise, and smelled an acrid smell. We passed venders counting their money, and I turned around to watch them, they winked at me—now there's a job I hadn't thought of; why not, maybe next summer—and when I turned around to find Moony, we were already out there, under a ledge, out, near the field. The baseball diamond, the players, the bloody dirt basepaths, the grass, everything scrubbed and shorn and raked as clean and perfect as Mickey Mantle's crewcut. Everything trim as pinstripes, oh it was so lovely. I got dizzy, walked into Moony, who had stopped to get his bearings again. Seats and tiers rose everywhere, people were standing, it must have been the middle of a rally. I heard the crowd roar, and didn't know if I was screaming too, or not.

"I used to like the third base side," Moony said. "That OK with you?"

It sure was. We walked toward left field, along the aisle just above the reserved box seats. We walked until we were at the foul pole, to a pretty deserted section. Moony picked out two seats from which we could see right into the Yankee dugout. Couldn't be better. I had a perfect view of that water cooler.

Next surprise—when the vender came by Moony ordered two beers. "Don't tell your grandmother," he said. "Go ahead, drink up." I took a sip. Moony just sat there, holding his, as if he wanted simply to feel the heft of the brew, the spongy wet plastic.

"How'd you get us in here?"

"I used to know all those guys. We came here nearly every afternoon, after work, in the summer. With Mike Acre and Johnny Sparrow. This is between you and me, you understand."

I nodded. "It's so quiet here." I couldn't put my finger on what was missing.

"The Voice of the Yankees, that's what's missing," he said. "No one announces here. You have to keep your own score."

"What inning is it? What's going on?"

"I don't know," Moony said. "It never matters as much, once you get here. That's the beauty of the thing."

"Well the Yankees are behind by three," said the man sitting in front of us. "Where have you birds been?" Moony and he, Conklin, chewed over the game—Moony was interested after all, I knew it—and I sat back in my seat, looking around. Mickey Mantle's in center field. If I yelled to him he would probably hear me. His neck and thighs were really tremendous, just like they said. But for some reason, everything looked distant, almost more distant than things did on TV. I mean, there I was, in concrete stands, full of city filth and grime—beer and mustard, the seats were sticky, my feet were sticky. And there on the field, on the grass and the most manicured dirt I'd ever seen, stood men dressed like boys, in clean uniforms which were probably dry cleaned in between innings, who never spoke to each other, or heard us. They were in the country and we were in the city, and what a country game it was. And in that country you talk to each other by spitting, by patting each other's tails, by taking long drinks from the water cooler, kicking it sometimes, by taking skinny spits, where you always say less than you mean and count on your body to say the rest.

"What's the matter?" Moony asked. "Aren't you having fun? Didn't you hear, this guy Conklin's son is up there, hitting. He was just called up from the farm team yesterday. This here's an exciting game."

The kid looked mighty nervous to me, up there at home plate. Even with his coaches and manager signalling to him, he looked alone and sweaty.

"Don't hit it to Mick," Conklin yelled.

"He's a bum," Moony said.

The kid ran the count to three and two. The runners, on first and second, would be going with the pitch. The kid took a deep breath, you could hear it throughout the stadium, and leaned into the pitch. It took off, rising steadily for enough seconds to lose track of how many. And he broke into a run. If the ball stayed fair he'd have a homer. If it went foul, he'd have another crack. The ball hung in the air for impossible seconds, and then took a turn in our direction. It's coming, I started to say, but never finished. Conklin's eyes widened. Moony stayed in his seat, and the ball came toward us, a gorgeous curve, and landed right in Moony's stomach. Right against his beer, which exploded like a bomb. Moony started gasping, I couldn't tell if he was choking or laughing. He turned blue, the wind knocked out of him, and I was afraid that he would die. On camera. We were on camera, they always turn the cameras to the guy who gets the ball. "Hey," I started yelling, "Hey there, hi." And I waved. And I pointed to Moony, and said, "He's all right," to Cassie and my mother, who I knew were watching. And soon Moony stopped choking, but he didn't stop smiling, and he clutched the ball to his stomach as if it was a baby.

Still, it was a foul ball, and the rookie went on to strike out and the Yankees couldn't get a thing across in the bottom of the ninth and lost. It didn't much matter, they'd already clinched the pennant. One of the things you have to get used to as a Yankee fan is that most of the normal excitement is gone from the game by about July. And here it was August, but I didn't mind. It was the best afternoon I could remember having.

When the game was over, we all stood up and shook hands with the kid's uncle, who stood around, expecting Moony to give him the ball, I think. But Moony was holding on to it, moving it from one hand to the other, clasping his hands around the seams and releasing them, rubbing it up as if he were going to throw a spitter. Finally, Conklin left, to see if he could get into the dugout. "Go with him, if you want," Moony said, "I'll wait for you right here." But I didn't want to go underground. I wanted to stand where I was and watch the stadium empty like a giant drain. I wanted to think about how it would be when we went home and Moony gave me the ball.

Maybe he would give it to Ivan. What then? I would be too jealous to speak. But Moony wouldn't do that. He was saving it for me. He was biding his time. Like at home, when we waited for the game to be completely, totally over. We watched the batboy, the last one in the dugout, disappear down the tube to the clubhouse. We watched the grounds crew pull the tarp over the bases, and the shadows grow longer in the outfield.

One of Moony's friends, in a cap, came and told us to move on. We started slowly down the ramp, up the aisle, back through the cavern to the street. We had a long, silent wait for the bus. People all around us were full of tips on how the Yankees could have won. Moony never liked to second guess. His only advice: don't change pitchers. It's a man's game to win or lose.

But something happened to Moony on the bus, he got a seat in the back, near the window, and started talking. "There was one night I came here, after work, a Thursday in 1954, 55. Me and Johnny and Mike, we had the bleachers to ourselves. It was late in the game. Maybe it was 56. Anyway DiMaggio was up. He hit a long ball, I mean a long ball, dead away center field, practically right to me. Watch out, they yelled, those guys, what a bunch of clowns, and they hid under their seats. Me, I wasn't afraid of the ball. As I watched it sailing to me, I thought that everything is about right, just as it is, now. I had a job, my family, a roof over my head, it was a late summer evening, I had half a pack of smokes left, and enough money for a beer and the bus home. I thought, That ball is gonna sail on outta here and we'll never have to worry again.

"The ball was caught," he said, "up against the center field wall. And for some dopey reason, nothing was the same after that."

"Really?" We were walking home now, from the bus stop. I could see the light on in Cassie's living room. I had just learned about his bad illness, that he had lost fifty pounds, then put on three times as much, that he had lost his own parents within a year—I knew events, I wondered if these were what he meant. I realized how little I knew him, how insignificantly I figured in his life, how I hadn't put in an appearance until he was two thirds of the way out. Suddenly he looked like a dinosaur trudging up the Kingsbridge hill. He was still holding the baseball.

"You should give that ball to Ivan," I said.

"No, I don't think so," Moony said. And then I knew he'd be giving it to me. We climbed the stairs, I went as slowly as he did, and Cassie and my mother met us at the door, telling us how they saw us, how great we looked.

Moony brushed them away, sank into the recliner. It whistled and moaned to welcome him home. He put the ball in his lap. Then he put it in a drawer of the table next to his chair. And I never saw him take it out.

JUDY GOLDMAN

◇

Endless Odds

And when the mother entered, as if in a dream,
a glass quaked in the silent china closet.
                              —Rainer Maria Rilke

The nature of parental love is what I'm after,
how it's bestowed, rationed, withheld. The father
calls out to his son on the mound,
just as the boy's leg is drawn up to his chest
and he begins the slow unwinding
which is a dangerous act of faith, the father calling,
calling his son's name as if each syllable will carry
the ball where he wants it to go. The umpire
holds up four fingers, letting the father know
his son has walked another batter.

The fifty-year-old daughter who finds
in her mother's handbag a diary the mother kept
before she died. Page after page, details
of fights, the daughter's fault,
doors slamming, people taking off
in the middle of the night. She reads in silence,
her mother's voice now engraved.

◇   ◇   ◇

Remember how Pinocchio was supposed to harden
into an obedient puppet?

Geppetto *said* he wanted a real boy
but what he really wanted
was someone made in his own image,
the paint barely dry
before wood turned to flesh
and the nose began to grow to a length
Geppetto could not measure.

When a baby is born, the small face is full
of possibilities. How clear it is
the parents' luck will turn,
they wish this part would last forever.
But the child will grow
as if he were driven by a restlessness.
His face, at first stolen from the father
or the mother, will eventually hold no trace
of either, the child dreaming himself
into a stranger. Years later
none of them will be able to recall
the instant of breaking.

◊   ◊   ◊

Everyone knows Rilke's mother wanted a girl,
how she gave him seven or eight middle names,
including Maria. When he was young
he'd stand alone in the hall
and knock on the living room door.
"Who is it . . . is it Rainer?" his mother would tease
from inside.
"No, that naughty Rainer is dead."
"Is it Margaret?"
"Yes."
"Well, then you can come in."
Rilke would enter the room, wearing a dress,
taffeta perhaps, or dark velvet
and he and his mother would have tea.
The years passed. Rilke fathered a daughter
whose wedding, you remember, he did not attend
for fear of losing his concentration.

◊   ◊   ◊

The part about the parents' luck turning
is straight from my own mother
who always said when a first child is born
it's good luck for the parents, the way, I suppose,
a lottery ticket is purchased and suddenly
there are endless odds. But at no time after that
are they so clear, so sure. Certainties
slowly sink back into the place
from which they came and we learn
they're merely promises to believe in
until they dissolve on the tongue like parental love.

Note: The information about Pinocchio is from *Parables and Portraits* by Stephen
Mitchell, and the information about Rilke is from *Selected Poems of
Rainer Maria Rilke,* translated by Robert Bly.

JEREDITH MERRIN

◊

Summer Before College

Since we've been to ballgames, I finally
noticed just last summer
how sweetgum trees are baseball-diamond green;
and because my daughter
would leave home soon, the long August sunsets
absorbed me like parting.

Late afternoon stratus spread out thick to
thin to disappearing—
sand strewn over a beach cabin floor;
then the sunlight lifting
a sheer, slow yellow curtain up buildings
(the low clouds now pastel,
too pretty, like unwound bolts of satin);
then the sentimental,
vaguely alcoholic display begins—
sangria, cabernet.
Grown maudlin (the whole sky now a wineglass),
a fond mother might say,
"just the right mix of fruit, tannin, pepper . . . "
—but my daughter resists
such coyness, as the wide red sky cannot
be contained in short lists.

                    Besides, we fought: over
nothing, or always, in some way, about
sex—my imposed order
like a formal French garden of players,

the start of an inning
having to give way to errors, and grace.

Both of us lingering,
pulling sometimes away (the bay sky now
is almost accomplished,
sober), our desirable, difficult
parting stays unfinished—
unlike a long ballgame or a sunset
and more like the knowledge
she'll add to, reading what others have said
in classes at college;
like, too, my own repeated attempts to
say what it is I know.

LINDA MIZEJEWSKI

◇

Season Wish

In turns of season
come exchanges,
transformations—daughters, even,
traded to gods for wheat or rain.
Rapunzel, before she was even born,
was traded away for cabbage leaves
on a risk her father took one night
for love. A man might think of dowry
on a night that pivots warmth and cold
during Indian summers, false
springs, sudden August cool.
A miller might say his daughter
can spin horses' straw to gold.
A man might offer in sudden hope
a crop, a dove, his youngest girl.

In spring, my father
took me out at dusk
to lots the boys had left,
seeing each year if I could spin
the winning curve ball back to him
and learn the catch, the grip and swing
of a missing son; hoping there was magic
in the glove or sneakers or wooden bat
like the power children found
in the legend in pauper's clothes
that created a man from balls of snow.
The cap, perhaps, might keep my hair

forever clipped; holding the glove
against my chest might stop
my breasts; and if I learned
the grip and stance, perhaps my wrists
would thicken, hard, around the bat.

My father made the diamond
out of stones he piled like altars
into three small mounds.
Pitching to him underhand,
sometimes I threw him winning runs
and watched him round our bases,
touch the stones and then
take home. He hoped
the season would never come
when something more important
would keep me on an April night
from trespassing with him into lots
till boys came back
to claim their ground
and kick our home and bases
into rocks again.

Year by year he built for me
the things he thought
a man one day would want me for:
investments, a name
the family business—stock
to insure a fair exchange
for a man who might try
to be a son. My father's
spring trades always failed:
I always came back being
still a girl who couldn't play
the way he'd hoped while he
built for me stone bases
on his knees there in the dirt.

ANN BAULEKE

◇

Heroes

Partway through the last homestand, when the doctor told us my father would probably not live another week with the cancer, the Twins' struggle to stay in the pennant race seemed unimportant. Kent Hrbek and I had planned to talk about his and the Twins' slump, but I missed the interview. For the first time in the month my dad had been sick, he'd asked me not to leave his side. I stayed with him until he drifted into a deep, morphine-induced sleep. Then I raced 60 miles from the hospital in Le Sueur and arrived late at the ballpark. As it turned out, Hrbek missed the interview, too. The shoulder he'd injured the night before needed treatment.

It's 10 years this September since Hrbek's dad, Ed, died at 53 of ALS, the central nervous system affliction known as Lou Gehrig's Disease. Hearing my father's prognosis, a writer friend suggested I talk with Hrbek about his father and write about our dads, who had given both of us baseball. Hrbek was willing, but we had no chance to talk until I finally reached him by phone in Detroit last week.

Eleven years ago Kent Hrbek was a first baseman on the Twins' A-ball team in Visalia, California, when his dad phoned to tell him he had ALS. "I didn't know what the hell it was," Hrbek says. "He told me it would kill him, but he didn't know when." Hrbek wanted to quit baseball and go home, but his father told him to stay put. "You've wanted to play baseball your whole life," his dad told him. "We'll come out to visit you."

At the end of August 1981, Hrbek was called up from Class A to the big leagues. "I was supposed to be happy and excited, and my dad was dying," he says. "What are you supposed to do? How are you supposed to act? I told a lot of people I went from the highest to the lowest." The next year, as the Twins' rookie first baseman, the dissonance he felt between his love for his father and his love for baseball continued. "It was weird, because I was living out a dream playing baseball," he explains. "I was getting a paycheck that jumped from $500 a month to $30,000 for a summer. That was like cloud nine. I was Kent Hrbek. I was king of the world, playing in my hometown, experiencing all kinds of things in one year. It wasn't easy."

His father made it easier. "The middle of the summer we were sitting on the bed in his bedroom," Hrbek recalls. "He told me, 'I'm proud of you and of what you're doing. Don't worry about me. Just keep on playing baseball and having fun. And take care of Mom.'"

Hrbek's father freed him to go on with his life. That's only right coming from the parent of a 21-year-old. At 42, I didn't need those words from my father. The truth is, I'd always forged ahead, sometimes against his silent wishes. Reluctantly, my dad had bid me goodbye on many adventures. I'd gone to Europe twice, once for school and once on a bike trip; I'd hitch-hiked to California and camped three weeks in the Sierras; I'd spent five months in the desert in Arizona, and lived a year in New Zealand.

This separation seemed necessary. I had grown up feeling responsible for my father's happiness. I never stopped wanting to make him happy, and I never ceased to believe it was a commentary on me when he wasn't. I real-ized only later that the pressure and guilt I felt as a result caused me to add something to the distance between us. After I started writing about baseball, I sent him my articles but warned him not to show them to people. Last week, after he died, I found out he'd ignored me. I'm told he rode his red moped around the neighborhood—this at the age of 80—sharing my sto-ries with his friends. I'm glad now that he didn't listen to me, and sorry I tried to censor the joy he took in my work.

The point is, I was used to living my life. When I learned that he was dying, it was hard to know how to stop. But I followed my impulses, an-swering my every urge to be with him, and never regretted it. My father and baseball comprised the past month of my life. He was a great Twins fan. When he stopped listening to the games and reading the newspaper, I knew he was terribly sick. But baseball still helped connect us. I brought him the pin the Twins gave away one night a couple of weeks ago, and he wanted to wear it on his pajama collar. During his last few weeks I always seemed to be telling him that the Twins had lost again while the A's had won. He'd draw his mouth in a line and slowly shake his head. When they fell seven games out of first place he said, "They're done."

By August of 1982, Ed Hrbek could no longer walk up the stairs in the Metrodome. But he continued to attend every home game. I remember see-ing him carried to his seat behind home plate. It was late in the year, while Hrbek was in Kansas City with the Twins, that he received the call to come home. He went to the hospital that evening. "He was staring into space," Hrbek remembers, "but he knew I was there. He asked me how my knee was. It had been bothering me, I guess. The next morning, two minutes after I got there, he was gone."

In Hrbek's locker at the Metrodome there is a photograph of Ed Hrbek. He's laughing with a friend at someone's retirement party. "It fits him perfectly," Hrbek says. "He always had a smile on his face, unless he was chewing me out for something." The picture captures Hrbek's one regret, too. "I never really got to know him as I wanted to," he admits. "I think you really get to know someone when you can sit someplace and talk. He was my baseball coach, and I knew him as my dad, but I never really was an adult hanging around with him. I never had a rip-snorting time with my dad. I know I would have liked to, because I've done it now with his brothers. We've had some serious laughs. They say, 'I wish Ed would have been here.' That's the thing I really miss." The times he feels the loss of his dad are many: He feels it when his teammates bring their fathers into the Twins clubhouse; he feels it when hunting and fishing opportunities arise during the off-season; and he feels it when he drives by the spots on the shore of Lake Minnetonka where they fished for crappies.

When I think of my dad I see him in Johnny's Red and White, the grocery store he owned for most of his years at work. He was a svelte 6-foot-1. He wore a long white apron and always kept a pencil behind his ear. We attended dozens of Twins games during the '60s, courtesy of the bubblegum salesman who visited the store.

Like Hrbek, my love for baseball comes through my father. For many years baseball and oil changes were the gist of our conversation. He had his larynx removed due to cancer 15 years ago, making talking even more difficult. The truth is, neither of us was much of a talker. We talked mostly in letters, writing once a week, ever since I left for college. If I should miss a week, he'd shake a veritable fist at me in his next note.

I was searching frantically the other night for any of his letters I might have saved. There they were, in a file with photos and other letters, distinguished by his unique squarish printing, which always made me believe he was an artist at heart. "Kinda glad baseball season is here," he wrote in one letter. "Something to listen to." Another time: "I really enjoyed Hrbek's comments on Viola's agent. Hrbie says he'll be here next year and won't be fighting for a couple of bucks. Hooray for Hrbie." He ended one letter by telling me, "Well, be calm."

Hanging up the phone after speaking with Hrbek, I went to be with my dad. His eyes were shut. His breathing was even more labored than it had been the day before. I pulled a chair up next to the bed and took his hand. I told him I was there, that I had just talked with Kent Hrbek and would be writing about us and our dads. At different times, two staff members from the hospital hospice program visited us. I had come to know them during the short time my dad was sick. This afternoon I talked with them about my relationship with my dad—and the little-girl vision of the relationship I had always thought I wanted. I wanted a more verbal relationship with my father; I imagined him divulging wisdom to ease a girl through life. But, I told them, I realize now that he gave me more than words. He gave me himself, a kind, simple, humble man. There were bad times, I admitted. There was alcoholism. But he hadn't had a drink in 20 years. During the month he'd been sick, whatever barriers remained had tumbled down. I realized how close we were.

When I was alone with him again I noticed his eyes had opened slightly. I stood up, thinking he had awakened. All of his energy seemed concentrated on taking a breath. I remembered sitting on his/lap when I was tiny. While he took a nap in his chair, I rode up and down with his breaths. "It's so hard to breathe, isn't it," I said, stroking his arms and shoulders. "It must be scary." Suddenly I knew he was dying. My hands trembled as I continued to stroke him. "It's all right," I told him over and over.

I felt panic but I stayed, holding his warm hand. I couldn't believe he was giving me this. I couldn't believe he was letting me help him die. "Be peaceful, Dad," I said. "You can let go." His chest stopped laboring, and his breathing grew shallow. I told him I loved him, and then I heard myself asking him to watch over me. A nurse stepped into the room. "I think he died," I whispered. My dad took two more quick breaths. Another nurse checked his heart and nodded. I sat there a while longer, not wanting to let go of his warm hand.

BARBARA GRIZZUTI HARRISON

◊

Red Barber

I loved him, and I heeded him. Whenever he spoke, he spoke only to me. That is what I thought. And that is what everybody else thought, too, each of his millions of listeners. He brought the gold of summer into an attic apartment in the bowels of Brooklyn; no kitchen has ever been so sunny as the kitchen into which the radio carried his singular voice. Summers have never been so benevolent, so bright, so merrily green and happily rowdy as they were then. He brought order and he brought joy.

When I listen to him now, on tape, it is still the summer of 1947, two out in the last of the ninth inning; Cookie Lavagetto, a Brooklyn Dodger pinch hitter, chunky and obscure, steps to the plate and doubles off the right-field wall at Ebbets Field, bringing in two runners, robbing New York Yankee Bill Bevens of a World Series no-hitter and winning the game for the Dodgers, "Dem Bums" (there never was such a happy noise in Brooklyn, and there never will be again). I hear Red Barber's voice, soft and clear, cadenced and authoritative, and the shadows lengthen on the playing field as they did in those days when tomorrow was all the future one needed. . . . We'd live to play another day.

So this is a love letter . . . a very respectful love letter . . . to a graceful, stubborn, prayerful, charming, wise old Southern gentleman in whom curiosity and ardor breathe as steadily now—he is eighty-two—as they did years and years ago when he was my eyes, the poet of my childhood, a man who instructed me in the beauties of creation and of order, the necessity of law and the transforming power of grace.

He didn't know he was doing all this—or, if he did, he is too modest or contained to say so. I didn't know he was doing this.

What I thought I was doing was simply listening to Red Barber announce a ball game, an experience that delighted both by virtue of its sameness and constraints and of its openness and unexpectedness: the rules never varied;

the play marvelously did. (This was the world when the world was safe.) For fifteen years, from 1939 to 1953, Red Barber broadcast games for the Brooklyn Dodgers, as feisty, heartbreaking, eccentric, contentious, beautiful and gritty a team as ever played the game of ball, perfectly matched with their fans: there were no fans more loyal, ardent, knowledgeable and vociferous – loud-mouthed – than Brooklyn fans; true believers, we knew (in part because Red told us so) that "if anything could happen it could happen here."

We were loud-mouthed – listening to baseball was a baptism into the melting pot for my generation of immigrants' children (the image and the experience of the melting pot are violent); he was courtly, impartial and civil. We were oddly matched. We took him to our hearts. He was ours.

Red Barber went on to broadcast for the Yankees; the man William S. Paley made head of CBS sports, the man who loved radio and became part of the Cooperstown Baseball Hall of Fame and the American Sportscasters Hall of Fame educated himself to broadcast on that totally other medium, television; he has written columns for the *Miami Herald* and the *Christian Science Monitor*; and now he's back on the air, with National Public Radio – and with legions of delighted new fans who have never heard of Cookie Lavagetto. But for many of us, the baseball announcer who was and is the consummate professional – the man who broadcast the first night game, the first game in New York and the first televised game – will always remain a part of a trinity enshrined in happy memory: The Dodgers, Old Redhead, and us: Brooklyn. From the moment Miss Gladys Gooding played the organ and sang the "Star Spangled Banner" (she was *ordained* to sing the national anthem; we didn't have opera stars or situation-comedy persons singing then); from the moment Shorty La Reese gave the downbeat to the Dodger "Sym-*Phonie*" – a bunch of guys with permanent reserved seats behind first base who couldn't play a note and played at every home game – from the moment Hilda Chester waved her cowbell in the right-field bleachers as a signal to Play Ball, he belonged to us . . . like Hodges and Snider and Pee Wee Reese and Leo Durocher and Carl Furillo and Ralph Branca and Jackie Robinson and gallant Pete Reiser who was always crashing into the center-field wall and injuring himself belonged to us.

When Cookie Lavagetto spoiled Bill Bevens' bid for a no-hitter, Red Barber, after calmly reporting the latter-day miracle, said: "Well I'll be a suck-egg mule." It's funny: a red-clay Southerner whose vocal rhythms were derived from *The Book of Common Prayer* and who liked to talk about magnolias spoke to the hearts of the stoop-ball, stickball-playing kids of immigrants who barely spoke English. He had what he called "the hottest microphone in radio" – he was the man on the spot when Jackie Robinson broke the color barrier in baseball. And he beguiled us with expressions like the "catbird seat" (his; or that of anyone on the spot), a "rhubarb" (a violent verbal exchange between an umpire and player, and a frequent happening in Brooklyn); "he's runnin' like he's goin' home for Christmas," he'd say; or, "he is tearing up the pea patch" . . . "you could say he's hollerin' down the rain barrel," he'd say. You could see the perspiration on the players' faces when he spoke, you could hear the "piping shrill voices of the infielders as they encouraged the pitcher" and see the grin on his face, "wide as a slice of watermelon," when the pitcher struck a batter out; you could hear the crack of a bat, "as sudden as a pistol shot," when a player "put one in the icebox when it was really needed"; you could see the third basemen "like a restless cat in a new house" on a perfect summer day, "not a cloud in the sky, air is soft, see the leaves and the birds just poppin' out of the trees." You could smell the hot dogs and the green green grass. Red Barber used metaphor; he never used hyperbole. He never said a careless word. The very truth is that you could see the game better when Red Barber was broadcasting it on radio than you can see it now on television, because, as Walter Lanier Barber says: "You see with your emotions." And all along in his folksy way, Mr. Barber was delivering little homilies—chatty, backfence asides on character, time, and fate, urging us to charity and understanding: "I don't want you to judge Pee Wee harshly," he'd say, in that persuasive drawl; "only pop fly I've seen him miss in eleven years." Or: "You know, the hardest thing in the world is for a man to beat himself. Southworth [a third-base coach, and an alcoholic] has my most complete admiration. He has had to beat himself twice. One time as manager of the Cardinals he went all the way to the bottom, started again in Class B ball, came back as a manager again and won the world championship. And if there was one thing on the face of the earth Southworth loved, he loved that son of his. And then, you recall, he went off a runway landing at LaGuardia field and his body wasn't found for months. And Southworth nearly was torn apart. He survived that. You gotta like a fella that spritely." You gotta like Red Barber, a master of metaphysics, sly guy, a preacher in the guise of a baseball announcer.

When Red Barber broadcast the ball games I was home safe, every time.

It didn't even occur to me, on the way to Tallahassee, where Red Barber and his wife, Lylah, now live, that it might be a mistake to visit a childhood icon. I never for a moment feared he'd disappoint me. I was right not to be afraid.

Since 1981 Red Barber has been on the air every Friday morning for National Public Radio. He gets fan letters from Mozart- and Beethoven-listeners who were in diapers when the Dodgers left Brooklyn. Barber has a four-minute conversation with NPR's "Morning Edition" host Bob Edwards. No telling what he'll talk about. Could be the squirrels getting into the bird feeder. . . . And if you think a conversation about squirrels and bird feeders can't be enlightening, you've never heard Red Barber. If you think four minutes isn't enough time in which to be seduced, you don't know the economical Mr. Barber. (He used, in the interests of brevity, to employ an egg timer to remind him that listeners needed to hear the score every three minutes, a cheap sixty-cent egg timer ["they break"].) . . . He gets dressed up to broadcast in his study before the sun comes up . . . everything, even a tie. . . . Do you think many men like this are left?

"I talk to the most powerful people in Washington every day of the week," says Cokie Roberts, ABC's congressional correspondent. "But the only interview that people ever ask me about is the one morning I sat in for Bob Edwards and talked to Red."

The morning I see him he is guest of honor at Florida State University, where WFSU, NPR's regional outlet, is celebrating its ratings success and the addition of another radio station. Affection surrounds him. This is the first time he's broadcast in the same room with Edwards, although the feeling between them, even long-distance, is sweet. (Red—that's what he likes to be called—doesn't rehearse and doesn't script; live he was and live he is.)

He's slightly stooped (he navigates steps delicately); he wears horn-rimmed glasses; and such hair as he has has faded to ginger. . . . I'd know him anywhere.

He vamps till broadcast time; behind the mike he comes to vibrant life. This morning he elects to talk about a textbook—*Connections: Using Multicultural, Racial and Ethnic Short Stories To Promote Better Writing*—written by his daughter, Sarah, a professor of English at New York's LaGuardia Community College. Isn't it nice; the daughter of the man who helped smooth the path for Jackie Robinson appears to be following in her father's footsteps. And isn't it nice; he's so proud of her. Along the way he quotes Saroyan and Burl Ives. . . . He answers questions from an audience that can't get enough of him: "Robinson physically was the most exciting player—especially on base. And the most tremendous player spiritually. Mr. Branch Rickey [owner and general manager of the Brooklyn Dodgers] told him the only way for the first black player is that for three years you must turn the other cheek. And he handled unbelievable abuse with dignity and grace. Turned his cheek so often he didn't have a cheek left to turn."

Should women reporters be allowed in the locker room? It's clear from his stance that the questioner expects Red to take a traditional, conservative position, which Red does not: "Of course women have the right of equal access and should have—the clubs will just have to accommodate them." Should the umpire have thrown out pitcher Roger Clemens in the 1990

World Series for using profanity, Clemens being crucial to his team's success? "You cannot curse an umpire or profanely abuse him. The umpire did what he should have done. It's not a question of the World Series—you're in a ball game and the rules are no different from any other ball game—or you wouldn't *have* a ball game." This is the Red Barber I remember, decent, fair, honey-voiced and stern. . . ."

And infinitely courteous to all, and (I don't know a better word for it) brotherly: "Well, now, I have to go home and fix Lylah some breakfast," he says, taking us into his life, "she's had an eye operation, you know, it's comin' along all right. . . . Now here are the directions to my house, let's see if the old man knows where he lives."

I think I'm in love.

Every morning Red and Lylah Barber read the last verse of the nineteenth Psalm: *Let the words of my mouth, and the meditation of my heart, be acceptable in thy sight, O Lord, my strength, and my redeemer.* He likes the Book of Psalms: "It's the only book in the Bible where man speaks back to God."

Red Barber once refused to review a baseball player's autobiography on the grounds that the player had behaved "unchivalrously" in discussing his marital breakup—he was, Red Barber said, "incredibly ungentlemanly." One of the lovely things about Red Barber—and so encouraging—is that he is in love. He is in love with his wife, Lylah. And she is in love with him. They have been in love for sixty years.

The feeling between them, Lylah says, "was very quick and it's been there ever since. At the time I met him, life was full and there for the picking." She was twenty-five when she met him, an independent young woman born into a matriarchal society of strong women (Lylah's father died when she was five, and for years she woke up screaming with night terrors . . . which her handsome young husband received with "kindly patience"). She was a nurse at Riverside Hospital in Jacksonville, Florida, where she got her Bachelor of Science in Nursing in 1929—one of the first five women in America to have been given that degree, Red says proudly.

They are watchfully aware of each other's needs; once in a while something like flirting occurs between them, it is pretty to watch. She is sometimes tentative, sometimes astringent. He is laconic, always assured. Their personalities have not melded into one; they complement each other and enjoy the mutual comfort that is the product of profound trust; they do not speak with one voice. One heart; two voices. . . .

He, when they met, in the midst of the Great Depression (when things were "bona fide tough"), was a janitor and a waiter at the University of Florida in Gainsville. They met when he was admitted to Riverside Hospital after crashing in a friend's bakery van on his way to get "shine whiskey." He was covered with pink and yellow and green icing, sand, and blood. (The next day he sent Lylah roses.) They were married on $135 a month. He had just started his broadcasting career:

"Well, I was sitting in this bachelor-professors' club where I was janitor, working on a paper, and Ralph Folger, one of the professors from the School of Agriculture, came in. Now, Folger put on a farm program on the campus radio station – 5000 watts, educational, daylight operated, no commercials. Folger asked me to go over to the radio station and read three ten-minute papers from professors who'd left town. 'No,' I said, 'I'm busy, leave me alone.' 'Well, I'll buy you dinner tonight if you'll read one,' Ralph said. 'Oh,' I said, 'for that I'll read all three.'

"I can understand why that prof left town. Very exclusive paper on bovine obstetrics.

"Money was something then. The director of the station offered me thirty-five cents an hour to be a student announcer. I said no. 'Well,' he said, how much would I have to guarantee you a month for you to come out here? Well, I thought very quickly: $20 a month I can eat, $10 a month I can get a room to myself. Another $5 will take care of laundry and incidentals and another $15 and I'll be rich. I'll ask him for all the money there is, and that will end it. I said, 'Fifty dollars a month.' He said, 'You start tomorrow.'

"So that's how I got into radio. And no convicted murderer ever walked to the death chamber more slowly than I walked to that radio station the next day, having to give up my hard-earned security of a room and meals to get into something I was not interested in and knew nothing about. . . . I soon became interested."

And so, by way of Cincinnati, where Red did the first play-by-play broadcast for the Cincinnati Reds, on to Brooklyn, where he established the most gorgeous symbiosis ever between broadcaster and fans.

His adored wife was never a fan. She was his constant critic, but she was never a fan. Red traveled with the Dodgers and later with the Yankees – he calls himself a baseball hobo, "sat with them on the plane, on the train, sat at the table. We ate together. But I didn't play cards with the players. And I never went to a player's room in a hotel. And I didn't have drinks with the players. I stayed to myself. I thought that was the thing to do. I wanted to be fair to everybody who was on the ball field out there. I tried to school myself not to care who won or who lost. Because I understood early that vision is as much emotional as it is physical and if you want to see your team win, you can't broadcast that game objectively. You can't."

Lylah, he has written, "sat in the stands close to where the players' wives sat—she was happy to have short visits with them—but she sat with her own friends, or she sat alone."

"Lylah," he says now, "spent many lonely years. In fact she tells me now she's just beginning to realize how lonely she was at times. . . . The work that I was in made it very hard for my family—for Lylah, and for Sarah, too. Lylah was a widow, a baseball widow, without a widow's prerogatives."

He dedicated his book *1947, When All Hell Broke Loose in Baseball*, to "Baseball Wives, Who have the hardest jobs . . . Rachel Robinson . . . Laraine Durocher . . . Dodger/Yankee wives . . . Lylah Barber."

There are two ways of loving a public figure, both of them selfish: One is to inquire into his life and know the minutia of it, fostering the illusion of closeness and placing queasy claims on his privacy; another is to allow oneself, in one's quiet self-absorption, never to think of the icon's private life at all, which is tantamount to believing that he exists solely for one's own pleasure. I loved Red Barber, when I was a kid, in this way: I thought only of what he gave to me. I retained enough of this proprietary attitude to be glad, therefore, to know that Lylah had said her fifteen years with the Brooklyn club, before internal dissent in the organization sent Red Barber packing to the Yankees, were the happiest of her life. "To me," she writes, "the Yankees were as cold as the triple-deck mausoleum in which they oper- ated." I am enough of a partisan, still (still crazy about Ralph Branca after all these years! still mad at the big bad Yankees after all these years) to be glad it was *our* team she preferred.

Does Red Barber miss New York?

"No."

"Ask me," Miss Lylah says, "ask me. . . . I miss it very much. Very much."

"The New York today . . . she doesn't really want to go back to that. The New York then is not the New York now."

"Everything in the world, it seems to me," Lylah says, "was there."

"She remembers the New York when we were young. Nothing takes the place of when you're young and know that you're moving on up. Oh my goodness. I knew that I was succeeding. And I'd sometimes look at that big city and think, my goodness, how in the world am I able to do this?"

There is the husband's story of the marriage and there is the wife's story of the marriage; there are two marriages, always. And the best one can ask is that each learn the story the other has to tell. In a good marriage—and theirs is good—the dialogue continues; and so do the vicissitudes. (But, "As Noah must have said, it can't rain *all* the time.")

"We have both wanted to be married to each other. We have both respected our marriage vows. When I was on the road, she was my strength.

I never worried about her. And I saw to it that she had no reason to worry about me."

She could depend on him to be faithful; he's a moral absolutist:

"*Bull Durham*? I don't have to go and see a picture like that. I read what it was about and I don't have to go. I know all about ball players. I know this: The greatest computer in the world is the human mind and nothing is lost in that human mind. It just takes the right stimulation to bring it out. And I don't want to put things in my mind that I don't want there. . . .

"I saw *Field of Dreams* and I couldn't figure it out. It confused me. But you see I have to be careful about criticism of motion pictures because there's so much that goes on that I don't hear. See, I'm stone deaf in my left ear and there's just a little hearing in my right ear. I hear you because I'm looking at your face. . . . I can put sound and lips pretty much together."

He went through hell and terror before he could say the word *deaf*. Like a pitcher losing the feeling in his pitching arm. He was afraid he'd lose his job. He looked strained when he first appeared on TV, for very good reason: He was straining to hear. He was a reporter; and he couldn't hear. That's past him, now. Saying the awful word—*deaf*—gave him the power to face the problem.

A lot is behind him, behind them . . . "And here we are. She's eighty-four and I'm eighty-two and we are living by grace. I'm grateful."

"Preparation, like creation, never stops."

His father was a locomotive engineer. His mother was a school teacher. There wasn't much money. From his mother he gained "an ear as well as a love for the language. There was no way I could have broadcast all those countless hours ad lib without my mother giving me the ear. And the love of the language.

"One of the greatest blessings that my father gave me was to say that I was free to do anything that I wanted to do as long as it was honest. And that's quite a leeway." Did he have to search his conscience to ask if he were being honest? "I didn't have to. I just knew instinctively." He is emotionally fine-tuned. And spiritually fine-tuned:

"I tried to do my preparation daily. The most important part of my work was the two hours before the game started. And the job of the broadcaster is not to talk in those two hours but to listen. . . . So, you'd stand back in the batting cage and just listen to what the players were saying. And you'd sit in the dugout and listen, and, before long, the manager would come out, and then he'd be at ease. Then you could ask him your questions. . . . I was prepared. I had the spiritual strength of knowing I knew. When I stepped to the microphone, I knew I was ready. . . .

"A very famous old hard-nosed football coach once said, 'There's no such thing as an upset if you know the minds of the players at the kick-off.' "

He's different in style and substance from today's broadcasters: "I felt that a statistic was only to be used if you needed it. If somebody was approaching a record—you may remember—I said, 'Well, I don't know if it's a record, now. I'll look in the book and let you know.' And that seemed to suit the audience. . . . No computers. I just had to say, 'I'll look it up.'

"In television, you don't do the job yourself. The director is putting all these pictures up and in fact if you don't want to say anything you can just let the picture speak for itself. An announcer on television can't sit there and talk about things, because the pictures are changing. You just have to say a quick word and go on. Now this new technique . . . you take Jack Buck, he's got Tim McCarver breathing down his neck. If Buck hesitates, McCarver's in there. And that ABC Television under Roone Arledge—remember they had three men in there. And they had a better contest in the booth than they did on the field most of the time. . . .

"I don't want to talk about other announcers."

He's only human. ("The game is played by human beings. It is watched by human beings. Human beings are not perfect.") He has in the past spoken of other announcers with a fair amount of vitriol and sarcasm, charging, for example, that they talked a lot of "aimless Amos 'n' Andy stuff on the air." "Broadcast jocks" earned his contempt and occasioned his embarrassment and anger: In the 1964 Series, "Garagiola kept interrupting Rizzuto on the air, cutting in on him, taking the mike away from him. It was as though Rizzuto wasn't good enough to detail a routine play—Garagiola had to explain it or make a wisecrack. . . . Rizzuto just let Garagiola cut in on him. . . . our little Phil let Old Joe run with it all he pleased. . . . Joe Garagiola is today the fountain of all wisdom and knowledge. Woe to the player who makes a mistake. Joe at length explains how the play should have been made, and how much the oversight cost the erring player's team. The 'dumb' play is meat and potatoes for Garagiola, and what he doesn't criticize, his partner does."

Joe Garagiola replaced him as announcer of the Yankee games. He says Garagiola was a "house man," willing to schill for the Yankees, which Barber was not; Barber was his own man and refused to be a crowd-pleaser and hype and holler.

One day in 1966 the Yankees, a ruined team, played to an almost empty ballpark. Barber asked his director for a picture of the stands. He didn't get the televised picture, but he had the microphone, and he told the story: "It is the smallest crowd in the history of Yankee Stadium . . . and this smallest crowd is the story." That week he was fired. It's hard not to see cause and effect in that sequence of events.

"I got dismissed by the Yankees without a word of explanation after thirty years of doing good work and I have yet to receive the first letter from anybody in baseball saying they're sorry. I'm not kidding you."

Resentment seeps through; but so does pride: "One time a Brooklyn taxi driver volunteered to a friend of mine, 'Well, the trouble with that Barber is, he's too fair.' I like that. I'd put that on my tombstone . . . except I'm going to be cremated."

His work seldom bored him: "Baseball is my favorite sport . . . because it is orderly. Football is organized confusion. Even the coaches don't know anything about it until they get it on film. And basketball is just fellows running up and down in their undershorts. . . . Boring? Well, I used at times to go to an institution called Rosary Hill out in Westchester—a home you qualified for if you had incurable cancer and were flat broke. The Sisters at Rosary Hill never had anybody there who was going to get well. I used to just drop by and talk with patients, you know; and I found out that their lives were so bleak, if a game was 20 to 0 it was still interesting to them because they didn't have anything else to look at. You know, when you have a game that's bang-bang-bang it carries you with it. But then you get those lopsided games, and that's physical work, you just want to get it done. But when I'd begin to get tired, I'd think of Rosary Hill and I'd say, Well, no. There's somebody out there that this is important to."

He seems a perfect angel. He was crucial, after all, in Brooklyn's acceptance of Jackie Robinson in 1947; it's unlikely that any other broadcaster could have handled that volatile situation. It's as easy to idealize Red Barber as it is to romanticize baseball—he seems to embody all the virtues of an idealized small-town America. I'm in love with him; he's not in love with himself (he prizes objectivity in all things): "I have said it many times, I have written it, Barbara: We are all creatures of heredity and environment. I was born in the deep south, in Columbus, Mississippi. My mother was Mississippi, my father was North Carolina. When I was ten, my family moved to Sanford, Florida, which is very very redneck—deep south, I mean redneck. As a boy I saw a black man walk the streets tarred and feathered. And I had never thought anything about the relationship between blacks and whites. There it was.

"And Lylah and I, our first year in Cincinnati, went to the symphony. Sat way up there where the seats were twenty-five cents. And one afternoon a black couple came and sat down beside us . . . and we just quietly moved. Just as simple as that. Without thinking. That was the way we'd been raised.

"Mr. Branch Rickey told me in complete confidence one afternoon in March of forty-five that he was going to bring in black players. He didn't leave any stone unturned, he meant to do it. This was before he even knew of Robinson.

"I came home and told Lylah I didn't think I could do it. The relationship between broadcaster and players was too close. And she said, 'Well, you don't have to quit tonight, let's have a martini.'

"So I mulled."

Branch Rickey had told him this story: When he was coaching college baseball at Ohio Wesleyan University, a young black player was denied entrance to the team's hotel; Rickey found him crying, sitting on the edge of a chair, "pulling at his hands as though he would tear the very skin off. . . . 'It's my skin, Mr. Rickey. If I could just pull it off I'd be like everybody else. . . . It's my skin.'" That was one of the things Red Barber mulled over.

"In a few days I came to the point of economic determinism: I had the best job in the world; where would I get another one? . . . Then I began to think more deeply: I had no control over the parents I was born to, so why am I getting so high and mighty about somebody else whose skin is different because of the parents they were born to? I finally digested that. And then I heard a voice from the past—the World Series, Judge Landis, Commissioner of Baseball, 1935:

" 'These ballplayers are the best in their business. You let them play—just report what they do. And the managers are the best in the business. Don't criticize their moves. You let them manage. You just report what they do. And the umpires are the best in the business. Don't be second-guessing any of their decisions. Just report. Report the reaction of the players, of course. Report the reaction of the crowds. But just report.

" 'What I mean is, if a ballplayer gets a mouthful of chewin' tobacco and walks over to the box where I'm sitting and spits it in my face, don't have any opinion. Report. Report his steps, the rapidity of his stride, report the accuracy of his ejaculation, if your eyes are that good. Report the reaction of the commissioner, if he has one. Leave your opinions in your hotel room. Just report.'

"And suddenly my dilemma was resolved. For goodness' sake. My job is simply to report. And that's what I did. I never once said that Robinson was black or a Negro. I didn't have to. Everybody knew it. All I did was, I just reported what he did—which was more than sufficient. Once he got on the bases and started dancing, we didn't need any more.

"Robinson did more for me than I ever did for him. He made me a better man, a cleaner person. He got these scales off my eyes.

"Terrible things happened. Robinson's life was threatened. It wasn't easy. But it was easy for me. I had no problem. I just reported.

"This was the most competitive ball player since Ty Cobb. His every instinct was to react to violence with violence. But he took abuse—he honored his commitment to Branch Rickey for three years. Robinson carried that heavy load." Barber believes that Jackie Robinson's death, on the twenty-fifth anniversary of his playing major league ball, is due, in part, to his having repressed so much anger for so long.

"It's a whole different enterprise."
The world has changed and baseball along with it and this is what the Old Redhead has to say about it all:
"Big money has changed baseball in a big way. It has to. I don't care what anybody says. You got all this money, your agent says, 'Don't go up against that concrete wall, don't hurt yourself. You're valuable.' You're not gonna play as the ball players used to play when they knew the only extra money they'd get would be if they hustled enough to get into the World Series. . . . Whoever is gettin' the most money is a prima donna. That goes for opera stars and anything else. There are very few people who can be on top and get all the big money and not be a prima donna. . . .
"A game with a designated hitter is a different game of baseball. Now, if you like the designated-hitter game, fine. . . . When pitchers have to hit in the National League, they're a little careful how they throw at opposing batters, 'cause those pitchers are gonna come up to bat and they're gonna get thrown at. The American League pitcher doesn't have that fear. He's not comin' to the plate. You know, that's a hard item, that baseball. And these pitchers are mean and selfish men, like Casey Stengel said. Have to be. They have the toughest job in baseball. . . .
"The very nature of the enterprise is, you get to be self-centered. You've got to be pretty self-centered to go up to play against these fastball pitchers. You've got to be self-centered to stand out there at shortstop and field a hard-hit ground ball. You've got to be self-centered to be out there in the outfield going up against a tough sky, a concrete wall—of course you get to be self-centered. . . .
"The best all-around baseball player I ever saw was Willie Mays. Oh yes. What was it that any other ball player could do better?"

"The blood of Brooklyn, in this broadcasting booth, washed over me when I sat down."
Everywhere he went, people hollered—Hey, Red!; he enjoyed the friendship and goodwill of all of Brooklyn, the strap-hangers, the apartment-dwellers. So when World War II came along, he was a natural to enlist in the Red Cross drive for blood . . . *blood*, which had been a taboo word on the airwaves, and the people of Brooklyn responded with a generous and steady supply. The women of my family lined up to donate blood and

that was the first act of civic duty they performed: They had become in deed American citizens.

What was it about the Brooklyn Dodgers that continues to exert such a claim on the imagination?

"The Dodgers," he's said, "belonged to the people of Brooklyn just as children do to their parents. . . . Brooklyn is a different place. Ebbets Field is a different ball park. . . . The Brooklyn fan was different. . . . In Ebbets Field the fans and players blended almost into a oneness."

Yes. We were country cousins. (We were sophisticated about one thing: The Brooklyn Dodgers. Our knowledge of them was encyclopedic.) The psychological distance from Brooklyn to Manhattan was immense. When we went to Manhattan we went, we used to say, to "the City." That city didn't belong to us. We belonged to the tree-lined streets and the stoops and the humble tenements of small shopkeepers and subway commuters. . . . I remember our first class trip into Manhattan: We went to the Museum of Natural History to see the dinosaurs. Subsequently all class trips took us to Manhattan. That was where everything *was*. We were left with the indelible impression that Brooklyn was where everyone lived and Manhattan was where everything happened. . . . "*Okay, where's the butcher? Where's the stoops?*" my third-grade boyfriend yelled on the steps of the great museum. He meant: If people live here, *how* do they live? They were different from us. In our imaginations there were no butchers—no shoemakers, no five and tens, no candy stores on Fifth Avenue, no back fences, no cellar doors. We were in exotic, alien territory. . . . The dreams of that city didn't belong to us. No one ever came to Brooklyn to nourish a dream. No one but the Dodgers. . . . "*And when the Dodgers played the Giants it wasn't play—it was blood on the moon.*"

"You had the small ball park—the fans and the players were almost interchangeable," he says. "You'd see the perspiration on them and you could hear everything a player said. . . . Brooklyn itself was a major city until 1898 when the state legislature forced it to become a member of the city of New York because of the development of the subways, the water system, the bridges, the electric system. And the people in Brooklyn didn't want to be part of Manhattan. And then Manhattan had all those tall buildings, Wall Street, the theaters. The people of Brooklyn had only one thing. They had the ball club and they used that ball club as a weapon against Manhattan . . . especially when they played the Giants.

"There will never again be the rivalry, the natural genuine rivalry in baseball that there was when the Giants and the Dodgers were in New York. And most of that passion came out of Brooklyn. Brooklyn loved its players. It really did. A player could be just a routine player someplace else; once he put that Dodger uniform on, something seemed to happen. Only the

Brooklyn people called them Dem Bums. Nobody else could call them that. . . .

"The people in Brooklyn didn't think baseball was business, and it broke their hearts when O'Malley took the ball club to Los Angeles. And if any of these broken-hearted Brooklyn fans had been in O'Malley's position, they would have made the same decision. Ebbets Field was about to fall down. It's a little small ball park. You couldn't enlarge it. There was no way you could get a parking space out there, no way. . . .

"It went against tradition and it went against sentiment, but baseball has always been a business. The owners always saw to it.

"I always knew it was a business. After all, I had to negotiate my contract. It was a very hard business for me." He made it look easy . . . "It took all my strength . . . "

I know it's a business. But my heart is still tender when I think of them. (I didn't know it was a business then; that was innocence. I wouldn't have had it any other way.) I've never again been able to love a team whole-heartedly—I try to transfer my love, but it doesn't happen. A couple of years ago, when the Yankees met the Los Angeles Dodgers in the World Series, I couldn't get enough of my brother; because we found ourselves on the horns of the same dilemma: as he said, How can you root for the Dodgers when they betrayed us? And how can you root for the Yankees when they were our enemies all our lives? We never outlive the loves of childhood, or the enmities, never . . .

And when I told my brother I was going to interview Red Barber, he said: "Red Barber! That was summer afternoon in Bensonhurst! That was our life!" . . . I've interviewed celebrities and politicians and my brother didn't much care. My brother is still Brooklyn and I'm still Brooklyn, though we don't live there anymore and you can't go home again, and: That was summer afternoon.

Red Barber's less nostalgic than we are. He has the pragmatism that comes with age. There are a lot of things about the world we live in that he doesn't like. He doesn't much care for television and "jock broadcasters" and bonus players and the designated-hitter rule and he doesn't much care for "ego-mad rich baseball owners" and when the Episcopal Church put *The Book of Common Prayer* into the vernacular "that hurt" him: "When you have got something right, leave it alone, don't embellish it, don't put extra stuff on it. If it ain't broke don't fix it. I couldn't figure what was wrong with the 1928 *Book of Common Prayer*." He's "quite aware of the evil that's in the world—just look at the front page of the newspaper. . . . I don't know whether the world has gotten worse . . . it's just gotten so many more people. . . .

"I don't feel sad about things and I don't look back. I'm like Satchel Paige:

'Don't never look back because somebody might be gaining on you.' I try and look forward and I try and appreciate the day: 'This is the day the Lord hath made. I will be glad and rejoice in it.'

"There's not very much I can do about this world. I have no control over what's over there in the Far East, over congress, over things in South Africa. I do what I can of things that come to me."

There is no mistaking his decency. One knows that whatever he puts his hand to, it will be good.

Did you know how loved you were?

"I knew that I was appreciated, let's put it that way."

You were loved.

"I knew that people believed me. . . . I wanted people to believe that if I said it, it was as close to the truth as I could get it."

If you had one thing to say to all those people who loved you and be-lieved you, what would it be?

"Thank you."

There is no baseball memorabilia in his modest house; everything has gone to the library of the University of Florida; these are the years reserved for Lylah . . . who never was a fan: "This is Lylah's house." But Lylah misses New York and Lylah says, bemused: "They're funny in this neighbor-hood. . . . They just nod. . . . " It is Lylah who sometimes misses the hurly-burly, the fans, so loud, fierce, and loving. . . .

The dialogue between them continues, and Lylah's restless dialogue with the past continues, here in a house surrounded by azaleas and camellias and fragrant herbaceous borders, the house so full of the past—pictures of Lylah's family everywhere, a dress of Sarah's framed. And their cat, Arwe (Coptic for wild beast); and a small pool and ancient live oaks and pines . . . and Lylah hates moss. . . . A house with Matisse rugs and sculp-tures Lylah chose and sculptures Lylah made and Steuben glass cats, and a lamp with a rearing bronze cat that was a gift from Mrs. Branch Rickey.

During World War II, the Barbers took in two Nisei-Japanese girls, Kimi and Michi, eighteen and sixteen, who had been in an internment camp on the West Coast. Lylah has never quite gotten over the feeling that she has not one but three daughters . . . So many years . . . They went back to Japan, she no longer hears from them. . . .

Standing next to the ornamental Japanese maple tree she planted, in front of the Japanese memory garden she designed, pretty Lylah Barber regards her still-handsome husband, and she grasps my hand: "Not for one second have I doubted the love," she says; I have to bend close to hear her whisper: "Not for one second of our lives."

Sometimes at night they listen to George Beverly Shea—"that magnificent light bass voice" and to Ella Fitzgerald—"she did an LP of hymns, have you ever heard about that one? Singers singing the songs. That's our form of worship." He doesn't feel the need of what he calls "corporate worship" now. "Between your creator and yourself, everything you do is a form of prayer. Goodness, I look at these trees—what complicated beauty! How in the world is this tree created and what sustains it? Everywhere you look it's a spiritual experience."

He used to talk about the muscles and sinews and dance of a baseball player . . . and I saw the hand of God in his creation. . . . He talked about the glory of a summer day; and it was a form of praise.

"I was always appreciative of the work that I was given. I didn't choose it. It's a form of grace. I was given this work." He looks at dear Lylah: "I was given this love." And Lylah says: "I didn't have a chance. I loved him so much so right away."

What is the meaning of grace?

"A realization that you're not so important. That things have been done for you out of all control. I'll tell you. I had a massive hemorrhage in Pittsburgh in 1948. The doctors at Presbyterian Hospital stood at the foot of the bed and said, Well, we don't know where he hemorrhaged from; we can't move him around and take x-rays, he might hemorrhage again. We just have to let him lie there. So I lay there in the bed and I heard everything they said. I had the knowledge that I was right at the brink, right at the edge. I could either go over into death or not. And then—and I make no secret of it—I knew there was a presence in that room. It didn't speak to me . . . I couldn't smell anything . . . I couldn't touch anything . . . but I knew; and I was told, 'Go to sleep; don't worry; it will be all right.' And I woke up the next morning and it has been all right."

"My father was the most Godlike, genuine Christian I've ever known. And he never went to church. But he did a powerful amount of thinking, good thinking—just living by the Book."

I've always thought a baseball field—a small baseball field, Ebbets Field, Wrigley Field—resembled a cloister: safe, enclosed space, a protected space of leisured ritual, in the world but not part of it. A place of exaltation and resolution.

It did not surprise me to learn (but not from him) that Red Barber, Presbyterian born, had for years been a lay reader in the Episcopal Church, entitled to read morning and evening prayer, the litany, and the penitential office, the offices of instruction, the order for the visitation of the sick, the burial offices. On road trips, he was often invited to deliver a sermon; and he did—in Cincinnati, Pittsburgh, St. Louis, Chicago, Philadelphia, New Orleans. He said something nice; he said: "Ball players are no different from anyone else. Every man is interested in religion and there have been times when ball players have come to me to talk about God. I never push it, and I want to make that clear. Maybe that's why I never once have been kidded on a ball park about being a lay reader. . . .

"In baseball, the good manager has made a careful study of each of his players. He knows their strength and their weakness. He only asks his players to do what he knows they can do best. And I don't believe the Good Manager is going to send one of us on an assignment that we can't do."

The "Good Manager . . . has created the universe, and the way his creation can continue is through human beings. . . . We have a job to do."

He did his job; he's still doing it.

"I sought perfection in my work," he told me; and it seemed to me I had been given a definition of a perfect world—everybody doing his job as he is supposed to on a summer afternoon.

The ancient oaks throw long shadows on the green lawn in Tallahassee; and Red Barber, holding Lylah's hand, says, "Wait. . . . Tell them . . . I would say this in all humility and all honesty: Looking back I have done good work and I meant to do good work."

O spare me a little that I may recover strength before I go hence and be no more.

SECTION II

◇

Why We Love It

LILLIAN MORRISON

◇

Fan Valentines

Yours till the pinch hits
Yours till the 7th inning stretches
Yours till pennant races
Yours till pop flies
Yours till the home runs
Yours till the line drives
Yours till the double plays
Yours till batters box

CAROL TAVRIS

◇

Why I Love Baseball

If you are at all like me, when you were growing up, baseball was a game for the boys. Long before the Equal Rights Amendment, they were babbling about ERAs (which turned out to be something called Earned Run Averages) and Ribbies (Runs Batted In) and all manner of arcane percentages. The effect of their passionate mumbo jumbo was to make the girls feel Out and the boys In.

Over the years I have seen women, myself included, react to this barrier in several ways. Some decide resolutely that they *like* being out—"It's a dumb old game anyway," they say. And others hate being out, but refuse to go to the games with their husbands or boyfriends and then resent the game for coming between them. And some go to *one game*, which they don't understand, and pronounce it boring.

To evaluate baseball on the strength of one or two games is like deciding about sex on the basis of one act of love-making. The first time doesn't tell you anything. Now, eventually you may decide you love baseball or hate it, just as you may love sex or hate it, but it takes experience to make a smart decision.

That's the first lovely thing about baseball: It isn't a fickle lover, a one-night stand. Like a good marriage, it's the long stretch that counts. This is why statistics are so important to the baseball fan—they provide *history* and *context* and a promise of the future. For instance, let's say you've gone to a New York Yankees–Boston Red Sox game and Chicken Stanley, of the Yankees, hits a home run. Nice, if you're a visitor. But suppose you know that Chicken Stanley, who is an excellent shortstop, is a perfect cluck with a bat. Verily, he is famous for not being able to hit. The opposing team, knowing this, has intentionally loaded the bases so their pitcher can strike old Chicken out and end the inning.

Under such circumstances, Chicken Stanley's home run is not just nice. It's a flaming miracle. And how many miracles do you get to see these days? But you wouldn't have recognized this one without knowing Chicken's statistics.

As a group, baseball players are beautiful to behold. They do not have to be padded or born to the size of the Incredible Hulk; baseball players wear simple, sleek uniforms that reveal the natural physique. ("The real reason I like the Mets," confessed one friend, "is Lee Mazzilli–what a tush!")

Baseball players, like the game they play, are truly democratic; they come in every size, shape, hue, age and temperament. Unlike basketball players, they need not all be nine-foot-tall string-beans. You can love Freddie Patek, who is five feet four, or Mike Torrez, who is six feet five. Maybe you'll go for the characters and comedians–Pete Rose, "Mick the Quick" Rivers, Al "The Mad Hungarian" Hrabosky–or maybe you'll get hooked on the movie stars–Steve Garvey, Bucky Dent, Carlton Fisk. Maybe you like them young and unseasoned; or maybe you go for older men–Luis Tiant, like Jack Benny, apparently plans to be 39 for the next ten years. The point is, you will find the man to love. Baseball is a game of individuals and personalities, each clear in his splendid isolation on the field. Yet like democracy, baseball is ultimately a game of teamwork and co-ordination.

A fan without a team is like a hog without truffles–she has nothing to root for. You cannot expect to feel any sense of appreciation for the game unless you are partisan. "This blind, chauvinistic belief in one's own team, often against all reason, is foolish and marvelous," says writer Art Hill. "It is the muscle and magic of the game's attraction, and you cannot crush it." Promiscuous fans who flirt with team after team and dispense their favors according to which team is on top, are regarded by true devotees as gold diggers. A baseball team, like a family, needs loyalty.

The beauty of baseball starts with the stadium. The infield is no mere rectangle or oval. It is a *diamond*, a jewel. The setting for this jewel is a geometrically perfect field shaped like a fan, and a fan will gain a different perspective on the game wherever she sits. At ground level near the infield, you feel as if you're in the game; you see the expressions of the players, hear the exchanges between umpires and coaches. If you sit behind the batter, the homeplate dramas (batters out, runners in) unfold practically in your lap. If you sit high up in the stands, you get the master plan of the game as a whole: the split-second timing, for instance, that determines whether a runner will get to third base before an outfielder hurls the ball there. And if you are out in the bleachers, steerage class, you see the game from the perspective of the fielders, lonely sentinels who cover an area that seems the size of Texas. (You might get lucky and catch a home run.)

Wherever you sit, you will hear the sounds of summer; the assorted cries of the vendors ("Beer here!" "Hey, hot dogs!"); the roars of the umpires ("Steee-RIKE!" "YerrrouuuTTT!"); and the eloquent commentary of the fans ("QBRXTYTRPM!"). But all these noises are merely background buzz awaiting the magic *tock* of the bat connecting with the ball—as startling a sound as an obscenity in a sermon.

The architecture of baseball is classically simple and elegant. Start with its core, the battle between pitcher and batter: a duel in the sun that is as American as the shoot-out at the OK Corral. Some pitchers have a cunning repertoire of pitches, with marvelous names such as forkballs, sliders, curves, knuckleballs, change-ups, all designed to fool the batter into swinging at mush. Other pitchers throw "smoke"—balls that are simply too fast to hit.

Batters have their own arsenal of tricks to unnerve the pitcher and build confidence, which is why they seem to be forever fussing with their bats and caps and cleats before settling into a glowering stare at the enemy. This duel is not frivolous. An entire game can rest on the success or failure of a pitch.

And then there are the gentlemen of the outfield, whose grace, co-ordination and skill rival those of any acrobat or dancer. It doesn't seem physically possible for them to make the catches they do, but they do it— backhanded, one-handed, two-fisted catches in which they pluck the ball from the air, the ground, the dirt, over the fence, hurling themselves vertically or horizontally to prevent a run from scoring. And Graig Nettles, who plays for the Yankees, is the Baryshnikov of third base. You won't see fancier leaps on any stage.

"Well, fine," some of my friends say, "but baseball is so *slow*. So *dull*." But any game will seem slow and dull to those who don't know the rules, the subtleties of strategy, the idiosyncrasies of the players or which team to cheer for. What they are really objecting to, I think, is an aspect of base-ball that I love most of all: its timelessness.

Baseball, in this mechanical age, is not mechanical. Each game consists of nine innings, or more if the score is tied, and each inning lasts as long as it takes to get three outs. There is no artificial nonsense of fake time, time-outs, overtime, and the like. (Football consists of four 15-minute "quarters." Hah! What football game did you ever watch that lasted an hour?)

Baseball lasts as long as it takes. Like life, like love, baseball exists in real time.

In the final analysis, you can't ever fully dissect the reasons you love something. You wouldn't want to. To me, baseball is nature's most nearly perfect game, but my reasons may not be yours. Give it a chance. Baseball will cheer you up when you're down (of course your team may let you down when you are up, as well), lend color when your mood is gray, provide poetry when your life is prose and introduce you to some of the handsomest, bravest, most comical, amazing, vivid characters you'll ever meet.

As the lady said in a different context, a diamond is a girl's best friend.

LINDA GEBROE

◇

No Particular Place to Go

When the game ended, I had nowhere to go. The Giants won on a pitching gem by Billy Swift, and it had been a pleasure to watch. Samurai baseball, he'd sliced through the batting order of the Mets several times over, each player returning forlornly to the dugout for lack of a hit.

I lingered a while, watched the bench players come out and congratulate the starters, the team congratulate itself, smiles on the field and then into the clubhouse. The grounds crew took over then, men in white coveralls, baseball's equivalent to the cleaning lady. One guy dragged the infield; that is, he drove something like a lawnmower that had a big rake on the end of it that smoothed out the infield dirt. This was one of the most sensual acts I'd ever witnessed outdoors. The man drove in curves, leaning to the left, then to the right, making sure he'd covered everything. The action approximated ice skating, first the right leg goes forward and glides, then the left forward and glide, all the while hands clasped behind the back. It was a very feminine thing to watch.

The public address system switched from big and booming to soft and mellow—the better to drag the infield to. The music was saxophone, the moves were soft, there was room in the stands, the sun was bright but soft in the late afternoon, the field was greener than it looks on TV, the seats were orange, the sky was blue. Like day care for grown-ups.

I stayed as long as I could and even as the usher approached, I stood my ground. I would not leave one millisecond sooner than I absolutely had to. He finally came within earshot and said, "Time to go," a little wistfully, because he understood that I was just where I wanted to be.

And so I turned and headed out, up thirty or forty rows, and when I reached the top, I turned to look back at my sanctuary, which stood still, green and blue and orange and a couple of other colors in between.

I reached the concourse, the concession area, where a few other fans were still making their way out of the park. The game seemed distant now, just leaving was becoming its own activity. I stood high atop the Candlestick escalator, overlooking Hunters Point, downtown, the Bay Bridge, the bay. I was on top of the world with nowhere to go.

MARY CECILE LEARY

◇

Why I Love It

Moms get crushes on Jim Palmer, and dads can still make their kids
swoon and their friends cheer as they shuffle through the paces,
beer foaming in sweaty hands,
but still they can do it, and
some of them can really hit, and the taste of dirt is
almost sweet, such a long-forgotten pleasure; the taste of
dirt in the mouth when you've finally landed at home plate;
a hero and
singer of
sweet songs
for the rest of the day.

If there is one thing that is beautiful it is baseball and if there
is one thing that is baseball, it is beautiful, and if there is one
thing that is a sport that is beautiful, it is all these grown men
wearing fetching uniforms, running like
hell's on their heels (You
think it's slow-moving!? Just the nervous twitch of the first
baseman's head toward the runner on his base, of the outfielder
nodding to the second baseman, imperceptibly, the glance
from the catcher to the pitcher is like *lightning*) and
they can all catch, you have to be able to
catch or they'll laugh at you but
in a good-humored sort of way, like,
"That guy may have no balls, but he's all right,"
not like football, where they'd eat you for breakfast and really

mean it, or work awful hard to,
that's a sport for men.

But baseball is where boys practice being boys and
men practice being boys, and
they get real good at it.

SARAH VAN ARSDALE

◇

Most Valuable Player

If I had a trophy
I'd put it on the middle shelf
of my bookcase. I'd dust
it every day
and polish it once a week.

It would have a statue of a woman
holding a bat, her golden arm
cocked up a little
waiting for the pitch.
When my friends came over
I'd stand next to the bookcase casual-like
till they said, "Is that a trophy?"
I'd read the inscription every morning.
I'd ask someone to take my picture
with my trophy.

My trophy would say
"Softball Player" on the bottom,
and everyone would know
that in summer I tie on my cleats

run onto the field,
slapping high fives.
They'd know I take third base,
put my glove to the dry dirt,
scatter dust in the air.
They'd hear the fans shout,

"Hey, some catch!"
when that white ball comes slamming
into my glove,
and, "Watch out, she'll steal home,"
as my cleats dig and dig.
They'd feel the weight of the little statue
and think, "I bet she's going out
with her team tonight,"
"I bet she could teach me how to throw,"
"I bet she plays softball,"
and I do,

I do.

SARA VOGAN

◊

from *In Shelly's Leg*

Summer light lasted until almost ten o'clock. On evenings when Margaret didn't have a game or a practice she and Woody would play ball with the children in the backyard. At the heart of the season Margaret felt her arm and shoulder tightening into a perpetual ache located somewhere beneath her muscles. She felt good and loose only when pitching and for a few hours right after. She wondered about professional pitchers; they must hurt all the time, their muscles bound in tight knots until the arm was being used.

Woody caught and called the imaginary hits. If the whiffle bat connected with one of Margaret's pitches, the ball dropped like a shot pigeon. The kids always swung past the pitch. Woody invented the plays for them, giving them a lot of triples and home runs.

Adam had been talking about trying out for Little League next summer and he started concentrating on hitting Margaret's curves, slowballs, and sliders. Sometimes he would just stand holding the bat and watch the arc of the ball as it left Margaret's hand and sailed toward him, across the car mat they used for home plate, and into Woody's glove.

Margaret pitched a riser. Adam swung. The bat whistled through the air. "A double!" Woody yelled, expecting Adam to run to the maple tree, first base, and pull up at the garage corner, second base.

Adam stood with the bat resting in his arms. "Don't do that," he said. "Do that for Allison, not for me."

Woody looked at him quizzically. "Don't you want to run?"

"No. I mean yes. But I only want to run if I hit the ball. Then you can tell me if it's a double or something."

"I get all the home runs!" Allison yelled.

"Okay," Woody said. "You sure? It'll be easier to hit a Little League pitcher than one of Maggie's."

"I know," Adam said. "But I want to really hit them. Not just pretend."

Woody studied the boy. He seemed to be measuring Adam's height with his eyes. "There's more to it than that," Woody said. "You got to lob them into holes in the outfield."

"Woody." Margaret didn't like Woody trying to dampen Adam's enthusiasm. In some way Adam's seriousness about pretend ballgames seemed to her an indication he was growing up.

"We don't have an outfield," Allison said.

"I'll tell you what," Margaret said. "I'll give you seven pitches."

"Seven?"

"Sure. Four balls, three strikes." Margaret smiled. "It will give you a chance to practice."

Adam grinned. "Okay!"

Allison pouted. "I'll never get to bat."

Woody touched her hair. "But you'll get all the home runs."

Margaret's first pitch was a nice, slow ball, directly across the plate.

Adam did not swing and stood to the side and watched the ball sail by. "That's a little kid's pitch, Mom. Do your regular stuff."

"You sure?" Woody asked. "It might take a while to get a hit."

Adam glared at Woody. "I'm not going to be a little kid forever."

Margaret pitched Adam three slowballs and four risers. He missed them all. As he handed the bat to his sister, Adam looked at Woody, over to Margaret, then back to Woody. "It's just kid's stuff the other way," he said.

Allison stood next to Woody, the whiffle bat held high in the air. She wiggled her butt the way she had seen the women on the Shelly's Leg team shift when they settled their feet into the box. "I'm ready," she said. Woody, crouched behind the car mat, looked to be exactly her height.

"This will be a double home run," Allison said. "I've got Billie Jean King on second."

Margaret practiced another slider. Allison swung after the ball landed in Woody's mitt. "A home run!" Allison yelled.

Woody played the announcer. "Look at that, folks! That ball's gone right out of the park! A cute little girl in the second bleachers is going to catch that ball and take it home as a souvenir."

Allison slapped her hand against the treetrunk. "We've got the second-base runner coming in," Woody called.

"Billie Jean King!" Allison screamed as she tagged the corner of the garage.

Woody tossed the ball back to Margaret. "Look at that girl run, ladies and gentlemen. In case you folks in the stands didn't know, Allison is also an Olympic short-sprinter."

Allison ran past the piece of cardboard at third.

"She's coming down the home stretch now." Woody held his hands up like a megaphone. "And here she comes! A home run for Allison and a run batted in!" Woody caught her up in his arms as she crossed the car mat and swung her as easily as an infant in a circle through the air. He kissed her loudly on the top of the head when he set her back on the ground.

Allison giggled and squirmed in his hands. "Too bad," she panted, "you can't kiss Billie Jean King too. She doesn't like boys."

Margaret worked on her knuckleball for the next seven pitches to Adam. She watched his small body standing by the plate, studying the first pitch as if he were concentrating for a test. He swung at the next five pitches, missing them all. As he watched the last pitch, he seemed to be memorizing its pattern through the air. Then he handed the bat to his sister.

"I'm going to beat you," Allison said. "I'm going to cream you." She told Woody she had Phyllis Schlafly and Gloria Steinem on bases this time.

"Christ!" Woody laughed. "You sure have one hell of a team."

"We're all famous," Allison said. "Even me. That's what makes us so good."

Woody gave Allison only a single, but allowed Gloria Steinem to score another run. "Just to keep things interesting," he told her when she looked disappointed. "You can't get a home run every time."

Adam varied his attack on the slowballs Margaret pitched. He lunged at the first two, studied the third, walked lazily through the fourth, and on the fifth slowball he tipped it. The ball dropped and rolled off toward Margaret in the center of the yard.

"Okay!" Woody said. "Mightyfine!"

Adam stopped running halfway to the maple tree. "What is it? What'd I hit?"

"A triple for sure," Woody shouted. "Maybe you can steal into home. There's a muff-up in the outfield."

Adam ran hard past the maple.

"Hurry!" Allison shouted. "They're gaining on you!"

Adam slapped past second at the garage and ran, head down, toward the piece of cardboard at third. Sticking his arms straight ahead of him, he dove to the ground five feet in front of the car mat and scrambled in on his hands and knees.

"An in the park homer, folks!" Woody called as he stood Adam up, dusted him off, and patted him professionally on the shoulder. "That was all right. Mightyfine!"

Adam beamed at him. "See? I can do it. Someday me and Mom will have a real game."

ALICE NOTLEY

◇

As Yet

Oh dear, how lovely it is &
so pure. To be lone, to be
hated, to be wrong. Or
to be right, in a prospect of
cabbage & fireweeds . . . So
its being despicable to be anything
look at Pete Rose's grin
today in the *News*, after
hit no. 3,772—with his wrecked
face & his stupid team lost the game
anyway—I wish I had some of his drugs.

VICTORIA GILL

◊

Hommage à George Brett

All their days, vanity? Each year I fall
in love with baseball & get burned by my
heroes. Better than mortal flowers
are the garlands of fifteen-minute fame
For who would want the burden of being
George Brett, whereat the dull world stares,
pedant & pitiful! Oh, how his rapt gaze wars
with their stupidity! & mine too. George, you were
my lamentable brother, mon semblable, mon frère,
before you turned into a kamikaze third baseman
whose dreams divine lifted yr. long, laughing reverie
like enchanted wine, like the surfer you were.
Hey, it's tough: the star-crowned solitude,
the oblivious hours spent watching Steve Balboni pop up,
the crash dives into walls and dugouts. Those years when you
should have won the MVP but didn't, I watched
you sadly sign flat autographs, tired at last
of the world's foolish noise. Don't worry!
Your team took the Series last year;
your silence & austerity shall win at last; your homers still look
effortless,
and you can dig
deserting vanity for the more perfect way.

ELOISE KLEIN HEALY

◊

Poem for My Youth/
Poem for Young Women

My eyes sometimes bounce up quickly I look away seeing
you see me and seeing me and seeing me and not knowing what to
   cover
I cover everything even imagining someday when I'm older

my eyes will anticipate and pick up quick the ball scooting
across a hard infield and knowing what to focus I'll focus
everything my body will move to it with the logic of strength
and good equipment and I will plant my feet knowing the slight
slide before the grab and hold and there will be no mistake

about it, the throw and I'll follow through with everything
my legs know about direction and the tight fit of muscles to skin
to the speed of reacting and reacting right my quickness
is about youth but already I see it is not young.

VIOLA WEINBERG

◇

Bunt Ball

He woke stupid and limp,
holding his teeth in his hand,
chewing mucous like a pitcher's plug,
certain that she'd done something
to his soul the night before
when he moaned and groaned
in the sheets, burning and babbling
in his troubled sleep.

This was serious.
The pennant depended on it.
Earlier in the season,
he'd been brilliant.
Later he was all hits and no runs,
choked up on the bat, angry,
throwing her around on the bed,
rubbing her skin off
with his hard beard.

Until there she was, covered
in fingerprints, swept by hands,
a bloody rut in the turf,
flung sidearm to the outfield,
while unfamiliar faces scorned—
a bleacher sea of chalk and screams.

In the top of the ninth,
there was an inside bet

as he grabbed her by the legs
and took her on the mound.
The Louisville Slugger.
Damp as bourbon,
twice as fast.

BERNADETTE MAYER

◊

Carlton Fisk Is My Ideal

He wears a beautiful necklace
next to the beautiful skin of his neck
unlike the Worthington butcher,
Bradford T. Fisk (butchers always
have a crush on me), who cannot even order veal
except in whole legs of it.
Oh the legs of a catcher!
Catchers squat in a posture
that is of course inward denying orgasm
but Carlton Fisk, I could
model a whole attitude to spring
on him. And he is a leaper!
Like Walt Frazier or, better,
like the only white leaper,
I forget his name, in the ABA's
All-star game half-time slam-dunk contest
this year. I think about Carlton Fisk
in his modest home in New Hampshire
all the time, I love the sound of his name
denying orgasm. Carlton & I
look out the window at spring's first
northeaster. He carries a big hero
across the porch of his home to me.
(He has no year-round Xmas tree
like Clifford Ray who handles the ball
like a banana.) We eat & watch the storm
batter the buds balking on the trees
& cover the green of the grass

that my sister thinks is new grass.
It's last year's grass still!
And still there is no spring training
as I write this, March 16, 1976,
the year of the blizzard that sealed our love
up in a great mound of orgasmic earth.
The pitcher's mound is the lightning mound.
Pudge will see fastballs in the wind,
his mescaline arm extends to the field.
He wears his necklace.
He catches the ball in his teeth!
Balls fall with a neat thunk
in the upholstery of the leather glove he puts on
to caress me, as told to, in the off-season.
All of a sudden he leaps from the couch,
a real ball has come thru the window
& is heading for the penguins on his sweater,
one of whom has lost his balloon
which is floating up into the sky!

EVE BABITZ

◊

Dodger Stadium

The way to make it rain is to wash your car, as everyone knows (you can make it drizzle if you do only your windshields, but rain requires a whole car), and the way to get invited to a fancy French restaurant is to have rustled yourself up a nice, cozy omelette so that just as everyone has decided to go out for dinner and calls you, you're sitting there in your pajamas, thinking how virtuous you are for being home. So, if you want to get invited to something not quite dinner, you could make scrambled eggs with no bread on the side but melted cheese in the scrambled eggs or something, to show God that you are serious about staying home and being virtuous. His interest is then piqued as He seeks to devise an appropriate temptation for you to succumb to.

I had just finished making myself some nice scrambled eggs in my brand-new Teflon pan with not only cheese but this newfangled great *whipped* chive cream cheese, and it was Saturday and only 5:30. (I had considered putting chorizo, that Mexican sausage, in, but chorizo has so much garlic in it that if you make anything out of *that* someone you barely know who's wildly attractive will turn up and I just wasn't up to one of those, Saturday night or no.)

I settled down before the television to a *Saratoga Trunk* rerun and had finished my last delicious fluffy bite (that cream cheese is so fluffy) when the phone rang.

"Listen," he said—he never had to say his name, our voices were imprinted on each other's aural hearts—"I've been in this damn town of yours for a week now and I've been locked in the studio from six in the morning until eleven at night and I've *got* to get out of here. The Dodgers are playing the Giants and I thought you might . . . "

"Baseball . . . " I correctly assumed. I had this immediate feeling that he was about to tell me he was going with some friends and that if he could get out of it later, he'd take me to dinner.

"Well, I know it isn't the type of thing you usually do, but . . . "

"You want *me* to go with you?"

"Yeah, well, I thought maybe we'd just . . . But if you'll be bored . . . "

"Baseball? *Me?*" I said, attributing the whole thing to the cream cheese. It *had* to be the cream cheese.

"But I'd love to," I said. "When do we . . . "

"I'll pick you up in fifteen minutes. Dress warm."

I've been halfway around the world in a plane and witnessed revolutions in Trafalgar Square, but nobody has ever asked me to see a baseball game in my whole American life. People take me to screenings of obscure films, they drag me along to fashionable new nightclubs, they have me meet them in a taxi, honey, and whisk me off to dangerous Cuban samba places to *bailar* the night away. The don't take me to baseball games—it wouldn't occur to them. No wonder I'm such a sitting duck for this man. He is the only one who could take me out to a ball game, but then *he* could take me to a flower show in Pomona, and it wouldn't be any stranger than the idea of us together is already.

I remember the first time I saw him. It was at a reception for a nouveau-wave actress in a bungalow behind the Beverly Hills Hotel, and everyone was making faded, jaded little French remarks at each other and being tiresome because the toast for the caviar wasn't buttered enough—when in he came, dressed like Johnny Carson and asking for Scotch.

I pounced on him and lured him off to the sidelines.

"Do you think these shoes are too purple?" I asked

"Too purple?" he said, looking down at my feet. "If they're not *too* purple, they're not purple *enough.*"

And there, on that cold marble floor in that tricky company, I fell hopelessly in love without a backward glance and wondered what a nice girl like me was doing in a place like that.

In this day and age of men and women ducking for cover until whatever results from radical feminism and the general gory corruption riddling the country from stem to stern, I fell right smack in love with an obvious American man. In my mind, from that moment forward, I always thought of him as The Last American. It was too bad Henry James couldn't have seen him, the way he wore his store-bought clothes with such lithe nonchalance that he put to shame the other men in the room with their narrow Parisian shirts and Milanese tailors. He was obviously too busy to think beyond a turtleneck and an all-right jacket, but he was so artlessly physical that he was Astaire himself. Very American.

He was even too busy for the outcome of the game between men and women. He probably hadn't even noticed it. And I understood everything perfectly after that: Men and women are stuck with each other. Men go to parties they don't really like because women want to go, and women in love go to baseball games and are graceful about it, though they never would have thought it up all by themselves. It's very relaxing being stuck.

And so there he was, fifteen minutes later, an impatient, suspicious man brought up in a tradition of being kept waiting by women.

"I'm ready," I said, and was.

"You going to be warm enough?"

"Fur coat," I answered, throwing it over my arm and following him out the door into a sunlit late afternoon. Once we were safely driving (after he opened the car door for me—he's from another era, too, not just the opposite sex), I asked, "Tell me about baseball, about you and baseball . . . "

"Oh . . . it's very boring," he said, maybe having doubts.

We took Sunset because the night before fifty thousand people had jammed the freeway around the stadium. His logistics were always elegant—a personality trait that saved the studio untold millions every year.

"It isn't even a very important game," he said. "It's only the eleventh of the season . . . "

"So it doesn't matter?" I wondered.

"Well, if you win the first one and the second and keep on," he explained, "it adds up." The way he drove a car was the most inexplicable thing about him; he drove with an absent-minded, almost puttering kindliness, as though when he was inside a car, the world got slower; it was time for reverie almost. "You know," he said dreamily, "I haven't been to a game in . . . five years. When I was a kid, I was a fanatic. We used to go out and watch 'em practice."

"Who?"

"The Dodgers," he said, as though there was no other team.

"Well, can't you watch on television?"

"The phone isn't going to stop ringing just because I'm watching TV," he said.

"Well, aren't you glad you don't have one of those little bleepers in your pocket like doctors?" I looked on the bright side.

"Oh Jesus," he cringed.

We arrived at the wide tollgate-looking parking lot by about 6:15 and into the vast circular maze of parkdom which was already more than half filled, and he nudged the car into a lot that sort of looked like it was the one under a sign that said anyone without a green sticker would be towed away, and there he parked. I had never seen him do anything reckless before.

"What if they tow the car away?" I hated to be a wet blanket, but, still . . .

"It's rented," he pointed out. "And, besides, it's no good and I was going to take it back in the morning and get another one."

"Well . . . O.K." I could just see us way up there with no car, tramping down to Sunset and trying to get a cab. I decided not to worry about it.

We walked upward toward the stadium with all those people. At first I hadn't noticed anything because the people looked like the hordes who frequented every gigantic event I ever went to. They were young, in their twenties, and they wore jeans and pea coats and they all had long hair (later, looking down from our seats at all that hair brought it home to me how much those shampoo companies must take in). The only difference was that there were a lot of little kids—a *lot* of little kids. The kids all had long hair, too. Wait a minute, I thought to myself, I thought baseball was . . . I mean, I thought people who went to places I never went, like baseball games, were all fat, middle-aged, blue-collar workers holding Pabst Blue Ribbon. Or, at the very least, the well-scrubbed Young Republicans with their crew cuts and their girlfriends with freckles. All *these* people looked like they were going to a Dylan concert.

"Look at these people," I gushed. "I thought everyone here would be . . . "

"*My* age, right?" He gave me a very calculated, cold look. Oh god, I thought, *now* what have I done?

"No, older," I tried to patch up. For the first time in my life I did not envy his wife in New York; penthouse, fur coats, anything. He had never been angry with me before, but now I saw he could be; it was scary.

But then the feeling of baseball coming closer did something to him, and he shrugged and put his arm around me. A close one.

We got our tickets and strolled inside the gates where music was playing and hawkers were hawking, and he bought himself a scorecard and became downright cheerful. The blissfully festive smell of mustard cut through the air dissolving any residual anger, and zillions of little kids with pennants and blue plastic Dodger caps raced through the young couples as we all gave ourselves up to the setting sun. The tempo of the organ music inflicted the reality so that everything belonged inside of these Vatican Stadium walls, and the studios, and phones, and death, and rented cars belonged outside if they wanted any claims on time or space.

I love hordes. They screen out free choice; you're free at last: stuck.

Our seats were way up. They were around third base so we could see over the tops of the bleachers on the other side and out to the green hills in the coming twilight beyond. The green hills had violent purple ice plants on them and looked like a scratch in the world bleeding purple blood. The baseball field below was gorgeous. It was the first I'd ever seen, but I'm sure other people must think it's a beautiful one. The grass all mowed in patterns like Japanese sand gardens and the dirt all sculpted in swirling bas-relief.

"It's so beautiful," I gushed.

"Not bad," he agreed.

All the people were beginning to fill up the seats around us and the whole event just took over; it became completely itself, in a kind of very loose tension like inside a love affair. You can care or not care at a baseball game, just so long as you're inside the gates. You can casually chat with your friend and know that if anything happens you won't miss it for the crowd will alert you and carry you through.

At seven o'clock, this terrible lady sang a moribund version of "The Star Spangled Banner" as we stood, and I saw one man, the only one there who looked like a blue-collar cartoon, remove his cap for the occasion. Otherwise, it was all long hair or blue plastic souvenir caps on little kids. Then we all sat down and waited.

Baseball is easy to fathom, not like football, which people explain to me at great length and I understand for one brief moment before it all falls apart in my brain and looks like an ominous calculus problem. The tension in baseball comes in spurts between long waits where everyone can forget about it, a perfectly lifelike rhythm.

"That's your team," he explained when we first sat down and guys were out in the huge field aimlessly warming up. "The home team always wears white and the other gray."

"*My* team?" I almost scoffed. I mean, I'll go along with him to a baseball game gracefully, but he didn't expect me to take sides, did he? But it was too late because somehow, before the thing even started, I had acquired an intense, fierce loyalty to the Dodgers, and I don't know how it happened. I never expected that my external personality, which had hardened into that of a blasé Hollywood lady of fashion, could rupture at the first sight of those Americans down there in their white uniforms, but there it was. I was hooked. Early in life I discovered that the way to approach anything was to be introduced by the right person. Like the first time I smelled caviar, I put it right back down on the plate and waited five years until a Russian countess offered it to me again with cold vodka in her exile's parlor and *then* I loved it. (I didn't want to be one of those people who don't like caviar.) I had always thought, however, that baseball was never going to happen to me, but I hadn't counted on The Last American making me a Dodgers fan, all of a sudden.

The game started just as night began to fall, and he tried to explain to me what was happening and would happen and why forty-seven thousand people grumbled and moaned one moment and forty-seven thousand people cheered or yelled "charge" the next. A great deadpan man climbed up and down the aisles catching quarters brilliantly and throwing ice-cream sandwiches back with amazing grace, while below us incredibly agile men caught high flies with similar but grander perfection.

"Watch how fast that guy throws," he told me about the pitcher, and I watched as this ball slammed through the air much too seriously for it to be only a game. The pitcher, I decided, was a strangely serious person in all of this hurry-up-wait to-do.

Over the top of the opposite grandstand was one lone palm tree trying to sneak in. That palm tree was all that existed of Los Angeles, or anything, outside – the only way you could tell you were even in Southern California and not just in baseballdom. He told me that the last game he'd been to had been arranged by the studio and that they'd sat in the loges behind home plate, the best seats. But, unlike Dylan concerts, it doesn't really matter where you're sitting in baseball, or even if you sit at all, because some of the little kids never sat – they barreled up and down the aisles totally absorbed in any action at all that should fall their way. And it doesn't matter if you yawn; yawning is a luxury that befits all that tension.

"No wonder everyone loves this," I told him. "It's so . . . "

"Awww, come on," he smiled disparagingly, "you don't really . . . "

But just then this damn Giant hit a home run! The forty-seven thousand people were riveted to that ball, the outfielder was running backward, and he almost . . . almost . . . But he didn't.

"Ohhhhhhh," we all remarked.

"How could those damn Giants *do* that!" I groaned. "They're not going to *win* are they?"

I was clutching his arm rather tightly.

"Calm down," he said.

"But they *can't* win!"

It had been a comfortable three-to-one in our favor, and now it was three-to-two! And now that it *was* three-to-two, the whole place came alive with worry. No casual chitchat now, by gum, I thought with my elbows on my knees and my thumbnail in my teeth. By the ninth inning it was still three-to-two and the damn Giants came up to bat throwing in cheating pinch hitters and anything else they had up their sleeves. If they got even one point the thing would be tied and it would go into extra innings (and it was getting cold). They had two men on base; the Dodgers had a pitcher who was very makeshift, since the other pitcher had collapsed in front of everyone after throwing just one ball. Most of the Dodgers, in fact, I learned were in the hospital trying to get well, and in the game I saw, two more fell apart. So this novice was pitching, and the damn Giants had two men on base and all they had to do was hit a home run and all would be lost. But, just as I was succumbing to glumness, a wonderful third baseman caught a third out, effortlessly, and so not only didn't we have to stay for extra innings, we also got out early and *won* to boot!

"We won! We won! We *won!*" I cried gleefully.

"Did you really like that?" he asked, finally believing me.

"Yeah. What'll we go to next?"

"Hockey, when they're playing . . . " he thoughtfully decided.

"Oh, goody," I said. We had joined the hordes in the exodus to the parking lot and the ensuing chaos of trying to get out of that otherwise well-designed place. We got stuck in the parking scene forever (twenty minutes), and he fell into another reverie.

"You know," he began, "when I was a kid, I tried out for the Dodgers."

"You did?" I tried to imagine him in white and could, perfectly. "You'd have been great, I think," I said.

"I made it all the way to the finals," he continued. "I was only seventeen. I might have made it in the next season, only the war . . . " (He meant World War II, when he was a lieutenant or something in the Army, and my parents were married to other people and hadn't even considered having me.)

"What part did you try out for?" I asked quickly, remembering that cold, calculating anger, which was to be avoided at all costs.

"Pitcher," he said.

"And so what happens when you're the pitcher?"

"Well . . . You have a pretty good life. You work six months a year, you practice a couple of months, and then you're off."

"It sounds kind of like your life now," I offered.

But he wasn't listening, and he went on, "And if you behave yourself and don't get into a lot of trouble, you wind up coaching a team or managing . . . " His wistful voice faded out and then returned to a more realistic tone. "Awww, but I probably wouldn't have been good enough."

"You know what I wish?" I said; the traffic had at last untangled and we were beginning to move. "I wish I had one of your double Scotches."

"You know what?" he said. "So do I. Where shall we go?"

"Well, luckily we still have the car," I said, "so we can go anywhere."

Later, as we sat in this hidden little French restaurant, having gotten our Scotch and ordered, I looked at him and thought he would have made a great pitcher, but if he had, I never would have met him; he never would have found himself in his Hollywood/New York life of studios and girls in bungalow receptions who take one look and find him exotically American enough to pounce on.

He turned his glass in his hands easily, innocent of the motions of a startled agent at the next table who leapt to his feet and was upon us, plunging us into the great Hollywood pastime: movie-deal talk.

"Jesus, I been tryin' to get ahold of you for two weeks . . . " the agent began, sliding down into our booth.

The anonymous freedom of the hordes had so stuck in The Last American's eyes that he blinked twice at this otherwise familiar face, trying to remember where they'd met, but it didn't take him long to recall what the deal was, only a few seconds for his strange boyish eyes to rise to the occasion. He laughed, patted the agent on the shoulder, and quickly managed to shrug off his amnesia.

I felt myself fading into the background and let their voices wash over me, well aware of my place in this traditional back-street romance. There was plenty of time to worry about who was taking advantage of whom in the war between men and women or the future of the country or any of that. I felt The Last American's hand reach under the table and come to rest someplace just above my knee, and I suddenly thought how fortunate it was that I hadn't had my car washed that afternoon.

LUCY KENNEDY

◊

from *The Sunlit Field*

Po was so small she was able to work her way through the crowd until she was in the front row. But, there was nothing there, only a large open space of clay, beaten down hard by many feet, circled by this great crowd standing about.

Just then, the people on the side where she stood let out a great shout. A string of men had come trotting out, one by one, from a little tent she had not noticed before. They were dressed alike, in long gray trousers, white flannel shirts, and hats peaked like a rider at the Fair. Their middles were circled by wide belts of white, lettered "Putnams."

From the other side, a second file of men trotted from a tent, and a second shout went up. At the tag end of this group, hurrying, and still fastening on his belt, she saw Restored. She spelled out, on his belt, the word "At-lantics."

There was a little silence, like in a church when some ritual is to begin. Then, stooping way down to come out of the tent, appeared one of the biggest men she'd ever seen.

He was bigger than Larry. As he sauntered out with a little jocular roll, the crowd gave a joyful moan as if it were clasping him to its breast. He smiled a little and raised an enormous arm in greeting. They yelled "Bull! Bull Bender!" After that, things began happening too fast for Po. "Sure," she thought, "It's like moving day in hell!"

At first she could make nothing of it. She did not know the why of the mad surges of delight, the fierce rages, the screaming exultations, the joyful frenzies. But suddenly, on that Sunday in 1857, in Fulton Street, in Brooklyn, Po felt tears come to her eyes.

She wanted deeply, urgently, for her father to be here. All her fears, in Fall River, on the ship, seemed washed away in a flood of sunlight.

On the field, the men flashed about, stretching their bodies in long beautiful arcs, or leaped into the air to catch the ball with easeful sureness in bare cupped hands. Yes, these were the tall men! And running with the full swinging strides he had told her of! And the men watching let out their entire lung content in complete anger, or threw an arm over the shoulder next them, in some feeling where no dregs of hate remained in their eyes.

And even if small squat row houses pressed close in around this open field, and it was no longer dewy morning, but afternoon, the feeling of joy, of exuberance, was here! Of a people, running, shouting, raging, anxious, but caught-up, possessed by the delight of their own activity. If they were gusty with anger, or screaming mad with joy, ready to fight or to embrace, they were also flashing, fleet, agile, boss of themselves. They seemed lost in a feeling of oneness.

She remembered the thin gray men like sheep sucked into and out of the thread mills in Fall River. In Ireland, such men had starved. In Fall River, they had food enough to keep alive, but it was as if they had been compressed into small flat molds. All the sap and color and change had gone from them. On a Sunday afternoon such as this, they sat in drab houses, too tired to move. Again she thought of her Da, and the cellar they'd lived in. But . . . no more of that! He hadn't made it. But, ah, wouldn't he be glad she had!

She understood about Larry and Restored now. She understood about this game of ball called base. Suddenly, at the next roar, she screamed too, in mad delight, not knowing what the play was, but happy to lose herself the way the crowd had. That big man they called Bull was standing out there, waving a club. She sensed they were all the mighty Bull, waving the club . . . or at least, his smaller brother.

She longed to know why the crowd was possessed with rage or delight. Next her stood a mild plump man in velveteen jacket, who smelled of beer and the long meerschaum he smoked. Suddenly, the crowd groaned, the mild man snatched off his peaked cap and jumped on it.

"Please! What happened?" she demanded of him.

He shrieked at her in German, as his eyes popped with rage. Po shrank back, half scared. But after a few moments, a player ran around the playing field, and the crowd seemed to be happy again. A thin dark man with beautiful mustachios kissed another mustachioed man next him. Po longed to share the general bliss. Timidly, she plucked mustachio's arm.

"What happened?" White teeth flashed, his hands made intricate gestures. She was inundated by a flood of Italian. She began to feel she'd gotten to heaven, but couldn't speak the language.

Then she saw a slender narrow-chested lad watching her with a smile. She remembered half-starved students around Trinity who looked like him. He had dark hair above a bulging white forehead, and dark eyes burned in an intense face. He leaned toward her so she could hear him above the crowd and gave her the glad tidings: "Twinkle-Toes made third base!"

Everything about this game must be learned as fast as possible. Maybe girls played it! Now it seemed all the players were walking on or off the field. There was a lull in the shouting. Po asked the dark-eyed one, "Is it far to a street called Pineapple?"

"No. Close. Looking for someone?"

"My cousin. Brian Brady."

"That runs Brady's Gardens? He's around. Saw him a while ago. My name's David Posen."

"I'm his cousin, Po O'Reilly, come from Ireland."

"Just stand here! I'll keep watching for him!"

But after a while, Po found herself looking, not for Brian, but Larry. Where had he gone? then she saw the blonde girl in the greenish-blue dress.

Most of the women had their eyes on some man's exploits on the field, but this girl was smiling with full red lips at someone sitting on the ground near by. She twirled her tiny blue ruffled parasol and wriggled about so the curve of her breasts showed above her low dress. Then the man she was flirting with stood up. It was Larry.

He crossed to her. Po could see that look of bursting out laughing on his face, his bright hair above the enormous shoulders. She had a strange sensation. Po guessed she was hungry or something. She felt empty. Then a kind of frozen rigidity settled in her, as if she had to keep her eyes un-waveringly on Larry. Dressed conspicuously, the girl still did not look like the street women in Cork. She was young, eighteen or nineteen, fresh, and yes . . . she was beautiful. Po could hear the girl's loud unself-conscious laugh, as she looked up into Larry's face invitingly.

"And who is that girl," Po asked Dave, "with that butter-y hat on her?"

"Who? Oh . . . there! That's Louise Denis!"

Intent as she was on what was happening between these two, Po sud-denly felt a strangeness in the air around her, like a cloud going before the sun. The people near her fell silent, became motionless, only their eyes turning to look at someone.

A big man was coming through the crowd. He was not as big as the Bull, but he was as massive as Larry, and in a certain way, built like Larry. His heavy shoulders, like Larry's, gave you the same feeling of power. But if they were built alike as two stony fountains, from Larry sunny water seemed to leap high in the air, while this man made you think of just the inflexible stone.

"And who is that, then?" Po asked Dave.

Dave stared at the man, with no fear, but a blank look. "William Hymes."

About thirty-five, Hymes's features were heavy and immobile looking, and under the new but dusty-looking beaver, his hair was dull brown and sparse. Po wondered why everyone seemed to look at him with such blank wooden expressions. He was common-looking as anyone here, his snuff-colored double-breasted tail coat no better than the crowd's. He looked even a little ill-kempt and his white stock was dingy. His glance was certainly not threatening. Indeed he paid no attention to anyone. He walked straight across the field, though, as if, seeing him, the game would suspend. It did.

Then Po saw Hymes was heading toward Louise Denis. Louise saw him coming, too, and made the great thing of flirting with Larry, laughing with wide sensuous red mouth up into Larry's face.

Then the clod was thrown. Po could not understand it. For what was the poor man doing but chasing some light-of-love, a thing accepted long since by the human race. The clod had landed in front of Hymes. In this crowd of expert tossers of balls, it could not have been meant to hit him. It was an expression of an emotion.

Hymes turned heavily, his massive shoulders hunched awkwardly. She felt a kind of admiration for him, for he stood, one against many, looking at the crowd with stolid courage.

By the time he turned, Louise had disappeared.

Hymes kept coming, though, straight toward Larry.

And then, it was a strange thing, but Larry seemed to lower his head with almost the same gesture as Hymes. You could think they were two great bulls, lords of the herd.

Then Hymes turned and walked off in the direction in which Louise had disappeared.

The game began again, quickly, as if some dark shadow, some apparition had appeared to claim all this sparkling zest, and they wanted to play again quickly, to forget they had seen it. They seemed to blink their eyes in the sun, to push the shadow back into their consciousness; as if they sensed it hovered, waiting to claim them; as if they feared the heady exuberance they breathed this day might evaporate like dew.

Po felt angry. She had been so caught up with the feeling of the free, happy, screaming crowd. She didn't want anything to spoil that.

"But—why—" she hardly knew how to ask Dave to explain. "You'd think he owned the place!"

"It's likely he does!" Dave's eyes looked over the heads of the crowd an instant, as if seeing the shadow. Then suddenly he gave a shout. "There's Brian! Brian Brady!"

Po felt herself trembling. The shadows that had dulled her at Fall River fell again. What if Brian did not want to be bothered with her? Or what if he did not like her?

Then she caught sight of the man Dave was bringing, and she knew it was all right. She wanted to laugh and cry, and guessed what she felt was homesickness. The thick brown hair, the deep-set gray eyes, were as familiar as a thatched roof. The cliff of his chin jutting between cascades of side-whiskers was as like home as a whiff of the green downs, or the mist off Ballybunian. Only he should not have been wearing a round bowler hat, a checkered vest and a blue coat with velvet lapels. Knee pants, gray wool stockings and a knit cap would have looked more natural.

A little boy of six clung to his coat tails, another lad about ten was at his side.

Then Brian grabbed her hands in great ham-like fists, and warmth ran all through her. "Hugh O'Reilly's girl!" Delight and surprise and love were all mixed up in his gray eyes. "Happy it is I am to lay eyes on you! Let me look at you now! Sure, darlint, your eyes are deep blue as the Lake of Shee-lin! And look at the face on her, Dave, pretty as a blushy rose!"

The little boys were not his sons. They were just friends, and they ran back to watch the game now.

"But your father? Where is he?"

"He's dead, Brian!"

"Ah, surra, it's that blaggard New England. If he'd but come to Brooklyn now, he'd be alive and singing! And Cousin Frank?"

Po looked at Brian's good-natured face. She could not speak. Then she said in a rush, "I ran away from there, Brian." She could not look at him or go on.

"It's all right, darlint. I'll not question you. You had reasons. And how was it you got here?"

"It was on a ship, and I stowing away!"

"Stowing away, is it?" Brian's eyes sparkled. "A slip of a girl! Well, that's done now! You'll stay with me. Mamie'll be glad to see you!"

At that moment, the crowd gave a great angry shout, and Brian dropped her hands and ran to the edge of the crowd, asking what had happened. Then she heard him yell in a dreadful voice: "The dirty dog! He tripped him as he went past! Didn't I see him with me own eyes? He oughta be hung!" After a few minutes, when the excitement died, he came back.

"Ah, poor Hugh," he sighed, "that lovely singer! I can hear him yet, singing 'Fair Athlone.' And to think he is dead!"

But just then there was the crack of a ball, the crowd yelled, and Brian was gone, screaming, red-faced. He came back soon, pulling his mouth down into mournful lines again.

"So poor Hugh is gone! I remember hearing of the crazy name he gave you!" But his eyes kept darting out to the field. A strident voice called, "Str—i-ke!" Brian's eyes blazed, and he ran off, screeching, "You're the blackest robber ever walked on Myrtle Avenue! Your mither was blind and your father an idjit!" Po thought it wonderful to hear him. When he returned again, he said, "Never mind me, darlint!" and he set his mouth in mournful lines again.

"Tis a game, this!" Po's eyes sparkled.

"You've seen nothing. Wait now till you see the Excelsiors play! That's the team Dave and I play on!"

Himself played! Ah, marvel! Somehow Po began to have the feeling these Excelsiors must be the wonder of the known world. The game had stopped while they hunted for a lost ball.

Some of the crowd, while they waited, clustered around a man, who was reading aloud to them from a newspaper. "There's Walt," said Brian. "Come on, let's hear what it is he's reading to them!"

This Walt was a big man, and though he seemed only in his late thirties, his beard was streaked with gray. The crowd was dressed in Sunday coats with high white collars and string ties, but Walt wore a red flannel shirt open at the neck, and a large round felt hat on the back of his head. He stopped reading a moment and looked up, and she saw his strange seer-like pale blue eyes. He began to read again in a deep resonant voice, and Po saw the print across the outspread newspaper, "New York Journal of Commerce." At first, she could make nothing of what he read, though in the crowd pressing in on him, she felt a gathering, outraged indignation. She listened, trying to understand why. Walt read on:

> "Since Mr. Cartwright founded the first ball club, the Knicker-bockers of New York . . . "

Someone let forth a sneering catcall, but Walt went on, saying each word as if he wanted them to miss none:

> " . . . there have come into existence three other clubs, the Eagles, Gothams and Empires of New York. These four clubs represent baseball today in America."

There was a second of silence, then a low hissing sound. A moment later, when it let loose, Po realized this had been the crowd drawing breath to let out a roar of outrage. Po had heard cursing along the byways of Ireland. It had been rich, too, but not so pointed or venomous as this.

"The low-flung sneaking pot-bellied plush-assed bastards!" a player near her yelled, red in the face. "They never even mentioned our names!"

Walt glanced around, and then he went on blandly, as though he were reading something mild and non-explosive.

> "Some of the most respected business men in New York play nowadays and the game threatens to supplant even the popular cricket.

> Our readers may remember Alexander Cartwright, who engaged
> in mercantile business on Fourth Street before he went to Califor-
> nia in the gold rush several years ago. It was this New York business
> man who invented the game about ten years ago. . . . "

"Aaeeyow!" The crowd gave an outraged incredulous groan.

"Invented the game!" Dave Posen yelled, indignant. "Why Bull Bender
played it upstate long ago as he can remember!"

Then Po caught her breath as she heard a familiar voice cry out from
the back of the crowd: "We played it in New England from way back!" It
was Larry.

Walt read on mercilessly:

> "The Knickerbockers make the rules and run the game since they
> were the first club and are generally recognized as the best. . . . "

Po was almost frightened at the feeling let loose around her. A chunky
player pounded one big fist into his open paw. "Champion of the world,
huh?" he said bitterly. "Because they're scared to play anyone else."

Walt went on:

> "The Knickerbockers are made up of some of the most solid and
> respectable business and professional men in New York. It is one
> of the tenets of this club, which has no doubt added to its strength,
> that no one can obtain admission to the club merely by being a
> good player. He must also have the reputation of a gentleman."

"So to play ball you gotta come on the *Mayflower!*" yelled the chunky
player, as the rest groaned and called imprecations.

"I come on the Cauliflower," a tall rangy Atlantic called, "and I'll play
'em any day!"

Walt was folding the paper blandly. "You boys ought to put a piece in
the paper yourselves! Maybe they don't know you're over here!"

Now Po saw, on the faces around her, the look she had seen on Restored,
in the cart. Cold, earnest, solemn. Then the tall rangy man said, slow,
heavy, grim, "They're gonna know soon!"

But now the game began again. Po kept demanding to know what it was
that made the crowd roar, and Brian or Dave would start to tell
her . . . until something else happened on the field, and they would become too excited to finish.

After a time, there was a great roar, and the crowd chanted like a litany:
"Bull, Bull Bender!"

"He's good, that one!" muttered Brian. "I gotta watch this, if the Excelsiors are to show they're best! Which we are!" A little man next to him took
exception to this, and began to argue hotly.

But the whole crowd hung motionless as the Bull swung on his great club. Then there was a terrific crack as the ball struck. It glanced off to one side, wild, over the head of the crowd, with electric speed and force. So quickly, she could not be sure it happened, she saw Larry, standing there, reach up a big arm, and as easily as if he were plucking a flower, pull the ball down out of the air.

She saw Dave Posen look at Brian and Brian at him. "Who's he?" Brian asked. "Never saw him before!" Dave said. They exchanged a glance, then Dave disappeared in the crowd.

Suddenly, there were shrill piping whistles. The crowd called out, not in the big roar as before, but in individual angry screams. They began to rush in one direction.

"The police!" Brian yelled. "Trying to break up the game!"

The peelers? Trying to break up such a beautiful thing as the game! "But why?" Po demanded.

"Blue laws! It's Sunday!" The police were all over now, in tight uniforms, brandishing staves.

"When else can they have time to play?" Walt cried as a policeman rushed by.

"I'll bet William Hymes put them on us!" someone screamed. Some of the crowd began to fight back.

Baseball clubs were swinging now, and fists. Po saw Brian, flailing away with his fists at a policeman, and as she watched, mouth open to yell, she saw another policeman, fat, start toward Brian, stave upraised.

At this sudden rude violent break up of the happiest thing she had seen in America, Po had felt a swelling of outrage pound up into her ears. She didn't know where the impulse came from. Maybe from long generations of rebels. She found her fingers closing around a piece of earth. Her impulses were always too strong for her. When she heard the clunk as the clod hit the policeman's neck, just as he was about to strike Brian, she was scared, but she felt good, too.

The policeman reeled off to one side, with a startled hurt look.

Brian ran toward her. He grabbed her arm. "Come along now." He breathed hard. "We better git from here!" They ran.

Down Fulton Street that Sunday afternoon, Brian and Po went.

And so Po arrived at her new home. "Running from the constabulary!" Po thought. "And what better way to arrive? Sure, I love this place entirely!"

JOSEPHINE JACOBSEN

◇

A Dream of Games

The game is dreamed for the rules:
when dusk takes the green diamond
set in dust, even the players' ghosts
are gone: the three-bat swing; the ghost

that hitched its belt, its cap; dipped
for the resin, hid its paw; leaned
like a pointer toward the tools-
of-ignorance crouch. In dark the rules wait it out.

The game we dream writes lines
where *love* means *nothing*, and *service*
is neither waiter, priest nor stallion,
and *let* is a net's whisper.

The game is dreamed for the rules.
Monte Alban's old rule dreamed
that ball-court from which the loser died.
Chaos, soft idiot, is close

as breath. But the games appear,
celestial in order; contracts we make
with light: the winner humbled,
the loser connected with his law.

GAIL MAZUR

◇

Listening to Baseball in the Car

for James Tate

This morning I argued with a friend
about angels. I didn't believe
in his belief in them—I can't
believe they're not a metaphor.
Our argument, affectionate,
lacking in animus, went nowhere.
We promised to talk again soon.
Now, when I'm driving away
from Boston and the Red Sox
are losing, I hear the announcer
say, "No angels in the sky today"—
baseball-ese for *a cloudless afternoon,*
no shadows to help a man
who waits in the outfield
staring into the August sun.
Although I know the announcer's
not a rabbi or sage (no,
he's a sort of sage, disconsolate
philosopher of batting slumps
and injuries), still I scan
the pale blue sky through my
polarized windshield, fervently
hopeful for my fading team
and I feel something a little
foolish, a prayerful throbbing
in my throat and remember
being told years ago that men

are only little lower than
the angels. Floating ahead of me
at the Vermont border, I see
a few wispy horsemane clouds
which I quietly pray will drift
down to Fenway Park where
a demonic opponent has just
slammed another Red Sox pitch,
and the center fielder—call him Jim—
runs back, back, back,
looking heavenward,
and is shielded and doesn't lose
the white ball in the glare.

EDNA FERBER

◊

A Bush League Hero

This is not a baseball story. The grandstand does not rise as one man and shout itself hoarse with joy. There isn't a three-bagger in the entire three thousand words, and nobody is carried home on the shoulders of the crowd. For that sort of thing you need not squander fifteen cents on your favorite magazine. The modest sum of one cent will make you the possessor of a Pink 'Un. There you will find the season's games handled in masterly fashion by a six-best-seller artist, an expert mathematician, and an original-slang humorist. No mere short story dub may hope to compete with these.

In the old days, before the gentry of the ring had learned the wisdom of investing their winnings in solids instead of liquids, this used to be a favorite conundrum: When is a prize-fighter not a prize-fighter?

Chorus: When he is tending bar.

I rise to ask you Brothah Fan, when is a ball player not a ball player? Above the storm of facetious replies I shout the answer:

When he's a shoe clerk.

Any man who can look handsome in a dirty baseball suit is an Adonis. There is something about the baggy pants, and the Micawber-shaped collar, and the skull-fitting cap, and the foot or so of tan, or blue, or pink under-shirt sleeve sticking out at the arms, that just naturally kills a man's best points. Then too, a baseball suit requires so much in the matter of leg. Therefore, when I say that Rudie Schlachweiler was a dream even in his baseball uniform, with a dirty brown streak right up the side of his pants where he had slid for base, you may know that the girls camped on the grounds during the season.

During the summer months our ball park is to us what the Grand Prix is to Paris, or Ascot is to London. What care we that Evers gets seven thousand a year (or is it a month?); or that Chicago's new South-side ball park seats thirty-five thousand (or is it million?). Of what interest are such meager items compared with the knowledge that "Pug" Coulan, who plays short, goes with Undine Meyers, the girl up there in the eighth row, with the pink dress and the red roses on her hat? When "Pug" snatches a high one out of the firmament we yell with delight, and even as we yell we turn sideways to look up and see how Undine is taking it. Undine's shining eyes are fixed on "Pug," and he knows it, stoops to brush the dust off his dirt-begrimed baseball pants, takes an attitude of careless grace and misses the next play.

Our grand-stand seats almost two thousand, counting the boxes. But only the snobs, and the girls with new hats, sit in the boxes. Box seats are comfortable, it is true, and they cost only an additional ten cents, but we have come to consider them undemocratic, and unworthy of true fans. Mrs. Freddy Van Dyne, who spends her winters in Egypt and her summers at the ball park, comes out to the game every afternoon in her automobile, but she never occupies a box seat; so why should we? She perches up in the grand-stand with the rest of the enthusiasts, and when Kelly puts one over she stands up and clinches her fists, and waves her arms and shouts with the best of 'em. She has even been known to cry, "Good eye! Good eye!" when things were at fever heat. The only really *blasé* individual in the ball park is Willie Grimes, who peddles ice-cream cones. For that matter, I once saw Willie turn a languid head to pipe, in his thin voice, "Give 'em a dark one, Dutch! Give 'em a dark one!"

Well, that will do for the first dash of local color. Now for the story.

Ivy Keller came home June nineteenth from Miss Shont's select school for young ladies. By June twenty-first she was bored limp. You could hardly see the plaits of her white tailored shirtwaist for fraternity pins and secret society emblems, and her bedroom was ablaze with college banners and pennants to such an extent that the maid gave notice every Thursday— which was upstairs cleaning day.

For two weeks after her return Ivy spent most of her time writing letters and waiting for them, and reading the classics on the front porch, dressed in a middy blouse and a blue skirt, with her hair done in a curly Greek effect like the girls on the covers of the Ladies' Magazine. She posed against the canvas bosom of the porch chair with one foot under her, the other swinging free, showing a tempting thing in beaded slipper, silk stocking, and what the story writers call "slim ankle."

On the second Saturday after her return her father came home for dinner at noon, found her deep in Volume Two of "Les Miserables."

"Whew! This is a scorcher!" he exclaimed, and dropped down on a wicker chair next to Ivy. Ivy looked at her father with languid interest, and smiled a daughterly smile. Ivy's father was an insurance man, alderman of his ward, president of the Civic Improvement club, member of five lodges, and an habitual delegate. It generally was he who introduced distinguished guests who spoke at the opera house on Decoration Day. He called Mrs. Keller "Mother," and he wasn't above noticing the fit of a gown on a pretty feminine figure. He thought Ivy was an expurgated edition of Lillian Russell, Madame De Staël, and Mrs. Pankhurst.

"Aren't you feeling well, Ivy?" he asked. "Looking a little pale. It's the heat, I suppose. Gosh! Something smells good. Run in and tell Mother I'm here."

Ivy kept one slender finger between the leaves of her book. "I'm perfectly well," she replied. "That must be beefsteak and onions. Ugh!" And she shuddered, and went indoors.

Dad Keller looked after her thoughtfully. Then he went in, washed his hands, and sat down at table with Ivy and her mother.

"Just a sliver for me," said Ivy, "and no onions."

Her father put down his knife and fork, cleared his throat, and spake, thus:

"You get on your hat and meet me at the 2:45 inter-urban. You're going to the ball game with me."

"Ball game!" repeated Ivy. "I? But I'd—"

"Yes, you do," interrupted her father. "You've been moping around here looking a cross between Saint Cecilia and Little Eva long enough. I don't care if you don't know a spitball from a fadeaway when you see it. You'll be out in the air all afternoon, and there'll be some excitement. All the girls go. You'll like it. They're playing Marshalltown."

Ivy went, looking the sacrificial lamb. Five minutes after the game was called she pointed one tapering white finger in the direction of the pitcher's mound.

"Who's that?" she asked.

"Pitcher," explained Papa Keller, laconically. Then, patiently: "He throws the ball."

"Oh," said Ivy. "What did you say his name was?"

"I didn't say. But it's Rudie Schlachweiler. The boys call him Dutch. Kind of a pet, Dutch is."

"Rudie Schlachweiler!" murmured Ivy, dreamily. "What a strong name!"

"Want some peanuts?" inquired her father.

"Does one eat peanuts at a ball game?"

"It ain't hardly legal if you don't," Pa Keller assured her.

"Two sacks," said Ivy. "Papa, why do they call it a diamond, and what are those brown bags at the corners, and what does it count if you hit the ball, and why do they rub their hands in the dust and then—er—spit on them, and what salary does a pitcher get, and why does the red-haired man on the other side dance around like that between the second and third brown bag, and doesn't a pitcher do anything but pitch, and wh–?"

"You're on," said papa.

After that Ivy didn't miss a game during all the time that the team played in the hometown. She went without a new hat, and didn't care whether *Jean Valjean* got away with the goods or not, and forgot whether you played third hand high or low in bridge. She even became chummy with Undine Meyers, who wasn't her kind of girl at all. Undine was thin in a voluptuous kind of way, if such a paradox can be, and she had red lips, and a roving eye, and she ran around downtown without a hat more than was strictly necessary. But Undine and Ivy had two subjects in common. They were baseball and love. It is queer how the limelight will make heroes of us all.

Now "Pug" Coulan, who was red-haired, and had shoulders like an ox, and arms that hung down to his knees, like those of an orang-outang, slaughtered beeves at the Chicago stockyards in winter. In the summer he slaughtered hearts. He wore mustard colored shirts that matched his hair, and his baseball stockings generally had a rip in them somewhere, but when he was on the diamond we were almost ashamed to look at Undine, so wholly did her heart shine in her eyes.

Now, we'll have just another dash or two of local color. In a small town the chances for hero worship are few. If it weren't for the traveling men our girls wouldn't know whether stripes or checks were the thing in gents' suitings. When the baseball season opened the girls swarmed on it. Those that didn't understand baseball pretended they did. When the team was out of town our form of greeting was changed from, "Good-morning!" or "Howdy-do!" to "What's the score?" Every night the results of the games throughout the league were posted up on the blackboard in front of Schlager's hardware store, and to see the way in which the crowd stood around it, and streamed across the street toward it, you'd have thought they were giving away gas stoves and hammock couches.

Going home in the street car after the game the girls used to gaze adoringly at the dirty faces of their sweat-begrimed heroes, and then they'd rush home, have supper, change their dresses, do their hair, and rush downtown past the Parker Hotel to mail their letters. The baseball boys boarded over at the Griggs House, which is third-class, but they used their tooth-picks, and held the post-mortem of the day's game out in front of the Parker Hotel, which is our leading hostelry. The postoffice receipts record for our town was broken during the months of June, July, and August.

Mrs. Freddy Van Dyne started the trouble by having the team over to dinner, "Pug" Coulan and all. After all, why not? No foreign and impecunious princes penetrate as far inland as our town. They get only as far as New York, or Newport, where they are gobbled up by many-moneyed matrons.

If Mrs. Freddy Van Dyne found the supply of available lions limited, why should she not try to content herself with a jackal or so?

Ivy was asked. Until then she had contented herself with gazing at her hero. She had become such a hardened baseball fan that she followed the game with a score card, accurately jotting down every play, and keeping her watch open on her knee.

She sat next to Rudie at dinner. Before she had nibbled her second salted almond, Ivy Keller and Rudie Schlachweiler understood each other. Rudie illustrated certain plays by drawing lines on the table-cloth with his knife and Ivy gazed, wide-eyed, and allowed her soup to grow cold.

The first night that Rudie called, Pa Keller thought it a great joke. He sat out on the porch with Rudie and Ivy and talked baseball, and got up to show Rudie how he could have got the goat of that Keokuk catcher if only he had tried one of his famous open-faced throws. Rudie looked politely interested, and laughed in all the right places. But Ivy didn't need to pretend. Rudie Schlachweiler spelled baseball to her. She did not think of her caller as a good-looking young man in a blue serge suit and a white shirt-waist. Even as he sat there she saw him as a blonde god standing on the pitcher's mound, with the scars of battle on his baseball pants, his left foot placed in front of him at right angles with his right foot, his gaze fixed on first base in a cunning effort to deceive the man at bat, in that favorite attitude of pitchers just before they get ready to swing their left leg and h'ist one over.

The second time that Rudie called, Ma Keller said:

"Ivy, I don't like that ball player coming here to see you. The neighbors'll talk."

The third time Rudie called, Pa Keller said: "What's that guy doing here again?"

The fourth time Rudie called, Pa Keller and Ma Keller said, in unison: "This thing has got to stop."

But it didn't. It had had too good a start. For the rest of the season Ivy met her knight of the sphere around the corner. Theirs was a walking court-ship. They used to roam up as far as the State road, and down as far as the river, and Rudie would fain have talked of love, but Ivy talked of baseball.

"Darling," Rudie would murmur, pressing Ivy's arm closer, "when did you first begin to care?"

"Why I liked the very first game I saw when Dad—"

"I mean, when did you first begin to care for me?"

"Oh! When you put three men out in that game with Marshalltown when the teams were tied in the eighth inning. Remember? Say, Rudie dear, what was the matter with your arm to-day? You let three men walk, and Albia's weakest hitter got a home run out of you."

"Oh, forget baseball for a minute, Ivy! Let's talk about something else. Let's talk about–us."

"Us? Well, you're baseball, aren't you?" retorted Ivy. "And if you are, I am. Did you notice the way that Ottumwa man pitched yesterday? He didn't do any acting for the grandstand. He didn't reach up above his head, and wrap his right shoulder with his left toe, and swing his arm three times and then throw seven inches outside the plate. He just took the ball in his hand, looked at it curiously for a moment, and fired it–*zing!*–like that, over the plate. I'd get that ball if I were you."

"Isn't this a grand night?" murmured Rudie.

"But they didn't have a hitter in the bunch," went on Ivy. "And not a man in the team could run. That's why they're tail-enders. Just the same, that man on the mound was a wizard, and if he had one decent player to give him some support–"

Well, the thing came to a climax. One evening, two weeks before the close of the season, Ivy put on her hat and announced that she was going downtown to mail her letters.

"Mail your letters in the daytime," growled Papa Keller.

"I didn't have time to-day," answered Ivy. "It was a thirteen-inning game, and it lasted until six o'clock."

It was then that Papa Keller banged the heavy fist of decision down on the library table.

"This thing's got to stop!" he thundered. "I won't have any girl of mine running the streets with a ball player, understand? Now you quit seeing this seventy-five-dollars-a-month bush leaguer or leave this house. I mean it."

"All right," said Ivy, with a white-hot calm. "I'll leave. I can make the grandest kind of angel-food with marshmallow icing, and you know yourself my fudges can't be equaled. He'll be playing in the major leagues in three years. Why just yesterday there was a strange man at the game–a city man, you could tell by his hatband, and the way his clothes were cut. He stayed through the whole game, and never took his eyes off Rudie. I just know he was a scout for the Cubs."

"Probably a hardware drummer, or a fellow that Schlachweiler owes money to."

Ivy began to pin on her hat. A scared look leaped into Papa Keller's eyes. He looked a little old, too, and drawn, at that minute. He stretched forth a rather tremulous hand.

"Ivy–girl," he said.

"What?" snapped Ivy.

"Your old father's just talking for your own good. You're breaking your ma's heart. You and me have been good pals, haven't we?"

"Yes," said Ivy, grudgingly, and without looking up.

"Well now, look here. I've got a proposition to make to you. The season's over in two more weeks. The last week they play out of town. Then the boys'll come back for a week or so, just to hang around town and try to get used to the idea of leaving us. Then they'll scatter to take up their winter jobs—cutting ice, most of 'em," he added, grimly.

"Mr. Schlachweiler is employed in a large establishment in Slatersville, Ohio," said Ivy, with dignity. "He regards baseball as his profession, and he cannot do anything that would affect his pitching arm."

Pa Keller put on the *tremolo* stop and brought a misty look into his eyes.

"Ivy, you'll do one last thing for your old father, won't you?"

"Maybe," answered Ivy, coolly.

"Don't make that fellow any promises. Now wait a minute! Let me get through. I won't put any crimp in your plans. I won't speak to Schlach- weiler. Promise you won't do anything rash until the ball season's over. Then we'll wait just one month, see? Till along about November. Then if you feel like you want to see him—"

"But how—"

"Hold on. You mustn't write to him, or see him, or let him write to you during that time, see? Then, if you feel the way you do now, I'll take you to Slatersville to see him. Now that's fair, ain't it? Only don't let him know you're coming."

"M-m-m-yes," said Ivy.

"Shake hands on it." She did. Then she left the room with a rush, headed in the direction of her own bedroom. Pa Keller treated himself to a prodi- gious wink and went out to the vegetable garden in search of Mother.

The team went out on the road, lost five games, won two, and came home in fourth place. For a week they lounged around the Parker Hotel and held up the street corners downtown, took many farewell drinks, then, slowly, by ones and twos, they left for the packing houses, freight depots, and gents' furnishing stores from whence they came.

October came in with a blaze of sumac and oak leaves. Ivy stayed home and learned to make veal loaf and apple pies. The worry lines around Pa Keller's face began to deepen. Ivy said that she didn't believe that she cared to go back to Miss Shont's select school for young ladies.

October thirty-first came.

"We'll take the eight-fifteen to-morrow," said her father to Ivy.

"All right," said Ivy.

"Do you know where he works?" asked he.

"No," answered Ivy.

"That'll be all right. I took the trouble to look him up last August."

The short November afternoon was drawing to its close (as our best tal- ent would put it) when Ivy and her father walked along the streets of

Slatersville. (I can't tell you what streets, because I don't know.) Pa Keller brought up before a narrow little shoe shop.

"Here we are," he said, and ushered Ivy in. A short, stout, proprietary figure approached them smiling a mercantile smile.

"What can I do for you?" he inquired.

Ivy's eyes searched the shop for a tall golden-haired form in a soiled baseball suit.

"We'd like to see a gentleman named Schlachweiler—Rudolph Schlachweiler," said Pa Keller.

"Anything very special?" inquired the proprietor. "He's—rather busy just now. Wouldn't anybody else do? Of course, if—"

"No," growled Keller.

The boss turned. "Hi! Schlachweiler!" he bawled toward the rear of the dim little shop.

"Yessir," answered a muffled voice.

"Front!" yelled the boss, and withdrew to a safe listening distance.

A vaguely troubled look lurked in the depths of Ivy's eyes. From behind the partition of the rear of the shop emerged a tall figure. It was none other than our hero. He was in his shirtsleeves, and he struggled into his coat as he came forward, wiping his mouth with the back of his hand, hurriedly, and swallowing.

I have said that the shop was dim. Ivy and her father stood at one side, their backs to the light. Rudie came forward, rubbing his hands together in the manner of clerks.

"Something in shoes?" he politely inquired.

Then he saw.

"Ivy!—ah—Miss Keller!" he exclaimed. Then, awkwardly: "Well, how-do, Mr. Keller. I certainly am glad to see you both. How's the old town? What are you doing in Slatersville?"

"Why—Ivy—" began Pa Keller, blunderingly.

But Ivy clutched his arm with a warning hand. The vaguely troubled look in her eyes had become wildly so.

"Schlachweiler!" shouted the voice of the boss. "Customers!" and he waved a hand in the direction of the fitting benches.

"All right, sir," answered Rudie. "Just a minute."

"Dad had to come on business," said Ivy, hurriedly. "And he brought me with him. I'm—I'm on my way to school in Cleveland, you know. Awfully glad to have seen you again. We must go. That lady wants her shoes, I'm sure, and your employer is glaring at us. Come, dad."

At the door she turned just in time to see Rudie removing the shoe from the pudgy foot of the fat lady customer.

We'll take a jump of six months. That brings us into the lap of April.

Pa Keller looked up from his evening paper. Ivy, home for the Easter vacation, was at the piano. Ma Keller was sewing.

Pa Keller cleared his throat. "I see by the paper," he announced, "that Schlachweiler's been sold to Des Moines. Too bad we lost him. He was a great little pitcher, but he played in bad luck. Whenever he was on the slab the boys seemed to give him poor support."

"Fudge!" exclaimed Ivy, continuing to play, but turning a spirited face toward her father. "What piffle! Whenever a player pitches rotten ball you'll always hear him howling about the support he didn't get. Schlachweiler was a bum pitcher. Anybody could hit him with a willow wand, on a windy day, with the sun in his eyes."

LULU GLASER

◊

The Lady Fan

Anyone with any real blood in his or her—as the case may be—veins cannot help being a fan, once he, or she, has learned to know the great national sport of America. Being a true American and being a fan are synonymous. There are exceptions to every rule, and once in a while you may find "a good citizen" who does not love the diamond game, but it's not often. It would not surprise me any to hear of some state legislature passing a law that would make it a crime for employers to keep their underlings confined to their tasks such time as the home team is in the thick of the fight. To be sure, all the employers would not favor such a move, but I have no doubt that you could find a good many of them who would be willing to side with the motion.

We will go out to the ball game. We enter and take our seats and look at the thousands upon thousands gathered there and wonder where they all come from. No matter what day it be that we are here, we invariably find the same enormous house. We gaze around. Such a great crowd would not make you wonder so much, if they appeared as though recruited from the ranks of the army of the unemployed. But they do not. We see a prosperous business man, happy and smiling—that is, if the team's in the lead—discussing the game with some leading light of the law. We can pick out leaders in all the professions and any number of clergymen. Here are representatives and senators, mayors and governors, all sorts of political bigwigs. The President and the Vice-President do not find it beneath their dignity to sit here and root like the veriest thirty-third degree fan: as a matter of fact, both of them [William Howard Taft and James S. Sherman] have stated that they thoroughly enjoy it. This baseball audience can be compared, with no loss of prestige to it, either, with any gathering of celebrities you might choose.

Now the game is in full swing. We are a couple of runs behind and it is the seventh inning. The end is coming. What beseeching supplications are poured out to the man at the bat. How his every motion is watched. But he fails. A sigh ascends to heaven, a sigh deep and heartfelt, and the eighth inning is upon us. More expectancy and despair, then the ninth. The enemy are done away with and we are having our last chance. A hit and all around us are on their feet roaring. Another, and hats and coats are wildly waving, while the din resembles a battle of artillery. But the next man, heedless of our wishes, strikes out. The uproar ceases for a moment and then breaks out louder than ever, as one of the stars steps up for his turn. But alas! He, too, succumbs easily and walks miserably back to the bench, while the great crowd remains quiet and chagrined. Here is our last chance. An eerie silence hangs over the field. Everywhere tense faces and clenched hands. In front of us, the senator, whose eloquent tariff speech had resounded through the country but yesterday, jumps to his feet, imploring, red-faced, and beseeches the batter to save the day. His voice alone breaks the stillness. We feel the blood pounding in our veins until we almost smother. We can hardly breathe. The pitcher shoots the ball, and involuntarily we rise up and watch it come to the man at the plate. He swings: We hear the crash of wood and leather. Far in the air it flies and we watch the outfielder desperately running back, while the men on the bases tear madly around. Now the crowd finds its voice again. The ball, they see, cannot be reached. It's a home run, and the game is over. Who can picture the glorious feeling that surges through one's body? You forget all but your joy. Some time after you will find yourself standing on your seat, wildly waving handkerchief or scorecard, weak almost to fainting. Then you depart, happy, most likely to wake up during the night and find yourself smiling and enjoying the day over again. Who wouldn't be a baseball fan?

I just love baseball. I think it's the greatest game in the world. Next to being a star on the stage, I think that there can be no other life as attractive and full of incident as that of a baseball player. If I were a man I would surely try to get out and make good with one of the big league teams. I know the game pretty well. In fact I feel safe in saying that there are very few women in the country who follow the game more closely than I do. In every big city in which I am playing I go out to the ball games every possible chance I get. There's nothing in the world, not even a first night appearance with a new play, that's so exciting as watching a man smash out a long hit with three men on bases. Why, it makes one feel glad to be living for days afterward. I was talking with a reporter in Boston a short while ago, and I have reason to think that I surprised him with my knowledge of what he called essentially a man's game. In fact, in his headline with the story of the interview, he declared that in my case the accident of birth had deprived the diamond of a great star. I believe that women, were it not for the conventionalities, would excel the members of the "stronger" sex when it came to playing ball. They have the high nervous temperament and the quickness of perception that go to make up a good ball player. Then they would be far more daring and willing to risk their chances on some sudden strategic move.

When I was a girl I used to play ball a lot and filled in every position on the diamond. It was in those days that I picked up whatever little I know about baseball. I remember that then the one great sorrow of my youthful heart was that I had not been born a boy so that I might be a great ball player. Even now, at times, I have the same feeling. Why, I'd rather sit on a fence in the burning sun and watch a crowd of youngsters playing scrub, with trees for bases and a bunch of string for a ball, than go anywhere else I know of.

From my experience I have come to the conclusion that to be a baseball fan, a person must devote all his or her time to it, and not let outside affairs interfere as outside affairs will surely suffer. For baseball fever is absolutely incurable, and once you catch it, you might as well resign to the inevitable; that is, your friends might, for you will be willing enough to stand it.

Traveling as much as I do, one meets all kinds of people and sees all kinds of sights. In the course of my wanderings, I have had occasion to meet quite a few of the big leaguers, and in every instance I have found them delightful gentlemen, by no means the rather uncultured beings that many people seem to consider them. From the members of the profession that I am acquainted with, I am sure that I was not wrong in my girlhood days when I thought that to be a ball player was one of the greatest things on earth.

ALISON GORDON

◊

Dream Game

A dream game is always played in the sunshine, memory omitting the lights or the cold of reality. It is watched from the boxes down the first-base line in Fenway Park in Boston or Royals Stadium in Kansas City, with a hot dog from Detroit in one hand and a beer from Milwaukee in another, surrounded by Baltimore fans waiting for the operatic vendor from Al Lang Field in St. Petersburg to pass by singing "East Side, West Side" in a ringing baritone. Dreams are like that, you remember the best.

The game proceeds at just the right pace: the one detractors call boring. It is gentle and relaxed, full of spaces for reflection or conversation, quiet moments in which to relish a play just made or a confrontation about to occur. What's the rush? The longer the game, the more there is to enjoy.

It's hard to understand people who hate baseball, but easy to pity them. Never to have felt the surge of joy watching a ball sail over the fence or a fielder making a running, leaping catch is to have missed a great pleasure indeed. For that matter, to have missed the anger and despair when the ball sailing over the fence beats your favourite team in an important game is equally sad, because the caring feels so good. To find baseball boring is to have missed drama and nuance, the laughter and the tears that come from joy or sorrow. It's a shame.

The unfortunate thing about baseball for the novice fan is that the more you know about it the more attractive it becomes, and there aren't enough teachers to go around.

It's not hard to find the excitement in a high-scoring game the home team wins, but the pleasure of a pitchers' duel is more elusive. To find the joy in a low-scoring game, you have to understand that the central confrontation of the game is being won by the pitcher, this time, but the battle is rejoined with each pitch.

That's what is at the core of the sport. Standing on a hill precisely ten inches high is a man who uses every bit of muscle and talent and brain he has to throw a ball harder or with more spin of one kind or another than anyone in the stands ever could. He has a lone enemy and eight accomplices on the field with him. His catcher is crouched behind the plate doing some (or occasionally, all) of his thinking for him, suggesting which pitches to throw. Seven other men, four in the infield and three in the outfield, are ready to make the pitcher look good. His enemy stands next to the plate with a stick in his hand, all by himself. It's as simple as that. The guy with the stick is trying to hit the ball thrown by the man on the hill, preferably out of range of the gloved accomplices.

The complications come in when we peek inside each man's head, the real battleground of baseball. The pitcher and catcher remember what they have learned from the scouts and from their own experience with the hitter. Does he have trouble with curveballs? Will he go for the slider low and outside? Does he swing at the first pitch or watch it? In short, is there an easy way to get this guy out? The fielders are remembering, too. Does the hitter pull the ball? Should the outfielders shade him to left or right? What's the pitcher going to throw?

The hitter, for his part, is reviewing what he knows about the pitcher and catcher, while trying to watch the fielders in case they open a hole he can hit through. All of the cerebration goes on in the time it takes the pitcher to get the sign from the catcher, wind up, and throw the ball, to the accompaniment of a hellacious hullabaloo from the paying customers in the stands.

Add a base runner or two and the equation becomes even more complex. The pitcher and catcher are worrying that the runner will try to steal and are trying to prevent it. The catcher will often call for a fastball with men on base to give himself a fighting chance.

That will please the hitter, because fastballs are easier to hit, but he has to worry about the base runner, too. He gets signs from the third-base coach to tell him whether he should swing or not, hit behind the runner into rightfield, or simply swing away. And, oh yes, he has to hit a round ball with a round bat, reckoned by some to be the most difficult endeavour in all of sport.

The experienced fans understand all of this, and even have some thinking of their own to do. Anyone can see the hitter's batting average on the scoreboard and guess at his chances, but the ardent fans know more. They might remember the last time the two players squared off, when the pitcher gave up a home run, or know that the hitter is in a three-game slump. They might even know that the pitcher's wife just had a baby and he's tired.

The numbers define the game, but so do human factors. These athletes, unencumbered (with the exception of catchers) by the padding, helmets, and masks of hockey and football, have faces, and their isolation on the field gives them no place to hide. This is one reason that newspapers and magazines profile these players more than they do those in football or hockey, and why readers are eager to learn more about them.

Their personalities also show clearly in the way they play. No one watching Pete Rose in action can have any doubt about the type of man he is. Compare the way Eddie Murray arrogantly approaches the plate with the excuse-me diffidence of Todd Cruz and see if you can figure out which is the slugger. This body language even shows what kind of a day a player is having. The difference between a relief pitcher struggling for control and the same one in command of his game is like watching two different men.

Sometimes the confrontation is classic, usually when it is the team's best pitcher against the other team's best hitter when the game is on the line. There's intimidation on both sides. The batter digs his spikes into the dirt and glares, saying with his eyes, "Throw the damn ball."

The pitcher responds. He throws it right at the batter's throat. "Out of my way, mother. Get back where you belong."

The batter picks himself up out of the dirt and laughs. The fans howl for the pitcher's head. The show goes on.

In Yankee Stadium on October 10, 1980, the confrontation was between George Brett, the Royal third baseman who had hit .390 in the regular season, and Goose Gossage, the Yankee reliever who had a 2.27 earned run average and twenty saves. The league's best reliever was up against the league's best hitter in the third game of the league championship series, but it was even more than that. It was also the fourth time the two teams had met in the playoffs, and the Yankees had won the three previous times. The Royals had never made it to the World Series but they had a 2–0 lead in games this time. They were hungry.

The score was 2–1 Yankees in the seventh inning and there were two men on when Brett came to bat, speedy Willie Wilson and U.L. Washington. Brett hadn't had a hit in seven at bats.

There were 56,000 fans in the stands, and every one of them was screaming: "GOOooooose, GOOooooose" echoed off the pillared façades of the historic park. They were banshees, drowning out the few voices shouting in the visiting dugout: "It's going to happen! It's going to happen!"

It was a moment so exciting, so purely dramatic, that years later it still gives me chills. In memory the two are frozen for an instant before Gossage threw his first pitch. Then whap, it was over in the blink of an eye—the delivery, the swing, and then the ball flying harder and faster than physics should allow into the third deck of the rightfield grandstand. There was no doubt about it. Brett was the Royals and Gossage the Yankees, and the series was won and lost on that single pitch.

OONA SHORT

◊

The Truth About Paradise

"*W*ill I have a good view of first base?" Evie asked.

The usher shot her a nervous look and fled to the top of the stairs, where he disappeared into the crowds of people pouring into the upper decks of the stadium.

Evie glanced down at the field, then turned to the man sitting behind her. "Is this the best possible view of first base?"

"Whoa! You got some hair!" he replied. He was naked except for running shorts and a can of beer in his hand. Evie tried not to bump her chin against his knees and repeated her question.

"Woof! What hair!" He got up from his seat and headed for the same stairway as the usher.

Evie turned around. The wind blowing in towards left field tousled her hair – dyed not the blonde she had hoped for but a shade that exactly duplicated the orange of the home team's color. She brushed some strands out of her eyes and peered lovingly at the field. It was beautiful. "I am here, you beautiful field," she announced loudly enough to draw stares from some of the arriving fans.

She settled into her seat and drew the folds of her black dress around her. The saleswoman had told her the dress was designed to be draped in a variety of ways. "What could those ways have been?" Evie wondered. There were always leftover hooks with no matching eyes when she did it at home, and she felt lucky when she identified armholes.

She did the best she could with it and thought today she'd achieved a fun-Gothic quality, although some people on the subway ride to the stadium had shied away from her and one woman had offered to give her some spare change.

"I am here," she repeated more softly. No more sitting alone in front of the television set for 162 games every year. The corners of her mouth turned upward. "When I cheer, everyone will hear me. People watching TV may see me." She smiled a roguish smile. She'd have this game on videotape, as she did all the others.

Three young women entered and sat directly in front of her. "And as for these *blonde people*," Evie thought, watching the new arrivals toss their manes, "these natural *blondes* will know I'm here and they'll be jealous."

A sudden cheer told her the athletes had taken the field. From her seat high behind the home team dugout, facing first base, Evie couldn't see the players. But she knew exactly where he was. "My presence will be known to all assembled here today," she thought, as the crowd rose for the National Anthem. "Me, Evie Berger, today . . . "

"O'er the laAND of the free-eee . . . " A low mad whistle, the cry of a fantastic bird.

"And the home (wait wait wait) of the (wait wait) brave."

The stadium erupted into cheers again, relieved that the preliminaries had ended and the game would at last begin. There was a confused creaking of seats being unfolded and the sound of bodies thudding into them. "Screw the Braves!" yelled a voice behind Evie, followed by a metallic pop, a slow fizz, and the pungent smell of beer.

"Now take it easy," Evie cautioned herself. She hyperventilated at the beginning of every ballgame. Anything could happen. A player could be standing out there in center field picking his nose and the next thing you knew the whole game depended on him. But the thing about these people—and Evie told her theory to anyone who'd listen—was that they knew what to do when an object was hurtling towards them and people were running every which way. They knew how to relax and pay attention at the same time! They had a gift, a precious gift, for getting to the heart of the game, where there was joy.

Her eyes went automatically to the muscular figure assuming first base: Roger Paradise, the captain of the team. He knew more about baseball than anyone. Every woman in the stadium was shifting to get a better view of him—dark and dashing, handsome enough to be a matinee idol, Evie had heard said, although she personally didn't go for that type. The girls in front of her pointed him out and giggled. Evie was offended. She leaned forward and tapped one of them on her tanned shoulder. "Excuse me," she said. "Try to remember that Roger Paradise is the epitome of baseball. And baseball is the epitome of purity."

All three girls turned and stared blankly. Evie wondered which word she'd used that they were hearing for the first time.

The lineup cards were exchanged. Evie had a good view of Paradise. She felt so close to him now, even though from where she sat he seemed not much larger than he did on TV. How unhappy he seemed, pacing around and muttering to himself at first base! Evie was puzzled, especially after what had happened the night before. For one disheartening moment, considering their relationship, she was almost put off. Then she smiled knowingly and settled back to wait.

The game was underway. Patterns of players formed, dissolved, reformed on the field, its grass lush and green with recent rain. Under the primitive blue sky, it was like watching wheat blowing, Evie thought — although she had never seen wheat — or waves whipped by the wind. The visiting team was retired quickly in its half of the first inning, and the home team prepared for its time at bat. Evie couldn't see Roger Paradise, who batted third, but she knew all too sadly what he was doing: sneaking a cigarette in the dugout.

She was right. He stomped the butt out quickly after the lead-off batter flied to right. He took his bat from the rack, inspected it, and headed for the on deck circle, where he knelt, as if in prayer.

"Screw airplanes," he muttered, his head bowed, as a jet began its roaring pass overhead. "Screw pilots who can't land or take off unless I'm batting. Screw the subway behind center field. Screw everybody who's gotta travel somewhere else the minute I gotta hit a goddamned ball."

There was a disturbed hubbub about a called third strike at the plate that turned to cheers when the name Roger Paradise was announced. He knew everyone was depending on him. He strode to the plate, the little nagging voice in his head growing louder: "Tap the head of the bat on the ground . . . tap the top of your batting helmet . . . hoist the bat over your shoulders and align the knuckles . . . look to see if they're aligned, don't leave it to chance . . . see if the goddamned knuckles are even there, some days you can't be sure . . . position the feet . . . knees . . . hips — not too open . . . shoulders — not too closed . . . "

The pitcher, sly and wiry in early middle age, gave Paradise a knowing leer.

"Nothing fast and inside, not this guy," Paradise thought, windmilling the bat. "It'll be a breaking ball, I know that — but does he know I know that?"

The pitch was low, for a ball.

"I wonder if he's remembering last night," thought Evie.

Paradise stepped back into the box, tapped the bat, tapped the helmet, checked his knuckles. He couldn't remember when these rituals had started. There had been a time, before he hit the big time, when everything had just seemed to happen on its own. He missed those days.

The next pitch was outside. Ball two. "Now something's gonna come over the plate," thought Paradise. "I just gotta connect."

"Maybe he's wondering where I'm sitting," thought Evie.

Low and away. Ball three. The crowd murmured its contentment.

"Connect!" thought Paradise.

The pitcher cursed himself as his fourth pitch went into the dirt behind home plate. Paradise flung his bat to the ground and cantered to first base like a landlord making an inspection. Thirty thousand people cheered him and he never heard a sound. He chatted with the visiting first baseman without hearing a word that was said. In a wary crouch, just wide of the base, Paradise was sad.

"Walked him; well, that's good," thought Evie, relieved he was on base where she could see him. Still, it wasn't quite the same to just walk there. Everyone must want to flail out and hit something. The thought led her to glance at the girls in front of her. Three young men in adjoining seats had noticed them, too. The girls seemed to be tanner now, if possible, than they had been at the beginning of the game. "Exposure to the sun makes you ugly," thought Evie, pulling a flapping length of fabric over her pale arms. "Eventually."

People of all ages streamed up and down the stairways, new arrivals carrying pennants or giant inflatable baseball bats; others with food: hot dogs, popcorn, sodas, leaving wet blotches against the thin cardboard boxes they were carried in. Evie leaned her head against the cool metal section divider. What a day. And it would get better. She looked expectantly down at the field. The second inning was about to start. She sighed with the knowledge that Paradise would sneak another cigarette before going out to play first base. She waited patiently for his sign.

Evie's invitation to the stadium had come the night before, during a long and hard fought game, twice delayed by rain. She lay in front of her television set in a baseball stupor, trusting the cries of an enthusiastic announcer to wake her if she fell asleep. Just before an expected double play, Paradise, playing first base, signaled to the second baseman. In a strangely hypnotic ritual, he touched his chest, his right ear, his left shoulder, and his chest again. Twice he did that: chest, right ear, left shoulder, chest. Then he looked directly at the camera and said the word "Evie." Evie jumped up and rewound her VCR. Maybe he had been saying "easy." But no, she played back the tape—a dozen times she replayed it—and he had said "Evie."

She could barely sleep. She arrived at work late, exhausted from a half-hour struggle to get into her dress. Her co-workers ignored her. Evie dove into a pile of materials on her desk, but her gift for putting things in alphabetical order seemed to have abandoned her.

"Up all night again watching baseball?" asked the woman in an adjoining cubicle, hearing Evie's sighs. The woman never looked up from the files she was stamping "Disapproved." "I don't understand it," the woman continued, "a young girl like you liking to watch men spit."

"Dorothy, there's more to baseball than spitting."

"You want my advice, give it up. Find a man who doesn't spit."

"I don't need any other man."

Dorothy looked up. "Other?"

"I have a very special, sacred relationship," mumbled Evie, turning back to her work.

"Yeah sure," chimed in Laurie, sticking her head out from a cubicle decorated with Strawberry Shortcake posters. She and Dorothy laughed together.

"As a matter of fact," said Evie loudly. "Roger Paradise has invited me to this afternoon's ballgame."

"No kidding—you know him?" asked Laurie.

"Not exactly. He . . . beckoned to me through the television screen last night."

"You don't say." Laurie swiveled in her chair and yelled to a young man wheeling baskets of interoffice memos. "Danny! Roger Paradise wants Evie to go to the ballgame today. He beckoned her on TV."

"Way to go, Evie! Mickey Mantle wants me to kiss his—"

Evie slammed down her files and headed out the door.

"Whoa, Paradise! Woof!" A knee slammed against Evie's shoulder. She joined in the cheering for the play at first base: a graceful leap and elegant throw impossible for anyone but Roger Paradise.

Paradise heard none of it. He circled his base, using his spikes to arrange the dirt around the basepath just the way he liked it. He couldn't get the old feeling back. Day after day, he tried to play better. Night after night, he had the dreams: botched plays from the past come back to haunt him. Dreams of the future haunted him, too. They were chaotic, acrobatic omens of the time he'd disappoint everyone who was counting on him by not being able to play at all.

The humid, buggy air blew against the stream of sweat trickling behind his ears and down his neck. He passed his forehead through the crook of his elbow, removed his cap, and ran his fingers through his hair, which still held the shape of his batting helmet. Goddamn bugs. And now what? A mosquito? Now there's mosquitoes?

He reached out to swat it. The mosquito flew around his body, Paradise swatting it everywhere: his chest, his right ear, his left shoulder, his chest again.

Evie sat straight up in her seat. There it was. That strange hypnotic ritual.

Paradise stood still as the mosquito hovered just in front of his eyes. "Okay buddy," Paradise muttered, catching it with a bold, upward wave of his hand. "NOW!" he yelled, and squashed it dead.

Evie bolted from her seat and headed for the field.

"Shall I call him Roger? I always call him Roger." She raced down a series of circular ramps. "I can't very well call him *Mister* Paradise, that sounds silly. . . . I can't help it if it sounds silly, that's his name."

She grabbed a railing just in time to catch herself from tumbling into the parking lot below. A young couple ambled by, saw Evie, and backed away hurriedly. "You'll see," she thought, resuming her run "I'm needed here."

She took the next two ramps at a steadier pace, until she emerged into the seating section level with the field. She could see him now. He was waving.

"Here I come," she whispered. She threaded her way through the fans moving to and from their seats and, before anyone could see what she was doing, slipped under a railing and onto the field.

"God, it's *dirty* down here," she thought. Her sandals were already filling with pebbles that would ruin her nylons. Paradise had his back to her and was farther away than he had looked. She ran towards him, feeling the full force of the heat accumulated in the well of the stadium. "Why doesn't he turn around?" she thought. "He *invited* me." Paradise, running the last play over and over in his head, was unaware of Evie.

"He must want me to surprise him!" Evie thought. "I'm special enough for him to want me to tap him on the shoulder. Then he'll spin around and hold me and twirl me in a little dance until the stars come out over the diamond and the crowd cheers."

She was close enough now to inhale the musty, smoky aroma of his uniform. "You don't get *that* on TV," she noted. Her hand reached up past the numeral embossed on his broad back, past his name, and hovered there. Paradise, sensing a presence, turned quickly to squash another mosquito. His eyes widened, his breath quickened, he reeled back in horror.

This was no mosquito! This was a bat! A black-winged creature with a deathly pale face and hair the color of his jersey! And it was on his base, like one of those three ghosts, the Ghost of Baseball Past, or worse—*much worse*—the Ghost of Baseball Yet To Come! "What do you want from me?" he asked, clutching his chest.

"Oh my God, I've killed him," thought Evie. It was becoming clear to her now. She was on television in a dress that didn't fit, her nylons in shreds, a freak at first base. And she was videotaping *this?* She felt tears start to roll over her lower lashes.

"She's so *sad*," thought Paradise, marveling at his urge to reach out and hold her. He fought it off. If word got out he was an easy hugger he'd have to embrace every weirdo in the stadium who was having a bad day. Still, he held up a palm to delay the approaching security guards.

The stands were absolutely silent. No jets roared overhead. No subway rumbled behind center field. "Goddamn-it!" thought Paradise. "Why isn't it like this when I'm batting?" He spoke. "Are you all right?"

Evie nodded.

"What are you doing here?"

"I thought seeing me would cheer you up," she blurted, wiping away a tear.

"Cheer me up! I don't need cheering up! I need to play better!" He didn't know why he told her that. He didn't know why he was talking to her at all. He was starting to like her. She was different from most of the people he met at first base.

"You play fine," said Evie. "You want to hear my theory?"

Paradise listened in bewilderment as the visitor spoke. It was something about a guy in center field picking his nose and something about how he, Roger Paradise, had a gift, and then she got to a part about joy, and something inside him went *click*, like the sound of a well-hit ball.

The guards, tired of waiting, headed towards them. The crowd was getting restless. Paradise longed to go back to playing baseball again, this game, and all the games waiting to be played, not to please the fans, the managers, the coaches, the writers, his teammates, but because he loved baseball so damn much. That was the God's honest truth, and here it took this strange, winged creature—this baseball bat—to remind him of it.

"What's your name?" he asked. "Eerie? *Evie* . . . Well, if I ever start forgetting the spirit of baseball, Evie, I'll think of you." He gave her a dazzling smile.

"Thank you, Roger," said Evie proudly.

The crowd stood and cheered as she was escorted from the field. "Everyone's so nice here," thought Evie, touched by the fans' support. She made a mental note to come out to the ballpark more often.

EILEEN MYLES

◊

American Baseball

I'm sick of baseball,
sick of the points
 & the players & the
averages, the endless
 voice droning,
 narrating the play.
I wish the players
didn't have names,
I hate the players,
 I hate the players'
 wives I never
 wonder if I'm
 good enough
 I hate baseball
Whenever I get
 invited I turn
 the offer down.
It's usually too hot & at night
 I just want to
get drunk in
 the stands &
 I could do
that anywhere.
I don't know
why everyone
loves it so
much, they
just love to watch.

They just love
the sound. I
   also admire
    the crack of
   the bat against
   the ball. I
love the desperate
little run the
outfielder makes
to catch it. He
never does. By

  now I've
  turned my head.

  I hate sitting in
   the stuffy rooms
with people watching
baseball. It's so human

everyone around
sipping & cheering
slipping in and
out, their

favorites stepping
on to the screen
this person
forgetting where she
is for some reason
so locked in to
no one that they
know just like
all the others

in the room
but I don't
care. I'm
  not devoted to a buzzing
   in the air to stampede the night
    that's closing in slowly

to suffocate us & no one
wants to watch *that*. The favorite

steps on the screen &
steps out. You've
got a few
stars doesn't
everyone?

No, I don't.
So I step outside
where it's cool
to smoke a cigarette
& someone comes
outside after me
and talks to me a bit
& then the bell rings
game's beginning

again & she says Wouldn't you
like to come

back inside?

ANNA QUINDLEN

◊

A Baseball Wimp

It was during the thirteenth inning, with it all tied up at 3–3, that I found myself hanging over the partition inside a Checker cab, my back end in the back seat, my front end in the front, twisting the dials of the radio to find the playoff game between the Mets and the Astros. My driver, who had been tuned to so-called easy-listening music, was a Thai immigrant who seemed to think that what he was witnessing was exactly what you could expect of indigenous Americans. His English was spotty, but moments before I finally picked up the game amid a ribbon of relentless static, he did manage to say feelingly, "You big fan."

Well, no. Actually, I am what is known in the vernacular as a baseball wimp. I ignore the whole season until, each year at this time, during the playoffs and the World Series, I become terribly interested in baseball. You've heard Reggie Jackson called Mr. October? I am Ms. October. Someone very nicely described it the other night as eating the whipped cream off the sundae. At home, not nicely at all, I am described as a disgrace to a noble sport, a fair-weather fan, a Joanie-come-lately.

I've always liked baseball, even as a child, when tradition dictated that I should be prohibited from playing, and my three brothers should be egged on. I like the sense of both the camaraderie and the aloneness of it, the idea of nine men working together in a kind of grand pavane—pitcher to catcher, shortstop to second baseman to first baseman—and the idea of one man looking down the loaded barrel of a pitcher's arm and feeling the nice clean solid thunk as he hits a ball that will fly into the bleachers. (I like basketball, too. I do not like football, which I think of as a game in which two tractors approach each other from opposite directions and collide. Besides, I have contempt for a game in which players have to wear so much equipment. Men play basketball in their underwear, which seems just right to me.)

But I like other things, too. I like a sense of drama, and I have to admit that I just don't find the question of whether someone is out at the plate in the third inning of the forty-eighth game of the season that inherently dramatic. I like a sense of continuity, and in today's baseball you don't get much. As soon as I take a shine to a player, he's gone–to another team or to run a car dealership somewhere in the Middle West. I have never fully recovered from the disappearance of a player from the Yankees called Chicken Stanley, for whom I developed an unwarranted affection some years back, not because of his playing or even his funny name, but because he looked somehow vulnerable and pathetic in pinstripes.

I like a sense of community, and in the early months of the baseball season it always seems to me that the community consists mainly of solitary men staring glassy-eyed at television sets and occasionally saying to befuddled three-year-olds, "Shortstop! That's a good position for you. Shortstop!" On the occasions when I try to join this community, I always blow it by doing something stupid, like screaming when Reggie Jackson hits a triple because I still think he plays for New York, or saying, when a player comes up to bat, "Boy, he's cute," which can throw a pall on the whole afternoon. Playoff games produce real community. I monitored the final National League playoff game in stages: first with an entire office full of people clustered around a television in midtown Manhattan; then in the cab with the radio; next in a commuter bus in which two people were listening to Walkman radios and reporting to all assembled, saying things like "They've tied it up" (groans) and "The Astros just struck out" (cheers), and then to a street being patrolled by a man in a white Pinto who kept leaning out and yelling, "Top of the sixteenth, still tied." I made it home to watch the last inning with my husband.

Baseball at this stage of the game offers just about everything I want. With only a handful of teams in contention, I can keep track of who's who and what they do best, of who can't run and who can't hit and who can't field. Each play is fraught with meaning, each loss a joy or a disaster. And each game is played before great communities of people, in bars, in rec rooms, even in offices, the ranks of the faithful swelled by those who have a passing interest and those who have no interest at all in baseball, but know a good cliffhanger when they see one–the same kind of people who watched the first episode this season of *Dallas* to see what happened to Bobby and then forgot about it. In fact, at this time of year baseball becomes a different kind of spectacle for me, something more along the lines of *As the Bat Swings*. Will Keith lose his temper? Will Lenny be a hero? Will Davey show emotion? Now we get down to the soap operas, and Chicken Stanley or no Chicken Stanley, I love soap operas.

◇

The Markoe Plan for Overcoming Boredom at a Baseball Game

Now that the baseball season is finally dancing gaily to a close, I can say it: I am not really a sports fan. I'm ashamed to admit it—in fact, I'm so ashamed that I added the word *really* to the previous sentence to make it sound as if I'm on the fence about the whole thing. I only wish I were.

I feel as intensely embarrassed about this as I do about my love for over-size, parasol-laden tropical cocktails in primary colors, with names that have a noun and more than one adjective or adverb. And I know I should be different. These are exactly the kinds of female stereotypes that I'd like to be able to sidestep. But now, after several decades of giving it the old college try (usually in the name of love), I am beginning to abandon hope.

Over the years I have attended a wide variety of sports events and logged countless hours in front of televised versions of same—each time hoping that *this* will be the magical moment when the veil lifts and I will be able to detect exactly what it is that I am supposed to relate to emotionally. But no payoff.

So why does this whole thing still concern me, you ask? Because it has become increasingly obvious that most appealing men are fanatical about at least one ball sport. And it becomes necessary for a woman who wishes to be with such men to develop, as I have, a reasonable strategy for survival. Since I trust I am not the only person still struggling with this, I offer you:

The Markoe Plan for Overcoming
Boredom at a Baseball Game

1. SNACKS. Eating and drinking play an important part in this survival strategy. You will want to make many, many trips to the various snack bars. Think of your visit to the stadium as a stop at a giant open-air cafeteria that

has a really awful ambience. People are shouting, there is a continuous selection of terrible short songs on the electric organ, and the menu is very limited (to say nothing of the wine list). Which is why I advise you to try a twenty-four-hour fast before attending any game. This gives you permission to indulge in the wide variety of poisonous meat and fried-dough snacks you might otherwise avoid. Be sure to buy at least one of everything and exercise your every condiment option. Tempting indigestion is just one more way to keep yourself awake and amused.

I personally recommend a hearty consumption of beer, but for those of you who usually abstain, an alternate beverage will do. The resulting trips to the rest room will be a welcome distraction and the best aerobic exercise available under the circumstances.

2. SHOPPING. Souvenirs at a ball game can be a real disappointment to any seasoned shopper because most of the clothing items are 100 percent polyester. And, let's face it, those dolls with the spring-loaded heads are depressing, even to tiny children. Nevertheless, this remains one of your few viable diversions, so inspect each item carefully. And, for extra fun, ask the salesperson if he or she can give you any information about the Korean or Taiwanese villages where these items were manufactured. The resulting reactions will look like moments in a David Lynch film, so bring your camera.

3. LOOKING FOR CUTE GUYS. As soon as you enter the ballpark, be sure to purchase a program. This will enable you to begin your game-long search for cute guys. When you spot one, memorize his name and number. Now you're all set to follow him, not just in today's game, but in life, as he travels the traditional road from sociopathic relationships to nasty paternity or palimony suits, and then on through assorted felonies and underwear modeling.

4. A DANGEROUS SEAT. Since it may not have been your idea to attend the game in the first place, you probably won't be consulted about seating. But if you do have any influence, request a seat between home plate and first base. Here you will encounter a steady flow of popup and fly balls as they rain down upon the spectators. This works to your benefit because nothing can keep a dulled brain fresh and alert like the very real threat of a broken face.

5. CONVERSATION. Something is called for during those long stretches of time when you have nothing relevant to say and you have wisely decided not to embark on a discussion of your relationship. So memorize the following question and ask it with an air of quizzical bemusement: "Honey, what was the difference between the batting average and the slugging average again?" Now sit back, relax, eat, start an art project or even take a nap — there will not be another conversational lull for hours and hours.

6. Self-Hypnosis. Perhaps you're at a point in the game where you have eaten a lot and drunk a lot and maybe even purchased some cheap souvenirs. You look up and realize that you still have six innings to go. What to do? Well, this is where the simple technique of self-hypnosis can become your friend.

Start by imagining that you are on a beautiful island in the Caribbean, the sun caressing your dewy skin, a warm breeze blowing peacefully through your mane of golden-yellow hair. Now consider how much this is costing you. Not just hotel bills, airfares and eating out, but new swimwear, new evening wear and the money it cost to bleach your hair golden-yellow. Next, remember that you are flirting with skin cancer and premature aging. Realize that this is *not paradise but a nightmare*, and then, gently, gently, bring yourself back to the wonderful stadium, where the worst thing that can happen to you is that you will have to stay until the very end of the ninth inning. You are a very, very lucky girl, and I think you know it.

7. Develop Team Loyalty. This may be the best answer to your problems, since it is considered reasonable to have a maniacal devotion to one team. And there is no better choice, year in, year out, than the Cubs, because they usually get eliminated early in the season. This legitimizes your desire to pay only minimal attention. "I'm just not into it anymore this year," you say ruefully. "Not since the Cubs got beat." Believe it or not, everyone will understand and respect you, even offer you sympathy.

Ideally, the responsibility for keeping the non-fan amused would be shared voluntarily by the concerned fan. And so, on the remote chance that the current Mideast turbulence makes people treasure their loved ones with renewed enthusiasm, I offer the fan some suggestions for helping the non-fan stay alert and cheerful.

1. Point Out Tawdry Personal Details. Regale your foggy friend with sleazy tales of Steve Garvey, Wade Boggs, Pete Rose, Jose Canseco, *et al.* Number 18 suddenly becomes a lot more interesting to the non-fan if he turns out to be the guy whose girlfriend was on Oprah because she is suing him.

2. Secret Messages. I don't know what kind of muscle it takes to pull a thing like this together, but if you could inform the non-fan that you've arranged for special messages to play amid the barrage of statistics on the Diamond Vision screen, I guarantee you will be sitting beside someone who is suddenly paying rapt attention, filled with an intoxicating mixture of excitement and nauseating anxiety as she waits to discover what endearing or hellish sentiment you have chosen to share with her and a stadium full of thousands of people.

3. Seventh-Inning Stretch Treats and Surprises. Honoring the tradi-

tion of giving the non-fan something to look forward to, agree in advance that when everyone else gets up to sing "Take Me Out to the Ball Game," you will submit to a quality-time discussion of where the relationship is headed. (Come on. You know you don't really want to sing "Take Me Out to the Ball Game" anyway.) Add to that a spontaneous presentation of lovely gift items, and there's no reason why the seventh-inning stretch can't be restructured into a miniature version of Valentine's Day. (There's no real reason why it can't be modified into a scaled-down version of Thanksgiving or Easter either, but let's just leave it at Valentine's Day for now, and, if it seems to go well, we'll see about adding other holidays later in the year.)

4. PERSONAL BETTING. I know this is strictly taboo and that players get tossed out of the game, etc., etc., for this sort of thing, but in my opinion there is no better way to keep a brain-dead female awake than by making the score a direct route to a better social or sexual life. I suggest bets along the lines of "If we lead by at least six in the bottom of the fourth, I'll let *you* pick what we do next weekend, and I won't whine even if it's a foreign film with subtitles." Or, "If the Mets are winning by more than six points at the bottom of the seventh, I'll attend at least a month's worth of couple therapy. *And* I'll try to remember to initiate foreplay."

SECTION III

◇

Analysis of Baseball

MAY SWENSON

◇

Analysis of Baseball

It's about
the ball,
the bat,
and the mitt.
Ball hits
bat, or it
hits mitt.
Bat doesn't
hit ball, bat
meets it.
Ball bounces
off bat, flies
air, or thuds
ground (dud)
or it
fits mitt.

Bat waits
for ball
to mate.
Ball hates
to take bat's
bait. Ball
flirts, bat's
late, don't
keep the date.

Ball goes in
(thwack) to mitt,
and goes out
(thwack) back
to mitt.

Ball fits
mitt, but
not all
the time.
Sometimes
ball gets hit
(pow) when bat
meets it,
and sails
to a place
where mitt
has to quit
in disgrace.
That's about
the bases
loaded,
about 40,000
fans exploded.

It's about
the ball,
the bat,
the mitt,
the bases
and the fans.
It's done
on a diamond,
and for fun.
It's about
home, and it's
about run.

INA ELOISE YOUNG

◇

Petticoats and the Press Box

It doesn't seem strange to me that I should be able to comprehend baseball better than the average man because I have known the game since I was a small girl. I only appreciate the fact that I am regarded somewhat as a freak when I meet old ball players.

It is funny to watch the expression on an old league player's face when he is told to go to me when he wants a decision on the score. He usually takes it as a joke and when I hand my score book to him or answer his question intelligently he departs with a bewildered look that plainly says he believes there's a fake somewhere—that someone must have told me.

The older men in baseball are always extremely kind to me, however, and are first to give me credit for having mastered an intricate problem.

When I first assumed the responsibility of official score keeper for the Trinidad team—a team that is made up of old leaguers who have passed usefulness in fast company and of youngsters just trying out for recognition in the leagues, I used to be driven almost to tears by the players who invariably had some objection to make on my decisions.

I soon discovered that the pitchers hated to have a man credited with a hit if it were possible to give one of the fielders an error and that the other players were just as anxious to keep up their fielding and batting averages, and when I learned that my own judgment was more dependable, being unbiased, I laughed at their protests and quit worrying.

It is hard for the average man to understand just why women comprehend so little of the finer points of the game and the cartoons that annually appear ridiculing women's knowledge of baseball are most always justified. It was forcibly brought home to me one day last summer.

I had given up my seat in the press box to some visiting newspaper men and was sitting with a bunch of girls that I knew in the grandstand. The game was a close one and at one of those points where the pitcher is in a hole and the fans are screaming themselves hoarse under the delusion that they are helping the man in the box to pull himself out; when I was trying not to bite a piece out of my lead pencil and swallow it, the girl sitting next to me nudged me violently and said:

"I just wish you'd look at my hands. They are getting so tanned that my diamonds look like rock salt on them."

My mother has been attending games religiously for the past three years and yet she never fails to heave a sigh of regret when a long high one drops square into the hands of the fielder who has been tearing up the grass to get under it and hold it. She says that the batter has tried so hard to hit the ball that she thinks it's a shame not to let him run when he does hit it. There is no science to her in anything but "butterfingers."

Still I have found many intelligent women fans outside the wives of players. Trinidad is one of those places where the first word the babies say is "Slide." There is a population of some twenty thousand souls, and if a presidential candidate ever wishes to make the acquaintance of the entire city, he needs only to drop into town on the day of a ball game. They will all be there, and he could hold his reception in the grandstand—if the crowd had patience to let him do it. When a league team plays an exhibition game here, the stores all close and only the Sisters of Charity and the patients in the hospital stay at home.

Two-thirds of that crowd wears white dresses, too, and therefore I have hopes of some day training up a successor for my place.

MARIAH BURTON NELSON

◇

On Trying to Watch Baseball Without Watching Players Scratch Their Crotches

Suzie said I couldn't write a story about the baseball game because I didn't pay enough attention, by which she meant that I didn't keep score, as she did—on a special score sheet she drew in the car on the way to Baltimore to save herself $2.

I said, I'll write a story for people who might want to go to a game but don't want to feel obligated to notice such details as who's pitching.

It was my first pro baseball game. I don't hate baseball the way I hate football, but it never occurred to me to go until the Orioles amassed such a marvelous early season record; then I got curious.

The first game I ever watched on TV was their twenty-second, which you may remember happened to be their first victory of the season; it was also the one in which Bill Ripken got beaned, which started a feud between the two announcers, one of whom wanted to speculate morbidly on what bad shape Bill's head must have been in while the other kept saying, "I'm sure he's fine, let's just enjoy this win." Since the O's also won the game I attended in person, I've never seen them lose. Statistics nerdos have no doubt already noted this: I'm probably the only person in the universe to have a perfect record with the Orioles.

During the in-flesh game, Billy got hit again. First he hit himself with his own bat, then he fell to the ground, and the ball rolled into the infield. The pitcher retrieved the ball and threw it home, presumably aiming for the catcher, but instead hitting Ripken on the shoulder. As you can see, I paid attention at least some of the time.

Most of the time I ate. Suzie brought popcorn and grapes, I brought apples, and we got a workout running up and down stairs to buy french fries and pretzels, which had identical consistencies and flavors, except one tasted more like ketchup, the other more like mustard.

I also gabbed with Nancy, Rich, Leslie and Brooke, the rest of our little cheering section—all of whom were vastly more experienced at baseball-watching than I and who kindly cued me as to when to stand for the seventh-inning stretch, when to cheer at the end of the national anthem and when not to cheer for Seattle, the enemy team, even though they had some gorgeous hits. And they taught me baseball lingo, including, "Last time at bat, he pop flied." (Pop flied?)

Our seats were in row 26 UPR, behind home plate, and they were not benches but real plastic chairs with backs—an unexpected treat. No one was near us so we spread out, draping our feet in row 25 and our elbows in row 27. Suzie brought binoculars, but every time I looked through them I caught one of the men scratching his crotch, so I handed the binoculars back to Suzie and settled for the aerial view. The baseball field was pretty, with its neat dirt lanes and the criss-crossed pattern of cut green grass in the outfield. Every once in a while a white ball would soar up over the grass and into someone's glove.

Brooke went to high school with rookie right fielder Keith Hughes and after the game she offered to introduce us, which is when Nancy suggested I write a story about the game and Suzie said "No." We walked down a lot of stairs until we reached the Fan Assistance Center, outside the locker room. There we told the guard that we were the Keith Hughes Fan Club, which was true—it was just a very *new* club—and he let us in.

Having not spent much time peering through the binoculars, I was unprepared for the appearance of Keith Hughes. Not only was he not fat, as one expects baseball players to be, but he was not chewing gum or tobacco, not short of six-four, and not shy about flashing his thirty-two white, orthodontically arranged teeth. In other words, Keith Hughes is overwhelmingly, distractingly, disconcertingly *cute*.

I asked him everything I've ever wanted to know about baseball players.

"Are you in good shape?"

"Not really."

"Do you need to be in good shape to play this game?"

"Not really. About like a golfer. It's not too strenuous."

"When you're at bat, do you try to hit the ball anywhere in particular?"

"Not really, I just try not to strike out."

On our way to the car we walked past about three hundred small children, each holding a triangular thing called a pennant, which I hadn't seen since hanging out in my brother's bedroom twenty years ago. We pretended that Rich was a baseball player but they weren't fooled, maybe because he didn't tug at his groin. I asked a happy, pennant-waving little boy who his favorite player was, and he said he didn't know—which goes to show that I wasn't the only one who didn't have a clue what was going on, and that lack of savvy does not disqualify one from enjoying a baseball game or, I hope, from writing about it.

SUSAN McCARTHY

◊

Uniform Comments

What men wore when they played the game of baseball in the early days now seems quaint and a little odd, but their dress reminds us of the great luxury of beginnings, the freedom from tradition. Not that baseball was the first organization of its kind to need a uniform. Baseball men undoubtedly looked to other sports, such as cricket and horseback riding, as a guide to appropriate dress, and were also influenced by military uniforms of the day. Once the uniform was established and accepted, though (as it was in about 1910), change came slowly through a series of gradual refinements—with a few exceptions.

Small town teams or college teams of the 1850s dressed very simply and practically in long dark pants, with long-sleeved light-colored shirts. The club teams of the period seemed intent on designing a suit of clothes that designated the members as ball players, but was still stylish in the fashion of the day. With this in mind, they disregarded completely the fact that a close-fitting collar with a bow tie and shirt with long sleeves and cuffs was just not very comfortable for playing ball.

A few examples: The Lowells of Boston wore what looked like leftover military trousers from the Civil War—a white, long-sleeved, bibbed shirt (that is, a large oval area on the shirt front extended from the collar down to the midsection, detachable, with button closures all round); a small bow or ribbon tie; high leather-top shoes and a cloth cap. The 1864 Mutuals of New York looked smashing indeed in all-white dress—long pants, long-sleeved and collared shirts, with a dark belt at midsection spelling out "Mutuals."

In contrast, the 1867 Niagaras of Buffalo were not a very homogeneous group; it looks like they borrowed from each other's closets. A few wore ties, some wore long-sleeved shirts with bib closures, while others wore button-up shirts with no collar. Long trousers were common to all, but some were checked, while others had checked tops.

By 1875, the style was just about set for the rest of the century. Teams wore baggy knickers, long stockings, lace-up high-top leather shoes, long sleeves with cuffs; shirts had stiff-looking collars, which gradually relaxed and were often turned up to sort of fan the face. A tie was worn in the early years, but when incidents of players choking to death while trying to make plays increased, the custom soon faded. [Ed. note: That's a joke.]

Albert Spalding in 1876 put different colored hats on the players to designate positions, making the team look like a "Dutch bed of tulips." The first instances I found of teams using a descriptive symbol on their uniforms, rather than the initial or name of the city, were the Skull and Bones team from Massachusetts and the Maple Leafs of Guelph, Ontario, both in 1876. The two teams later joined to form the Cemetery League. One more little tidbit: Will White was the only player of the nineteenth-century to wear glasses.

There was time in the nineteenth-century when all-women teams were in vogue as a small-time entertainment. And what did women wear to play baseball? A photograph of one such team, the "Young Ladies Base Ball Club No. 1" of 1890–91, has the team posed like any all-male counterpart. The women are wearing regular striped baseball caps, knee-length dark- and light-striped dresses, gathered at the waist and held there with a wide clasp belt. The sleeves are long and the neckline is tightly fastened shut with a big polka-dot bow. They wear long, dark, heavy-looking stockings and pointed, ankle-high leather shoes with a small heel. (Smart to put those dress heels in the closet, ladies.) The team members look relaxed, with several holding bats and a ball in the foreground. Women who played baseball around this time were called "fair base ballists."

S. W. M. HUMASON

◊

Madame Southpaw

Fred Collins stood in the door of his hardware shop and looked at the pale spring afternoon without giving it much attention. The sun glinted prettily through new leaves, and a noon shower had left a sudden lake in a depression in the gutter. A small boy sailed twig boats up and down it and from time to time created glittering spray for the pleasure of watching it rise and fall.

"Get your feet wet, Benny," said Fred mildly. Nothing happened. Benny wasn't Fred's boy or responsibility. Fred was thinking about the coming baseball season. He was manager of the local village team, and he gave that job all the time he could spare away from his business—according to his wife, more than he could spare. His after-school assistant, Eddie Parrish, came and stood beside him leaning on his broom. Eddie was thinking about baseball too. He seldom thought much about anything else. He was a newcomer to town, but he was already bat boy as well as Fred's assistant, so he could talk about baseball through most of his working hours.

"There," said Fred, "you see the fella who stopped the greatest sensation in baseball history—woulda been the greatest, anyways. Mighta changed the whole course o' baseball."

"Where?" asked Eddie, staring at the empty street.

"Right there."

"Benny?" said Eddie. "He ain't moren' four years old."

"He was even younger then," said Fred. "Ain't you never heard about his mother?"

"I only lived here three weeks."

"Was a time," said Fred, "when nobody talked about much else. But folks forget."

He rubbed his hand across his jaw with a slight scratching sound, and

Eddie put away his broom. He knew the signs. With one accord they went to the back of the store and sat down on two unopened kegs of nails.

" 'Bout this time of year it was," began Fred, "five years ago. I was here in the store just kind of thinkin' about the baseball season. It looked terrible. Four boys was in the Army, and two in the Navy, and Floyd Jones worked in a war plant over around Binghamton. He used to come home sometimes to play, but it cost us five dollars for his bus fare, and it run the treasury down. I couldn't play on account of my finger what I busted in nineteen twenty-seven, and it don't bend good. 'Bout this time of year, like I said, 'bout this time in the afternoon, Rufe Peters come in. I got up from where I was thinkin' to see what he wanted. He didn't want to buy nothin'.

" 'Fred,' he says, 'I wish you'd come over and see my wife Mildred.'

"I laughed. 'I seen your wife Mildred all my life,' I said. 'I went to school with her.'

"His wife Mildred used to be Mildred Shields, and she always lived here. Rufe, he come here 'bout ten years ago. Him and Mildred got married 'bout three years after he come. They hadn't had no children this time I'm talkin' about. They felt bad about it. Rufe, he's a great baseball fan. Well, he says he wants me to come over and see his wife Mildred, and I said what I said I said.

" 'Something funny's happened to her left arm,' he says.

" 'Well, hell, Rufe,' I says, 'I ain't no doctor.'

" 'She can throw things,' he says.

"I laughed again. 'You c'n dodge, can't you?' I says.

" 'I don't mean that,' he says, 'I mean she can throw good. Fred,' he says, 'I b'lieve she can pitch.'

"Well, then, o'course I thought he must of been drinkin', but I never in my life seen him take a drink.

" 'Rufe,' I said, 'except for that soft-ball team them tough girls from the canning factory in Oneonta had, which wasn't too bad, you know you never seen a woman can throw without lookin' like she was reachin' for a clothes-pin on the high end of the line?'

" 'Mildred can,' he said. Then he told me. Seems the night before this day I'm talkin' about he'd been mendin' a hinge on the kitchen door. He asked Mildred to toss him the screw driver what he'd left on the other side of the room. Next thing he knew something sang past his ear, and the screw driver is stuck deep in the doorjamb. He turned around. 'How'd you do that?' he asked when he could get his breath.

"Mildred looked scared. She didn't know. She hadn't meant to. She's fond of Rufe. She'd felt something slip in her shoulder, she said. He asked her if it hurt, and she said it didn't, so he asked her to try it again, getting well out of the way himself. She let go, and he swore he couldn't see the screw driver goin' through the air at all, but it stuck in the doorjamb again. He made her do it four times more, and she did it every time, and then she said she had ironin' to do and she didn't want to throw no more screw drivers that night. But the next day Rufe quit work at noon and went home and took Mildred out in the yard and got her throwin' stones and then a baseball, and then he comes over to get me. Well, sir—"

Fred had neglected to lock the door, and a customer came in. Fred and Eddie both looked at him with disapproval.

"It ain't five thirty yet," said the man, "an' you're supposed to be open until six, and I need a couple of bolts the worst way."

Fred got him the bolts in disapproving silence and rang up the money. This time he locked the door. It was getting dark, and Eddie started to turn on the overhead light.

"Leave it out," said Fred. "Folks will think there's nobody in here.

"So," he said, "I put a note in the door to say I'd be back in an hour, and I went over to Rufe's house, which he lives in just two doors down the street—"

"I know," said Eddie. "Green roof."

"Mildred was in the kitchen," said Fred, "and she come out on the back porch when Rufe called her.

" 'I want you should show Fred how you can throw,' he said. But Mildred said she was busy and had other things to do than throw baseballs around. She's stubborn, Mildred, like all them quiet ones. I remember one time—"

"No!" said Eddie suddenly.

"What say?"

"I mean—excuse me," said Eddie, "but I want to hear what happened."

"Oh," said Fred without malice, "yeah. Well, she didn't want to come out, and she wouldn't come out. But all this time I was thinkin', and I went up to her and said quiet kind of, 'Rufe's a little off his head, ain't he? He'll prob'ly get over it. Want I should call the doctor?' That fetched her down off the porch because she's fond of Rufe.

"Rufe give her a ball and told her to throw it at the shed. She swung around and her left arm come out kind of sideways, and the ball busted right through a board on the shed and went inside and scared the hens. She busted another board on the shed and a window, and she hit an apple tree so hard the ball bounced back and stuck in a gutter on the porch roof. Rufe went to climb up there and get it and Mildred said now I could see that Rufe's head was all right, and she didn't want to play no more.

"Rufe got the ball out of the gutter and come down and him and me come over here to the store. We sat for quite a while, just thinkin'. At least, I was, and I guess he was. I think a lot—have to, bein' manager.

" 'Rufe,' I said fin'ly, 'Nobody could hit those balls. Nobody. You can't even see them, hardly,' I says.

" 'I know,' he says. 'Maybe,' he says after a little, 'I ought to take her to Doc Wilson to see what happened to her arm.'

" 'Gosh sakes, Rufe, no,' I says. 'He might fix it. If it don't hurt her none, leave it be,' I says.

" 'Can she aim 'em?' I says. 'Can she control 'em?'

" 'She hit that tree on purpose,' he says. 'She might be a little wild yet, but she can learn to control 'em, I bet.'

" 'If she can control 'em,' I says, 'the Clarkton team ain't ever gonna lose another game as long as she's got her strength. Can't any team win a game without it can hit the ball once in a while, and the Babe himself couldn't hit what he can't see comin'.

" 'Only thing is,' says Rufe, 'you know how Mildred is.'

"So we both sat and thought about how Mildred was, and we couldn't think of nothin' to do about it. What we both knew was that Mildred most likely wouldn't want to play baseball. Fin'ly Rufe went home, and we hadn't thought of anything. We was right, too. He come back the next afternoon and said, 'She said nope.'

"We just sat here for an hour feelin' low. Then Rufe came up with an idea. It sounded good. Turned out good, too.

"Rufe had had a girl back in Berry where he used to work before he come here, and when he first started goin' out with Mildred he used to go back to see this girl once in a while, and Mildred didn't like it. Never has liked to hear him mention that girl since. Well, by this time I'm talkin' about, this girl is married to Tom Pierce, and he pitches for the Berry team, and Berry won the championship last year. So Rufe talks it up how baseball is a kind of rivalry between pitchers, and that if Clarkton won the championship Tom Pierce would feel bad and so most likely would his wife. So Mildred says maybe she owes it to the home town to do what she can.

"So then we had to start in trainin' her. Now Mildred didn't want to be laughed at, and neither did we. We were both still in kind of a daze about this thing like we was in some kind of loony dream. We decided we'd keep it a secret until we were ready. Only person we told was Bart Bellows, the catcher. We figured we needed him to help us. Rufe couldn't catch a sofa pillow with glue on it, and I can't catch or throw too good on account of my finger—it don't bend good, see? So we told Bart, and we agreed to go up to a piece of pasture Bart owns 'bout two miles up Boonton road.

"Bart thought we was both prob'ly crazy, but he's a good-natured sort of fella, and he said okay, if we said Mildred Peters was the best southpaw in America he'd at least come along to be shown. Rufe and me went up to the pasture and built a backstop in the far corner and put down a home plate and marked out a pitcher's mound.

"Then the next Sunday afternoon Bart and Rufe and me and Mildred went up there. Bart had his catcher's mitt, but he didn't have no shin guards or mask or chest protector. Rufe told him he'd better get 'em, but he only laughed. 'What's she gonna do, fire 'em out of a cannon?' he says. We didn't say nothin'.

"Bart stood behind the home plate and held up his hands, standin' kind of easy and lookin' like he wanted to laugh. We showed Mildred how to stand on the mound and give her a ball, and she took that half-turn and let go. Lucky for Bart it was wild. It went by him and smacked against the canvas of the backstop with a noise you could of heard in the next county. Bart gave one yell and got out of there. Then he started to swear. He can swear good. It wasn't all mad swearin'. Some of it was surprise, and some of it was plain admiration. But he was mad, too.

" 'Want to kill me?' he says.

" 'I told you,' said Rufe, 'I told you to bring your chest protector and stuff.'

" 'Stuff to you,' said Bart, 'I wouldn't stand in front of one of those things without I was inside a tank.'

"So then we got Mildred just firin' 'em, and we let 'em hit the backstop. I stood behind it (I tested the wire and the canvas good first) to see if I could tell when they went over. The ball was just a kind of white blur when it traveled, but after a while I got so's I could see it, and so help me heaven two out of three was goin' straight over.

"After a while I figured everything was so good it might as well be better. I showed Mildred how if she pinched the ball a certain way so's it would slide off her fingers or her thumb, or if she turned her hand over and snapped her wrist, the ball might curve. Mildred hadn't said a word all this time. She never did seem very interested really, but she stood there and listened to what I said like a good little girl, then I went back and watched some more.

"She must of done everything I told her and added a few frills of her own because I never saw curves like that before or since, and neither did you. It was like the ball would start to go way wild in a north-northwest direction and then change its mind at the last minute and come back home. Bart was standin' beside me, and he begun to swear again and we could have stood there all day watchin' those balls doin' barrel rolls and stuff and then hittin' the backstop amidships, but Mildred said the first thing she'd said all afternoon and it was that she wanted to go home. We all went home. I asked Bart and Rufe to come over that night.

"Seemed like every night we had some kind of a problem to settle. This time it was Bart. He just went on sayin' he wouldn't try to catch those balls.

" 'Leave 'em go back and hit the backstop,' he said.

" 'What about the umpire?' I said.

" 'Leave the umpire take his chances,' he said. 'If he don't want to stand there—which he won't—leave him stand behind the backstop.' "

Eddie's mouth worked, and he seemed about to speak.

"Yeah, yeah, I know," said Fred. "We was dumb for a while, but we was kind of in a daze yet. It come to me pretty soon what you're about to say. What were we gonna do about the third strike? If the umpire and the catcher both got out of the way and the ball hit the backstop, Bart couldn't never get it to first in time, and it might as well been hit. So we just sat there kind of glum because it looked as if we was just about back where we started from.

"Then Rufe and I kind of pulled ourselves together and started in on Bart. We told him where his duty lay. We put it to him. We said how Jerry and Joe and Fatty Brown and Grover Cleveland Dawes and others was all off fightin' in a war and they was countin' on the folks at home to keep the home team at least somewheres near the top of the league.

"Bart said that was all right, he'd of gone to war without kickin', only he was over age and had five children, and it was one thing to get wounded in a battle and another to get wounded by a baseball throwed by Mildred Peters. He said why didn't one of us catch if we were so all-fired patriotic. I told him I couldn't on account of my finger, and Rufe couldn't on account of he just couldn't, and to tell you the almighty truth, Eddie, I don't b'lieve either of us was very anxious to. Bart said I only had one finger that wouldn't bend, and I wanted him to go out and get ten that would be likewise. And we had to leave it like that for that night.

"But a couple days later Bart come over to see me and said it did seem a shame, and he still wouldn't try to catch those balls, but if he could put on enough protection he'd be willin' to stand in front of 'em and let 'em bounce off him.

" 'But I don't know what would be enough protection,' he said, 'without it's a suit of armor like I saw once in a picture in a book about knights.'

" 'That's it!' I said, a picture comin' into my mind as clear as if it was there in front of me.

" 'What's it?' said Bart.

" 'Never mind,' I says. 'You'll see.'

"The next day I went up to the Hildreths' house—you know that big house where those summer people live?"

"Yeah, yeah," said Eddie impatiently.

"Well, they weren't there o'course—they don't come until July—but old man Bowers lives there, a caretaker like, and I told him I wanted to borrow the suit of armor what stands on the stair landing. I seen it once when I went up to fix a lock on the bathroom door. A green tub, they got; I ain't foolin' you. Old man Bowers didn't want to lend me the suit. I promised I'd have it back by the time the Hildreths got there (I figured I'd buy one by that time if they're for sale anywhere), and I promised we wouldn't hurt it none, though I wasn't too sure of that. And I told old man Bowers I'd give him ten dollars when I brought it back. Well, he'd of let me take the green tub and the grand piano for that, so I carted that thing down to my car, and the next day Rufe and me took it out to the field.

"It took quite a time to get Bart into it, but we did. It worked perfect, at least, partly. Partly perfect. It worked perfect for protecting Bart. It even had a headpiece with a kind of feather in it–and a hinged piece over the face so you could close it up except for a little slit for the eyes. Well, Bart was safe enough. He'd stand in front of the ball which would go clang–and bounce. Trouble was it bounced too far. Bart couldn't run, and he couldn't bend over, let alone throw. It was all goin' to be no good if the runner was goin' to get to first anyway. Mildred was no help, except that she kept on clinkin' balls off that fancy suit. But you couldn't hardly expect her to have ideas as well as a trick arm. She didn't ever say nothin' except when she wanted to go home.

"Well, naturally, I was thinkin' about this business day and night, and I come up with another idea that night, and if I hadn't had all this hardware business to attend to I'd of made it sooner. This meant takin' more people into our confidence, but we figured that before long the whole world would hear about it.

"The next Sunday we took the rest of the infield out to the lot with us. We didn't tell 'em what they were goin' to see, just told 'em they wouldn't b'lieve it when they saw it. O' course they laughed their heads off when they saw Mildred walk out to that pitcher's mound, and when Rufe and me started gettin' Bart into his iron pants there were tears in their eyes.

"Mildred pitched one and Bart stood in front of it, and it conked against that tin union suit and caromed off and hit Cracker in the ankle. He didn't move, didn't rub his ankle or nothin'. He just stood there. So did the others. You've read about people bein' rooted to the spot. They was.

"I threw the ball back to Mildred, and she flung another one just as good as the first. The boys started talkin' then, and bein' as you're young yet I won't repeat it. Rufe fin'ly pointed out to them that Mildred, though a pitcher, was a lady, and they apologized. Said the occasion just ran away with them. Then I explained my plan, which was simply that since nobody was goin' to hit the ball they was no reason why they shouldn't all play in close to the plate and get the third strike ball and fire it over to first.

"We left Cracker on first, and the other three lined up like I said. It worked pretty good, but the ball bounced so fancy that they couldn't always get it.

"So next time we practiced we got all the outfielders there, too, and after goin' through the same procedure of laughin' and swearin' we got them lined up, and so there was six men to get the ball, and we seemed to have it sewed up. We practiced out on that hidden field all spring, lookin' forward to springin' things at the proper time. We kept Archie Bryden, the bat boy, out by the gate, but nobody ever come.

"Well, it wasn't long before the first game of the season come along."

Fred stopped to light his pipe.

"Night before it, I spent a lot of time thinkin'. But I wasn't worried none. Didn't seem to me there was anything could go wrong, and I was more than lookin' forward to the excitement. The first game was a Sunday with Bear Crossing. Nice day, too. Just right.

"We'd give Mildred a regular uniform, but she didn't think the pants looked good on her, so she wore her own slacks and one of our shirts on top and no hat. You could see she was a girl right away, as she stood there, glove on her right hand, tossing a ball in her left. The stands buzzed like Farraday's saw mill, and then you could hear the laughter begin. One loud-mouth on the Bear Crossing team kept yellin', 'Hey, Madame Southpaw!' Mildred, like always, was just calm and quiet, and she looked kind of pretty in that blue shirt and slacks. Then Bart come across the bench in his outfit, movin' real slow of necessity and soundin' kind of like a tin peddler's truck goin' down hill. Well, sir, if the fellas that writes radio comedies ever get one laugh like that they'd make their fortune. The Bear Crossing manager, Larry Flynch his name was, comes up to me and says, 'What is this a joke,' and I says it's no joke, and I says our pitcher don't want no warm-up and I tells Biff Giles, the umpire, to say 'Play Ball' and he does.

"The first batter was a fella named Johnny Court, left-hander–works his own farm. He stepped up, and you could hear the laughter in the stands and bleachers kind of die away into curiosity, and by the time Mildred got the ball everything was so quiet you could hear Ned Tomes puttin' the new shingles on his barn half a mile up the clove. Well, Mildred hurled one of those smoking loop-the-loops, and it popped off Bart with a noise like cymbals. Biff, when he could get his breath, said 'One strike,' and all hell let loose. Women screamed and everybody in the bleachers climbed down to watch. Biff chased 'em back again.

"Mildred pitched another strike, and you could hear one of those noises that hits a crowd sometimes, something between ah and oh and a groan and like everybody made the same noise at the same time. Then I signaled to the boys, and the whole team come up and spread across the infield, leavin' just an aisle from the pitcher to the plate, like they was gettin' ready to square dance or something'. After Biff, who was still havin' trouble with his voice, said 'Strike three' Joe Turner scooped the ball up from where it had rolled and threw it to first.

"After the end of that inning I seen the Bear Crossing manager gettin' out a rule book and talkin' to Biff, and Biff motioned me to come over and the boys all gathered around to see what was comin'. I wasn't a bit surprised. I'd kind of got ready for this.

"Larry Flynch was pointin' to the rule what says: 'Glass buttons or polished metal must not be used on uniforms.' He was makin' a case—and he had somethin'—that Bart was dressed up in polished metal and nothin' else, and I pointed to the rule that said: 'No player who shall appear in a uniform not conforming to the suits of the other members of his team, shall be permitted to take part in a game.'

"I asked Biff to take a look at the Bear Crossing team. Five of 'em had on uniforms that they'd bought with their own money, as I knew, but three of 'em was gray and two white. The third baseman had on blue jeans and a polo shirt. Two fielders had on sweat shirts that said Acme Aircraft on the backs, the first baseman's said B. O. H. S. on the front, and Marty Carraway who played right field was playin', as usual, in his undershirt. I said we'd take the oversize sardine tin off Bart if they'd all play in the same uniform.

"Biff is an easy-goin' fella, slow-spoken, but firm. After a while he said he guessed we were both infringin' (I think that's the word) the rules, and we could either both mind 'em or go on this way.

"The Bear Crossing boys were kind of mad, but they couldn't do nothin' about it so we went on that way. We went on just that way, except Bart took the plume outa his helmet because Biff said it swooped back and tickled him. 'Course Mildred had to bat. We'd shown her how to hold a bat so she wouldn't look too funny, but we told her to just stand there and not try to hit anything. She did that, backin' away a little each time because she was afraid of the balls though gosh knows, compared to hers, they was underhand tosses . . . We got two runs in the sixth inning and that was that.

"The boys and Mildred come over to my house that night for a celebration and some beer, only Mildred went home early and didn't like beer. After the boys were gone my wife wanted to know if I thought now I could take up the hardware business again, and I said yes because as far as I could see we wouldn't even have to practice any more—just go to the games Sat'dys and some Sundays and let Mildred take us to the championship. Except for one thing. Except that I'd still got to think a little because as soon as word got around all the other teams were sure enough goin' to show up in regular uniforms, and I'd got to think of somethin' else to protect

Bart. But I wasn't really worried, I was so happy. I was pretty sure I could think of somethin' if I gave my time to it.

"The next day was Monday. A stranger come into my store about ten o'clock in the morning. Big fat man named Keeley, with a fancy necktie and his shoes shined. I thought at first he was a new salesman from a wholesale place, but he wasn't. He was a scout for baseball—for a big league baseball club—and he'd happened to be drivin' through town the day before, and he'd stopped to watch the game because he said he sometimes picked up a rookie from sand-lot baseball. I ain't gonna tell you, Eddie, which club he represented because I promised on solemn oath I wouldn't. He didn't want the publicity, he said. He said as soon as he could get back to his manager and talk to him they'd be ready to sign Mildred up, or it might be he'd have to bring his manager down here on account of they wouldn't believe him. He wanted me to sign an option that I wouldn't deal with nobody else.

"I said I couldn't sign no option for Mildred, her not bein' my wife or anything, and he said he'd like to go over and talk to her. I went with him. Mildred said she wouldn't be a bit interested in playing baseball for anybody except the Clarkton team, and she didn't even like that much, but she'd promised. Mr. Keeley asked me if he couldn't talk to Rufe, and I said Rufe was out to the Compton's place helpin' plough, and we went out there and got Rufe, and he got Mildred somehow, and we all come back here. Then this Mr. Keeley mentioned some figures, and Rufe turned white as a sheet, and even Mildred looked surprised for the first time and said, 'Who do you think you're kiddin'?' But this Mr. Keeley wasn't kidding, and he said he knew his manager wouldn't hesitate once he saw Mildred, and he offered to write out a check for a thousand dollars right then on his own responsibility. But Mildred said she'd have to think it over, and that's all she'd say except to say that over again. So Mr. Keeley left, saying he'd be back shortly, and Rufe went back to ploughin' and Mildred went home, and I went back to thinkin'.

"I was feelin' kind of low because it didn't seem likely that even Mildred would stay stubborn in the face of all that money, and there went my pitcher and my ball team and my championship. But the more I thought the more I cheered up. I know even from little business that when somebody wants something bad enough you can get most any price for it, and I saw right then, like a picture, that if Rufe and I got together, we could put it so's this ball club would have to hire us if they hired Mildred. They could find something for us to do even if only to keep score, and we could see all the games we wanted for nothin' and not have to bother with farmin' or hardware any more at all.

"The next day was Tuesday. I come down to the store and sat there thinkin' about who I'd sell out to and that I'd have to take a inventory, which is a job, but worth it in this case, and wonderin', but only a little, about how my wife would like the idea of movin' away. Old Mrs. Travers called up and said a pane of glass was gone out of her parlor window and she was cold, and would I bring up another one right away and put it in? So I cut a pane and I was takin' it up to Mrs. Travers when, just as I went by Doc Wilson's office, I met Mildred comin' out. I stared at her an' she smiled at me as cheerful as could be, and I felt so weak in the knees I put Mrs. Travers' pane of glass down on the grass and leaned against a lamppost. 'Mildred,' I said, 'you been in to see Doc Wilson?'

" 'I sure have,' she says.

" 'About your shoulder?' I said when I could swallow.

" 'No, not about my shoulder,' she said. 'About something else. I'm going to have a baby,' she says, 'and I'm so happy I could kiss somebody, and it might as well be you,' so she kisses me on the cheek and she says, 'So no more baseball,' she says, just like that, and goes off down the street.

"I forgot the pane of glass—just left it there—and went back to the store. But there wasn't any use thinkin' about this one. I could tell that as soon as I began. So I sent a wire to Mr. Keeley, and I took Bart's suit of armor down to the blacksmith's to get the dents taken out of it, and I took it back to old man Bowers and paid him the ten dollars, and then I come back here and went on waitin' on customers.

"Mr. Keeley turned up in great state two days later and said he'd told the manager all about it before my wire come, and now he was the laughin' stock of the club which I could well believe. But then Mr. Keeley had lived long enough and been around far enough to have an eye to the future, and he said after all this was only one baseball season and by this time next year the baby might be big enough to be left, and he'd take Mildred down himself to show her to the manager, and he went away and left me thinkin'.

"We was at the bottom of the league that season, and the next February Mildred's baby was born. She went all the way over to the Barrows hospital to have it. Rufe drove me over there one day. Rufe was happier than he'd been even when Mildred was clinkin' those balls off Bart's iron suit. I said all the things there are to say about a baby, which ain't many, and I asked Mildred how she felt. She said she felt fine. I said, kind of cautious, 'Along about May you ought to be rarin' to throw some of them fast ones of yours,' and she said, just like she wasn't changin' her whole future (and mine), 'Oh, no. It slipped back, I think, Fred. I was reaching for the bellpull over my head, and I felt something. Besides, he wouldn't want his mother to be a ballplayer.'

"I wasn't so sure of that, but I couldn't ask him. I didn't b'lieve what she'd said because I didn't want to b'lieve it. When she got home and was strong enough I got her to come out in the yard, and I gave her a baseball. Rufe was there, too, but he wasn't nearly as interested now. He'd got something else to be interested in. Well, Mildred took the ball, and I told her to hit the shed which had got a new board where the old one was busted. Her arm come up over her shoulder, and she twisted her whole body around with it the way all women do, and the ball made a silly little arc and come down with a plop in the grass about four feet away.

" 'That the best you can do?' I says.

" 'That's the best I can do,' she says. 'I told you. Go on home now.'

"I went home and wrote a letter to Mr. Keeley and put in a big order to the wholesalers for I saw where my future lay, as you might say, and it wasn't in any big-league ball parks.

"Good gorry, Eddie, it must be almost suppertime. I guess I been payin' you overtime for half an hour."

The two of them got up slowly and got their coats and opened the front door. In the light of the street lamp the small boy was still playing in the lake.

"Benny!" said Fred severely. "It's late, go on home. Your mama wants you."

Benny stuck out his tongue.

"You want your hind side paddled?" said Fred. "Go on home. Shoo." He pushed the little boy in the direction of his house. Benny moved off slowly. Fred and Eddie walked in the opposite direction. They had gone some yards when a stone whistled past Fred's ear. They stopped and turned.

"Benny!" said Eddie sharply. "It musta been Benny. Ain't nobody else in sight."

"D'you throw that, Benny?" asked Fred gently.

"N'yah!" said Benny.

"C'm here, Benny," said Fred. "I ain't mad. C'm here. I'll give you a stick of gum." He held out the gum, and Benny approached with caution. Fred picked up a good-sized stone from the gutter. He handed it to the boy.

"See that street light—the second one from the corner?" he said. "Let's see you hit it."

The stone broke the globe on the second street light from the corner. Benny ran away fast from the tinkle of falling glass. Fred and Eddie looked at each other.

"He ain't only four years old?" said Eddie.

"That's right," said Fred. "Four years old last February." His jaw worked up and down several times.

"You go on home to supper, Eddie," he said finally. "I'm goin' back to the store. I've got some tough thinkin' to do."

ELLEN COONEY

◊

from *All the Way Home*

"*There's nothing in* the world like the game of softball," Gussie told the Spurs, who had gathered in Evelyn's front room. It was nearly time to leave for the game at the prison. The women were doing their best to ignore the excellent smells coming from Evelyn's kitchen. She was slow-roasting a chicken for her family.

"I bet you all find it hard to believe sometimes. Especially on those mornings when you wake up so sore you can hardly move."

There was a murmur of agreement. Avis Poli, living for the past month on a diet of lettuce, baked fish, and unbuttered vegetables, was starting to look pinched. Her nose kept aiming toward the kitchen.

"Smells good," whispered Avis. "Parsley and onions, just the way I like it."

Birdey Nolan reached into her purse for a small plastic bag filled with celery sticks. She handed Avis a long one.

"Little bites and long chews," Birdey advised.

Gussie cleared her throat. The effort at speech was pinkening her with embarrassment. Evelyn had a good idea what Gussie was trying to say. Good luck, team. Give it all you've got. Go, team, go!

"Remember that movie about Helen Keller?" said Gussie. "Remember when Annie Sullivan is trying to teach her about the word for water? She has the water running over one of Helen Keller's hands while she spells out the word in the other one. Remember how Helen finally gets it?"

"I cried for a week," said Birdey, putting the bag of celery back in her purse.

"I felt the same way the first time I ever saw a softball game," said Gussie. Birdey's eyes filled.

"Why softball?" Gussie let her eyes linger over every face in the room. "Who knows? All I can say for sure is that it feels good when you play it, and it feels good when you watch it, and it feels good when you think about it. With softball, see, it's all in the *team*. It's all in the *idea* of a team. Most people think it's just a different version of baseball. It's not. Playing baseball is like playing with bullets. In softball, you've got a ball you can really get your hands around. You've got more of a chance at the plate and you've got something that's real beauty when you do it right. I was only about four or five years old when I found out about it. My father took me to Lowell for a tournament the mills were sponsoring. The guys who were playing were factory workers, the kind of guys I'd seen all the time, but out there under the lights they looked different. It was almost like they were dancing in a ballet. We saw four games that night. Papa had to drag me away. After that, I was gone. I guess I never spent much time thinking about anything but softball. Softball was *it*."

Flushed and self-conscious, Gussie looked down toward the floor. "I guess what I'm trying to say is that, this being our first game against anybody but ourselves, I just hope you have a good time. You know the rules, you know pretty much what you're supposed to be doing. I just wish it wasn't so damn cold."

It was the first time Evelyn had ever heard her say so many sentences at once. For a long moment, no one spoke. The only sound was the steady crunching of Avis's celery.

Gussie looked around again. She opened her mouth in a big broad glow of a grin.

"Let's go!" she said.

Avis was the first one out the door. As the women headed for cars, Gussie stopped Evelyn.

"My mother came to see you," she said flatly. "Look, you don't have to try concealing anything. I already asked Rio about it. I had a feeling she might be trying something. I suppose it makes sense she'd try it on you. What did she say?"

"It's not important."

"Ev! Please!"

"She's not exactly crazy about the team. About softball. About the *idea*." Evelyn mimicked Gussie perfectly, but she didn't seem to notice. "Gussie, forget about it. She doesn't mean any harm."

"Pah! The only thing my mother *ever* means is harm."

A familiar jolting look came into her face. Evelyn knew it well. It was her I-am-about-to-curse-someone-in-Italian look. Evelyn gave her a nudge toward the car.

"Save it, Gussie," she told her. "Save it for the other team."

They arrived at the jail about an hour before the starting time. At the entrance they were stripped of all personal belongings, including all jewelry and hairpins.

Their gloves, bats and balls were confiscated.

In a small, windowless room with gray walls, somewhere deep inside the building, a female guard body-searched them. She led them through a maze of damp cement passages, each one narrower than the one before it. They finally came into an empty room no bigger than Evelyn's kitchen. They were told that this was the women's gym.

Linda Drago met them there. She wore a loose pair of insulated sweat-pants and an oversized shirt that said QUESTION AUTHORITY. She looked like she had just shot a quart of vitamins into her bloodstream. Evelyn wondered how the guards felt about her shirt. Drago threw out her arms to Gussie, cane and all, and looked at the Spurs over Gussie's shoulder.

"Welcome to our country club," she said with a laugh. "I was hoping they'd let us use the men's gym today, but no go. Looks like we'll have to play outdoors."

"No problem," said Gussie a little too eagerly. Most of the Spurs were already shivering.

They followed Drago outside to a small playing field completely sur-rounded with spiked steel fencing. Over their heads, the sky was sickly, emptily white. At their feet the ground was bare and hard. They looked from each other to the fences and back again, smiling uncertainly.

"Sorry about the bases," said Drago. "We haven't got any."

"No problem," mimicked Evelyn, and made them all laugh.

A door behind them swung open, and the prison women came out with a female guard who was a head taller and thirty pounds heavier than Gussie. As they came toward the field, Evelyn tried to guess who was in for prostitu-tion and who was in for drugs. She gave it up quickly. The women wore thick jeans and sweatshirts, and did not look any different from any woman on the Spurs.

The two teams shook hands as their coaches drew bases in the dirt with the tip of Gussie's cane. Gussie leaned on the female guard and Drago drew the baselines. The women's spirits were high. They went into the game with a great deal of noise and laughter but didn't keep it up for very long. It got colder and colder. Hannah Wally hit three home runs. Sandy Dorn played shortstop like an octopus and came up with four solid singles. Laura Brad-ley got two singles. Peggy Glazer got one. So did Karla Brown. Nancy Beth Campbell, the pitcher, hit a single that was called foul by the female guard, who was umping. The Spurs poured onto the field to protest the call but the guard held firm. Gussie let her have it. Birdey Nolan amazed everyone with a gorgeous line drive to left field but her shoe fell off as she was round-ing first base and she did not feel inclined to run without it.

At the end of the game, when the score was twenty-nine to three, Drago invited the Spurs to come back and do it again.

"Not a bad team you've got here," she told Gussie, thumping her on the back. "For a bunch of housewives." Drago flashed the Spurs one of her healthiest smiles, winked, and found herself flat on her back on the ground.

"You tripped her!" cried the guard, rushing forward. "With your cane!"

Gussie spread her arms apart, looking at her cane as if it were an abused pet. Spurs crowded around their coach.

"Must have been a rock," said Gussie. "Poor Drago must've tripped on a rock."

The guard looked all over, and could find no rock. Gussie did not find it surprising.

"Anyone who'd call that single a foul ball needs to have her eyes examined," said Gussie placidly.

The guard said, "Hey! Who you talking to like that?"

Gussie said, "What's the matter? You deaf too?"

Drago picked herself up off the ground and brushed herself clean, looking around for bruises.

"I'd like to hear you use that tone of voice if you were playing against the Belles," said the guard.

Pammy Flynn said, "Belles?"

"Best goddamn team on the Eastern seaboard," said the guard.

Gussie threw back her head and laughed at the top of her lungs. She laughed so hard she nearly fell over, and leaned on Pammy for support.

The guard stepped up close to Gussie. "You know what the Belles'd do to a half-assed team like yours?"

"Wh-what?" said Pammy nervously, with her eyes on the guard's hip. The gun in her holster was real.

"The Belles'd whup you so good you'd get fed to a toothless baby, that's what."

The Spurs leaned back as if they were trying to get out of the way. Evelyn stayed close to Gussie. She felt frozen to her bones. Her nose was runny and she was sniffing. She tried to think about her chicken dinner. The guard wore a pair of thick black leather gloves lined with brown fur. Her hands were enormous.

"Let's go home," said Evelyn.

Ignoring her, Gussie whispered in Drago's ear, and it was Drago's turn to laugh out loud. Gussie whispered something else. Drago put out her hand.

"You're on, Cabrini," said Drago. The two coaches shook on it.

Huddled closely together, the Spurs left the field and claimed their things from the guards at the prison entrance. In the doorway Gussie told them what she had done.

"We're going to play the telephone company. In May. I guess we've got some work to do."

Except for Evelyn's sneezing, they were quiet on the way home.

SUSAN FIRER

◊

A Night Game in Menomonie Park

A night game in Menomonie Park,
Where the ladies hit the large white balls
like stars through the night they roll
like angelfood cake batter folded through devilsfood.
Again, I want to hear the fans' empty beer cans
being crushed—new ones hissing open.
"You're a gun, Anna"
"She can't hit"
"Lay it on."
Oh, run, swift softball women
under the lights the Kiwanis put in.
Be the wonderful sliding night
animals I remember. Remind me constantly
of human error and redemption.
Hit
ball after ball to the lip of the field
while the lake flies fall like confetti
under the park's night lights.
Sunlight Dairy Team, remember me
as you lift your bats,
pump energy into
them bats, whirling circular as helicopter
blades above your heads.
Was it the ball Julie on the Honey "B" Tavern Team
hit toward my head that made me so softball crazy that right in the middle of a tune
by Gentleman Jim's Orchestra, here in Bingo/Polka
Heaven at Saint Mary of Czestochowa's annual Kielbasa

Festival, I go homesick for Oshkosh women's softball?
I order another Kielbasa and wonder
if Donna will stay on third next game or
again run head down wild into Menonomie homeplate.
Play louder, Gentleman Jim.
Saint Mary of Czestochowa throws a swell festival, but
Oshkosh women's softball—that's a whole other ballgame.

◊

Double Play

If Gertrude Stein had played second base
she would have said "there's only there there"
and putting thoughts in order.

The outfield is the place to dream,
where slow moons fall out of the sky
and rise clean over a green horizon.

The infield is tense as blank paper
and changeable as the cuneiform
of cleats along the path.

Stein would have loved the arc of arm
from short to second
and the spill of one white star
out of a hand.

VANALYNE GREEN

◊

Mother Baseball

"*Did it ever* occur to you," I recently asked a friend, "that baseball is played on the landscape of the female body?"

"Yeah, sure," he responded, "all those little men in the middle of a big womb, trying to inseminate the field with their balls, yeah. But you can't reduce it to that, you know."

Oh yes I can, I thought. Why not? Men do it. Baseball, they say, is America; or baseball is the individual versus the universe; baseball is statistics and ordering. Why can't baseball be seen as a pagan spectacle about the cycles of birth and death? Seasonal contests to promote fertility and the ripening of crops underlie most primitive ritual. The word pagan originates with the Latin *pagus,* or country – something to think about when sportswriters reminisce about baseball's pastoral beginnings.

Mother baseball. I enjoy speculating about its bloody beginnings as a fertility rite. Funny that with all the verbiage about the sport no one mentions the obvious structural relationship between a baseball stadium and a womb: in design, a stadium is both a circle and a "Y," two notorious female symbols. The curved and sloping shape of the stands is like a plush endometrium in which we fans cozy up to watch a lone batter square off against the universe. In the bowels of the mother, her reassuring presence presides over our humble attempts to reconcile the desire to live forever with hard, brutal facts.

But I do not worship at the altar of the Great Goddess. Unlike some feminists, I don't write *wommin* for *women* just to get rid of "men," and I'm not a member of a coven. The remarkable likeness that a baseball stadium bears to a womb means little in and of itself. But 50,000 people sitting in a monolithic uterus is an interesting notion to contemplate. I especially like to think about that when announcers describe players' bats as fast, corked, dead, quiet, live, or as loaded barrels – and pitches as high hard ones.

I went to my first game two years ago, at Yankee stadium. I hiked up the concrete ramps that encircle the stands and as I came out into the open, I saw a beautiful canyon of green, summer green, and light, the way it is at dusk, filling the basin of that space. And it was as if I'd just discovered a secret, but a secret that everyone else knew and took for granted. Why hadn't anyone told me?

Going to Yankee stadium was a more important experience than visiting the Grand Canyon—a fact that has to do with representation and with being a woman. I grew up with textbook photos and tourist snapshots of the Grand Canyon, so when I went there I wasn't moved. The potential shock of its grandeur had been diffused by countless two-dimensional representations; the real thing was like a living postcard. But as a woman not steeped in the history and culture of baseball, going to the game was a revelation. I didn't know its visual terms; I could possess it for myself for the first time.

I've since concluded that being female actually predisposes me to get more value for the price of my admission ticket. Unlike those men who were raised in the game and are more prone to associate it with their own oedipal struggles, I am freer to rethink its structure. Baseball can be the remnants of a sacrificial rite or it can reflect the nation's regressive, nationalistic mood. It can be a postindustrial outlet for cramped urban workers. Or baseball can be, as one woman friend describes it, an aesthetically pleasing opportunity to look at handsome men who don't talk back.

It should come as no surprise that baseball, of all American sports, draws so many female fans. First, baseball historically has attracted marginal people. Crazies. And women are, after all, marginal themselves—an economic and social underclass. Also the structure of the game involves elements traditionally associated with women: oral history, story-telling, and gossip. And although baseball has its own arcane language (for example, the box score), it's more accessible than football is because the slow pace of the game provides announcers with the time to call up relevant historical and strategic information.

At Yankee stadium, I sit in the "Little Tripoli" section, which is behind home plate in the upper decks. This is where the fanatics congregate, the ones glassy-eyed from the recitation of statistics. Sportswriters are critical of the sometimes dangerous antics of the fans. I certainly don't like the sexism and occasional mean-spiritedness. Yet compared to Manhattan—which is increasingly drained of its neighborhoods and ethnicity by gentrification and corporate hegemony—I find the unabashedly tribal rites at the stadium to be revivifying. I'm amused when men in suits and ties are told to go back to Wall Street where they belong. During the Yankees/Red Sox game, in which Clemens walloped the Yankees, a comatose Little Tripoli fan stripped, then twirled his clothes over his head and threw them out into the fans, I understood: defrocked, humiliated, and demoralized, he was acting out for all of us.

Family. Membership in the sports club is a calling card anywhere the language of sport is spoken. Being conversant breaks down sexual boundaries. To my surprise, most men have welcomed me into that circle where arcane memories of former heroes, great plays, and Freudian dramas are re-enacted. And if I don't talk to them about mother baseball, that's all right; I'm a spy in the house that Ruth built.

Watching baseball is an opportunity to decipher the now illegible handwriting of matriarchal culture.

In 1937, an Italian scholar, Gorrado Gini, traveled to North Africa to study a tribe of blond-haired Berbers. The blond strain was believed to be descended from Nordic invaders who had come to North Africa in the Stone Age. Gini was an Americanophile; he noticed that the Berbers played a game that was a remarkable mixture of elements resembling American baseball and earlier forms of European "baseball" (often called "cat" from catapult). The Berbers called their game "the ball of the mother of the pilgrim." When a batter struck out, they said he was "rotten," and "moldy." Considering this in light of the fact that in the Scandinavian game upon which baseball is based, players that were safe were called "fresh" may lend some credibility to the notion that baseball originated as a ritual battle between dying winter and burgeoning spring.

In the Berber game the runner's base is called "mother"; in the earliest games the batters were on the "father's side." Compare this with a related game, called "egg-carrying," which was played by women on the Estonian island of Runo. The ball represented seed and was placed in holes in the ground.

At first glance, contemporary American baseball, with its media coverage, advertising revenues, and millionaire players, appears to have wiped out all traces of primeval ritual. But this is not so. Consider the "rundown." A rundown is a kill; there is no other moment like it in baseball. It occurs when a runner is on second, say, and follows a batted ball, such as a ground ball to short. He heads to third, but the ball arrives first, having been picked up and thrown by either the shortstop or the outfielder. The runner heads back to second, but by now he's caught in a rundown. His only chance, almost always futile, is to try and beat the throws going back and forth and closing in on him. He will do anything—cheat, look ridiculous, even spastic, run like a doomed animal—to avoid the tag. His motions are wild, out of control, and a disturbing contrast to most of the otherwise routinized, repetitive gestures of the game.

Getting thrown "out" or being made a fool of (*Daily News* World Series coverage designated a "hero" and a "goat" for each game), continues to link baseball with rituals of sacrifice and scapegoating. Indeed the game of tag is "a survivor of rites going back to the labyrinth, to the scapegoat fool or sacrifice," according to Lucy Lippard. In *Overlay* she quotes Francis Huxley: "Tag is an 'endless game' that circulates the touch – a kind of infectiousness, reflected in a similar game in Madagascar where the chaser is called 'the leper.' He says that "children who end the day as 'it' are truly ill at ease, as if some racial memory of sacrificial victims operated." In this context, such words as "safe" and "out" take on special significance: baseball is a struggle between becoming *it* and returning home alive.

Modern baseball is a game of constantly shifting roles and signifiers, a delicate balance between randomness and order. It is a stage onto which we project our most primitive feelings about the seemingly random events that determine human fate.

A. Bartlett Giamatti, the president of the National League, illustrates baseball's ambiguities by analyzing the position of the catcher. Although playing defense, the catcher actually dictates the game by signaling to the pitcher what kind of pitches to throw. Further, his position behind the plate offers him the vantage point of the offense. Giamatti says that "part of the secretive, ruthless dimension of baseball, is the knowledge that an opposing player, crouching right behind him, signals wordlessly in order to exploit his weakness."

Since players are traded so often, it frequently occurs that a runner and a baseman know each other from a previous team. Yet later in their careers the two friends stand inches apart, each with the intention of causing his former teammate to lose.

Such a moment occurred in the sixth game of the 1986 playoff series between the Boston Red Sox and the California Angels. The game was characterized by miraculous turnarounds and history making plays. More important, the Angels had only to win this game to take the Pennant. During the 11th inning, Don Baylor reached first base when Donnie Moore's second pitch hit Baylor on the arm. His old friend and former teammate, Angel's player Bobby Grich, was playing first. "What do you think, Groove?" (Baylor's nickname).

Baylor turned to Grich and said, "This is the greatest game I've ever played in."

"Me too, partner," Grich replied.

If baseball is a game of surrogate kills, duels between men with clubs and men with rocks – primitive in its barely veiled murderous gestures – then moments such as this one may be interpreted as an astonishingly sentimental conversation between an executioner and his victim – because someone has to lose.

I have a diagram on my wall. It's a crude, stick-figure rendering of a base-ball drill, printed in a guide for little league players. Looking at it, the tiny narrow line that marks the baseball paths becomes the edge of the world. It's so easy to fall off. Sometimes, I just let my eye follow the base path, tracing all the things that can happen, like chapters in a novel or a person's life, from home plate and back around again.

A player is born when he steps into the batter's box. Once there, his job is to keep breathing. If the batter is able to foul off the ball on a count of two strikes, he is "still alive." He continues to live if he gets on base, where he enters the wilderness of the playing field.

On base, a batter is transformed into a runner. He struggles to stay alive for himself and his team (his species?). He is dependent upon his teammates to get him home. And if they don't, then he's "stranded," "abandoned," or "picked off."

The outfield is a black universe provoking the same endless contempla-tion of nature's mysteries that occurs when you look through a telescope. Consider the folklore surrounding the ball that was "hit into infinity." It was a home run that landed in a travelling truck on an adjacent freeway. It is still traveling, they say–the longest home run in the world.

My eye continues, back to the future coming home. But the purpose of the drill that's being illustrated is to show what happens when the runner misjudges the arm of the rightfielder throwing to home. He will be out. The ball sits in the catcher's glove, waiting. And that, surely, is the greatest tragedy, the most uneconomical of acts: to be thrown out at home plate.

And what is home, anyway? Home is a white surface in the shape of a house.

It's winter, the baseball season is over, and I, as every other baseball fan, go into hibernation. But I'll put myself down with machinations about the coming rebirth. In the twilight between my waking consciousness and dead sleep, I'll ask myself if Lou Piniella will have the horses next year, a twirler on the mound who can get the job done. And about the St. Louis Cards? Will they finally overcome the fatal Dave Denkinger call during the 1985 World Series and come back and be the team they should be? Have they been punished enough for their hubris? Is it possible that Bill Buckner could redeem himself in 1987? As I begin to sleep, the stadium filters into a dreamscape. I see it as from an aerial photograph. It looks like a Robert Smithson earthwork. Claw marks on the earth for space visitors to decode? America's answer to Stonehenge? Mother baseball. To sleep. In April the sun will come out again, and I shall be there to watch men with clubs and seeds stand on a green pasture and coax the sun to stay out.

MARIANNE MOORE

◊

Hometown Piece for Messrs. Alston and Reese

To the tune:
"Li'l baby, don't say a word: Mama goin' to buy you
  a mocking-bird.
Bird don't sing: Mama goin' to sell it and buy a brass
  ring."

"Millennium," yes; "pandemonium"!
Roy Campanella leaps high. Dodgerdom

crowned, had Johnny Podres on the mound.
Buzzie Bavasi and the Press gave ground;

the team slapped, mauled, and asked the Yankees' match,
"How did you feel when Sandy Amoros made the catch?"

"I said to myself"—pitcher for all innings—
"as I walked back to the mound I said, 'Everything's

getting better and better.'" (Zest: they've zest.
"'Hope springs eternal in the Brooklyn breast.'"

And would the Dodger Band in 8, row 1, relax
if they saw the collector of income tax?

Ready with a tune if that should occur:
"Why Not Take All of Me—All of Me, Sir?")

Another series. Round-tripper Duke at bat,
"Four hundred feet from home-plate"; more like that.

A neat bunt, please; a cloud-breaker, a drive
like Jim Gilliam's great big one. Hope's alive.

Homered, flied out, fouled? Our "stylish stout"
so nimble Campanella will have him out.

A-squat in double-headers four hundred times a day,
he says that in a measure the pleasure is the pay:

catcher to pitcher, a nice easy throw
almost as if he'd just told it to go.

Willie Mays should be a Dodger. He should—
a lad for Roger Craig and Clem Labine to elude;

but you have an omen, pennant-winning Peewee,
on which we are looking superstitiously.

Ralph Branca has Preacher Roe's number; recall?
and there's Don Bessent; he can really fire the ball.

As for Gil Hodges, in custody of first—
"He'll do it by himself." Now a specialist—versed

in an extension reach far into the box seats—
he lengthens up, leans and gloves the ball. He defeats

expectation by a whisker. The modest star,
irked by one misplay, is no hero by a hair;

in a strikeout slaughter when what could matter more,
he lines a homer to the signboard and has changed the score.

Then for his nineteenth season, a home run—
with four of six runs batted in—Carl Furillo's the big gun;

almost dehorned the foe—has fans dancing in delight.
Jake Pitler and his Playground "get a Night"—

Jake, that hearty man, made heartier by a harrier
who can bat as well as field—Don Demeter.

Shutting them out for nine innings—hitter too—
Carl Erskine leaves Cimoli nothing to do.

Take off the goat-horns, Dodgers, that egret
which two very fine base-stealers can offset.

You've got plenty: Jackie Robinson
and Campy and big Newk, and Dodgerdom again
watching everything you do. You won last year. Come on.

HILMA WOLITZER

◊

Jackie Robinson

The first subversive act of my young adult life occurred in the mid-1940s, in a school playground in Brooklyn, where I was just hanging around with a few friends. Someone a little older, a skinny boy with glasses and a clipboard, approached and asked us to sign a petition to allow Negroes to play in organized baseball. Although I had grown up in what I'd always thought of as a "liberal" family, the kid with the clipboard had to explain what all the fuss was about segregated baseball. The subject had never come up at our dinner table.

My friends refused to sign the petition, and one of them even muttered something about "Communists." I was, in those days, sheeplike in my conformity to the crowd—a pretty common adolescent affliction. "If your friends all jumped off a cliff, you'd jump, too," my mother would frequently complain. This time I decided to jump first, but no one else followed. While I scrawled my name and address on the petition, another girl hummed "Red Sails in the Sunset." I remember how rapidly my heart was beating, what a big deal it suddenly all seemed.

I was *almost* a baseball fan in those days, largely because my father and my favorite uncle were, and I enjoyed their animated, male company when they sat near the radio and listened to a game. So I often listened with them, especially to the Dodgers' games, and gradually I learned the ground rules and the various players' names and positions. If I wasn't quite sure what a balk was, and didn't really understand the logic of the infield-fly rule, I liked the background excitement of the crowd, Red Barber's soft drawl, and even the affectionate, amusing nicknames of some of the players—Cookie, Pee Wee, Frenchy, Pistol Pete. I cheered when the Dodgers were winning and booed when Walker or Reiser was "robbed" of a hit. But it was only after Jackie Robinson came down from the farm team in Montreal to join

Brooklyn that my interest in baseball became instantly, sharply focused, that I became a dedicated fan.

One of the beauties of listening to baseball, rather than seeing it played, is the work of the imagination. A similar analogy might be made between reading and watching television. Radiocast baseball depends a lot on the style of the sportscasters and the ability of the listeners to visualize the players and the action. I remember thinking of Pee Wee Reese as an agile midget, of Frenchy Bordagaray as romantically, languidly handsome—something like Charles Boyer. In 1947, when Jackie Robinson became the pioneer black major-leaguer, I imagined that he looked exotically different out there, and I thought I heard a difference in the crowd's response to him, a jeering among all the cheering. I experienced something like anxious pride whenever he came up to bat. Hadn't I put him there practically by myself?

I didn't actually *attend* a ball game until the middle of that 1947 season. It was a night game at Ebbets Field, and the Dodgers were playing the Giants. The look of the diamond itself surprised me. It was like a stage setting under the lights; even the infield grass seemed unnaturally green. And the actors! Like all celebrities, they were both wonderfully glamorous and disappointingly ordinary in person. Pee Wee Reese wasn't nearly as short as I'd imagined, and Duke Snider was impressive, but not particularly regal, as his name suggested. Jackie Robinson *was* conspicuously dark among all the white players, but what you soon fixed on was his quickness and grace, in the field and at bat. Baseball, I saw, was a kind of ballet, with continually improvised movements, and Robinson was its premier danseur. His stance at the plate was deep, the bat held high. He'd rub one hand on his hip, then grip the bat again, and I wondered if this was a nervous habit, if he was only wiping off his sweaty palm. After he reached base, with a hard line drive to left, he dodged and danced and bluffed going, to the crowd's delight and the pitcher's distraction. And he eventually did steal second, running swiftly in his distinctive, pigeon-toed gait, then sliding in to just beat the throw. So *this* was baseball! By the time the game was over (with the Dodgers winning, naturally), I decided that Robinson's hip rubbing wasn't a nervous gesture at all; no one who played that well could possibly be nervous.

It was only much later that I read the details of Jackie Robinson's historical passage into the majors. I learned about owner Branch Rickey's decision to integrate the Dodgers, his choice and summoning of Robinson, and the proposition that included one crucial edict: *Robinson must not overtly react to racist attacks.* It was understood by both men that such attacks were inevitable—during their legendary meeting, Rickey even acted out a series of probable abuses, in a kind of minipsychodrama. Robinson is reported to have said, "I get it. What you want me to say is that I've got another cheek." He finally agreed to Rickey's terms, but the concession must have been agonizing for him; he was an aggressive, hot-tempered man, one hardly inclined to be passive in the face of bigotry.

I learned that there had been other petitions besides the one I'd signed with such youthful fervor in the playground. One of them, circulated by a Dodger player, demanded that Robinson *not* be brought down to join the team. Volumes of vicious, threatening letters were sent to both Robinson and Rickey. And Red Barber, the southern-born announcer, almost decided to quit broadcasting for Brooklyn when he heard of Rickey's decision to break the color barrier. By his own admission, Robinson's palms *were* often sweaty at least during that initial season. As expected, there were taunting insults from the stands, and savage physical assaults by opposing players during the course of the game. The segregation of travel and recreational facilities incurred further indignities. Despite the growing support of his teammates, and the extraordinary bond between Robinson and his wife, Rachel, he must have suffered moments of profound loneliness and rage. But he endured it all, somehow, with astonishing self-control; his only revenge was the superb playing that led to his being named Rookie of the Year.

Five years later, I voted in my first presidential election. Pulling the switch in the voting booth, I was reminded of the thrill I had felt—a sense of participating in history—when I signed that baseball petition in the playground. I'd realized a while back that the signature of a minor in such a major controversy probably hadn't mattered at all, except to me. And my official vote, for Adlai Stevenson (in 1952, and again four years later) didn't carry the day, either. Yet I continue to vote and to sign petitions, often with a feeling of deep frustration, if not complete futility. And I know that Stevenson wasn't a lesser candidate for losing those elections—it takes a kind of valor just to run, especially against the odds.

Jackie Robinson ran against the odds, too, and against the grain of intense and disgraceful public opinion. Of course, he was a winner in every sense of the word—a brilliant athlete, a man of remarkable willpower and integrity, the groundbreaker for all the gifted black players who followed him. He kept his word to Branch Rickey, under brutal circumstances, and the integration of organized baseball was accomplished. But ultimately he *stopped* turning the other cheek—on and off the ballfield. He became an ardent and outspoken activist for civil rights, instead of relaxing in the comfortable climate of his own success, and that was his truest heroism.

VERONICA GENG

◇

What Happened

September 29, 1986

Dear:

We are fine. Please do not worry about us. I know it must have come as a shock to find your wife and children gone when you got home from work, but there is nothing to worry about. We are still the same loving family we were before. Nothing has changed. I will send you a post-office box number where we can be reached just as soon as I know where we'll be, but at this point I don't know when that will be. All I can say is that any concern or anxiety on your part would be premature and alarmist.

Still, I know you can't help asking yourself: What happened? And the answer is: Nothing. Doc hung a curveball a couple of times, that's all. It could happen to anyone. There's no more to it than that. The Mets are still a winning team. What matters now is to take things one day at a time.

Please try to understand that although nothing has changed, nothing can stay exactly the same, either. No sane person could possibly have expected Doc to sustain the incredible greatness of last year. To expect that would be to expect superhuman perfection. Even Doc himself would admit that. But it's no reason to suspect that there's some hidden explanation for why things don't seem to be going as well as they used to (which doesn't mean things have changed, just that they're not going as well). Knowing you, I can tell that your mind is already racing with all sorts of gloomy scenarios based on little things that have happened in the past and now, in retrospect, loom as significant—like the ankle sprain before spring training. Believe me, I have searched my heart about the possibility that maybe the ankle sprain (without my even consciously realizing it) might have something to do with this, and I feel it's highly unlikely. Also, I hope you won't be tempted to dwell on some distressing generalization like "overthrowing" (because there is no such thing). I pray that other people won't encourage you in this line of thinking. There's always someone who will play on your nerves by saying, This is not as good as it was yesterday, so there must be something wrong. When, in fact, that's a contradiction. If anything, there's reason to think the opposite. If things are not as good as they were yesterday, isn't that all the more reason to believe that chances are they will be better next time? Especially for a young man with Dwight Gooden's extraordinary poise.

Now, dear, I want to confess something that I'm sure you're unaware of. For the past few months, every night after you've fallen asleep, I've been going downstairs and watching hundreds of hours of videotapes comparing Doc's pitching motion last year and this year. I didn't tell you about this, because I didn't want to upset you. But you know what I discovered? There is absolutely no difference! It's just that now he's not getting as many batters out. In other words, this is a more *mature* Doc. That's all I'm trying to explain.

But I can just hear you saying, What is the problem, then? Why has she gone away with the children and refused to tell me where she is? I can assure you with every bone in my body that there is no problem. Last year was the greatest year I've ever known, and I feel confident that future years will fulfill that potential, which may necessitate a few minor adjustments in Doc's mechanics, something that a number of qualified people are helping him with. Above all, I beg you not to pin any blame on Mel Stottlemyre, who doesn't even know us.

There's one thing I'm sure of. If you really have something, then almost by definition there are going to be certain times when you don't have it. If I didn't believe that, I wouldn't be so convinced that at this very moment you and I are closer than any two people could possibly be. Someday we'll look back on all this and, with the complex understanding that comes from placing great demands upon ourselves, we'll be able to say, It was nothing.

—*Love*,
Kay

P.S.: And Doc? He's better than ever.

CAROLYN KIZER

◊

One to Nothing

The bibulous eagle behind me at the ball game:
"Shucks a'mighty!" coming through the rye
And Seven-Up, "I didn't mean to kick you, lady.
When you go to the Eagles' convention, you just *go!*"
Then he needles the batter from Sacramento:
"Too much ego!" he yells. "The old ego curse,
That'll hex him. The old ego never fails.
See?" he says to his phlegmatic friend,
"The bastard fanned!" And "Shucks a'mighty!"
Says again, an American from an English novel,
Named Horace or Homer, a strange colonial bird,
A raw provincial, with his outmoded slang.

"Say!" he cries to his friend, "just now I opened
One eye, saw the catcher, then the batter
In a little circle. And everything went brown.
What happened?" *"Nothing!"* says his friend.
He leans beside me, proffers the open pint.
My ego spurns him. "Fly away!" I say
To the badge on his breast. Eagle flaps down,
Confides in the man on first: "Just once a year
I have fun—see?—at the Eagles' convention.
Later I meet the other dignitaries
At the hotel. Forgive me. I'm from a small town."
He sighs, puts his head in the lap of his friend,

Listens to the portable radio, as the announcer
Makes sense of a blurry ball game

When batters turn brown, curl at the edges,
Fan and fan, like girls in early English novels,
And you can't tell the players, even with a program.
The count is two and one. We hear the *crack!*
Bat skids across the grass. The runner's on!
But eagle sleeps; he dreams away the ball game.
The dozen wasted hits, the double-plays
Are lost on him, as we lose, by one run.
Having his inning curled in a little circle,
He emerges, sucks his bottle; his badge mislaid

In the last of the ninth. We surge to the exits
While this bird claws among the peanut shells
In search of his ego. Carry him, friend,
To the dignitaries, to the eagle's aerie,
Where his mate will hone her talons on his breast.
As D. H. Lawrence wished, he has cracked the shell
Of his ego, but devoured it like a nut
Washed down with rye. And he finds oblivion
Like the lost hero of a Modern English Novel.
What happens? Nothing. Even the brilliant infield
Turns brown. Lights out. The circle fades below.
Shucks a'mighty. If you're an eagle, you just go.

LINDA PASTAN

◊

Baseball

When you tried to tell me
baseball was a metaphor

for life: the long, dusty travail
around the bases, for instance,

to try to go home again;
the Sacrifice for which you win

approval but not applause;
the way the light closes down

in the last days of the season—
I didn't believe you.

It's just a way of passing
the time, I said.

And you said: that's it.
Yes.

GAIL MAZUR

◇

Baseball

The game of baseball is not a metaphor
and I know it's not really life.
The chalky green diamond, the lovely
dusty brown lanes I see from airplanes
multiplying around the cities
are only neat playing fields.
Their structure is not the frame
of history carved out of forest,
that is not what I see on my ascent.

And down in the stadium,
the veteran catcher guiding the young
pitcher through the innings, the line
of concentration between them,
that delicate filament is not
like the way you are helping me,
only it reminds me when I strain
for analogies, the way a rookie strains
for perfection, and the veteran,
in his wisdom, seems to promise it,
it glows from his upheld glove,

and the man in front of me
in the grandstand, drinking banana
daiquiris from a thermos,
continuing through a whole dinner
to the aromatic cigar even as our team
is shut out, nearly hitless, he is

not like the farmer that Auden speaks
of in Breughel's Icarus,
or the four inevitable woman-hating
drunkards, yelling, hugging
each other, and moving up and down
continuously for more beer

and the young wife trying to understand
what a full count could be
to please her husband happy in
his old dreams, or the little boy
in the Yankees cap already nodding
off to sleep against his father,
program and popcorn memories
sliding into the future,
and the old woman from Lincoln, Maine,
screaming at the Yankee slugger
with wounded knees to break his leg

this is not a microcosm,
not even a slice of life
and the terrible slumps,
when the greatest hitter mysteriously
goes hitless for weeks, or
the pitcher's stuff is all junk
who threw like a magician all last month,
or the days when our guys look
like Sennett cops, slipping, bumping
each other, then suddenly, the play
that wasn't humanly possible, the Kid
we know isn't ready for the big leagues,
leaps into the air to catch a ball
that should have gone downtown,
and coming off the field is hugged
and bottom-slapped by the sudden
sorcerers, the winning team

the question of what makes a man
slump when his form, his eye,
his power aren't to blame, this isn't
like the bad luck that hounds us,
and his frustration in the games

not like our deep rage
for disappointing ourselves

the ball park is an artifact,
manicured, safe, "scene in an Easter egg,"
and the order of the ball game,
the firm structure with the mystery
of accidents always contained,
not the wild field we wander in,
where I'm trying to recite the rules,
to repeat the statistics of the game,
and the wind keeps carrying my words away

JOSEPHINE JACOBSEN

◊

Deaf-Mutes at the Ballgame

In the hot sun and dazzle of grass,
The wind of noise is men's voices:

A torrent of tone, a simmer of roar,
And bats crack, bags break, flags follow themselves.

The hawkers sweat and gleam in the wind of noise,
The tools of ignorance crouch and give the sign.

The deaf-mutes sit in the hurricane's eye,
The shell-shape ear and the useless tongue

Present, but the frantic fingers' pounce-and-bite
Is sound received and uttered.

If they blink their lids—then the whole gaudy circle
With its green heart and ritual figures

Is suddenly not: leaving two animal-quick
Wince-eyed things alone; with masses and masses

And masses of rows of seats of men
Who move their lips and listen.

While secret secret sits inside
Each, his deaf-mute; fingerless.

PATRICIA HIGHSMITH

◊

The Barbarians

*S*tanley Hubbell *painted* on Sundays, the only day he had to paint. Saturdays he helped his father in the hardware store in Brooklyn. Weekdays he worked as a researcher for a publishing house specializing in trade journals. Stanley did not take his painting very seriously: it was a kind of occupational therapy for his nerves recommended by his doctor. After six months, he was painting fairly well.

One Sunday in early June, Stanley was completing a portrait of himself in a white shirt with a green background. It was larger than his first self-portrait, and it was much better. He had caught the troubled frown of his left eyebrow. The eyes were finished – light brown, a little sad, intense, hopeful. Hopeful of what? Stanley didn't know. But the eyes on the canvas were so much his own eyes they made him smile with pleasure when he looked at them. There remained the highlight to put down the long, some-what crooked nose, and then to darken the background.

He had been working perhaps twenty minutes, hardly long enough to moisten his brushes or limber up the colors on his palette, when he heard them stomping through the narrow alley at the side of his building. He hesi-tated, while half of his mind still imagined the unpainted highlight down the nose and the other half listened to find out how many there were going to be this afternoon.

Do it now, he told himself, and quickly bent toward the canvas, his left hand clutching the canvas frame, his right hand braced against his left fore-arm. The point of his brush touched the bridge of his nose.

"Let's *have* it, Franky!"

"*Yee-hoooo!*"

"*Ah, g'wan! What d'yuh think I wanna do? Fight the whole goddam. . . .*"

"Ah-hah-*haaaaaaaah!*"

"Put it *here*, Franky!"

Thud!

They always warmed up for fifteen minutes or so with a hard ball and catchers' mitts.

Stanley's brush stopped after half an inch. He paused, hoping for the lull, knowing there wouldn't be any. The braying voices went on, twenty feet below his window, bantering, directing one another, explaining, exhorting.

"*Get the goddam bush outa the way! Pull it up!*" a voice yelled. Stanley flinched as if it had been said to him.

Two Sundays ago they had had quite an exchange about the hedge bushes. One of the men had tumbled over them in reaching for the ball, and Stanley, seeing it, had shouted down: "Would you please not go against the hedge?" It burst out of him involuntarily—he was sorry he had not made the remark a lot stronger—and they had all joined in yelling back at him: "What d'yuh think this is, your lot?" and "Who're you, the gardener?—Hedges! Hah!"

Stanley edged closer to the window, close enough to see the bottom of the brick wall that bounded the far side of the lot. There were still five little bushes standing in front of the wall, forlorn and scraggly, but still standing, still growing—at this minute. Stanley had put them there. He had found them growing, or rather struggling for survival, in cindery corners of the lot and by the ashcans at the end of the alley. None of the bushes was more than two feet tall, but they were unmistakably hedge bushes. He had transplanted them for two reasons; to hide the ugly wall somewhat and to put the plants in a spot where they could get some sunshine. It had been a tiny gesture toward beautifying something that was, essentially, unbeautifiable, but he had made the effort and it had given him satisfaction. And the men seemed to know he had planted them, perhaps because he had shouted down to watch out for them, and also because the superintendent, who was never around and barely took care of the garbage cans, would never have done anything like set out hedge bushes by a brick wall.

Moving nearer the window, Stanley could see the men. There were five of them today, deployed around the narrow rectangular lot, throwing the ball to one another in no particular order, which meant that four were at all times yelling for the ball to be thrown to them.

"Here y'are, Joey, *here!*"

Thud!

They were all men of thirty or more, and two had the beginnings of paunches. One of the paunchy men was red-headed and he had the loudest, most unpleasant voice, though it was the dark-haired man in blue jeans who yelled the most, really never stopped yelling, even when he caught and threw the ball, and by the same token none of his companions seemed to pay any attention to what he said. The redheaded man's name was Franky,

Stanley had learned, and the dark-haired man was Bob. Two of the others had cleated shoes, and pranced and yelled between catches, lifting their knees high and pumping their arms.

"*Wanna see me break a window?*" yelled Franky, winding up. He slammed the ball at one of the cleat-shod men, who let out a wail as he caught it as if it had killed him.

Why was he watching it, Stanley asked himself. He looked at his clock. Only twenty past two. They would play until five, at least. Stanley was aware of a nervous trembling inside him, and he looked at his hands. They seemed absolutely steady. He walked to his canvas. The portrait looked like paint and canvas now, nothing more. The voices might have been in the same room with him. He went to one window and closed it. It was really too hot to close both windows.

Then, from somewhere above him, Stanley heard a window go up, and as if it were a signal for battle, he stiffened: the window-opener was on his side. Stanley stood a little back from the window and looked down at the lot.

"Hey!" the voice from upstairs cried, "Don't you know you're not supposed to play ball there? People're trying to sleep!"

"*Go ahead'n sleep!*" yelled the blue jeans, spitting on the ground between his spread knees.

An obscenity from the redhead, and then, "Let's go, Joey, let's *have* it!"

"Hey!—I'm going to get the law on you if you don't clear out!" from the upstairs window.

The old man was really angry—it was Mr. Collins, the nightwatchman—but the threat of the law was empty and everybody knew it. Stanley had spoken to a policeman a month ago, told him about the Sunday ballplayers, but the policeman had only smiled at him—a smile of indulgence for the ballplayers—and had mumbled something about nobody's being able to do anything about people who wanted to play ball on Sundays. Why couldn't you, Stanley wondered. What about the NO BALLPLAYING written on the side of his own building and signed by the Police Department? What about the right of law-abiding citizens to spend a quiet Sunday at home if they cared to? What about the anti-noise campaign in New York? But he hadn't asked the policeman these questions, because he had seen that the policeman was the same kind of man the ballplayers were, only in uniform.

They were still yelling, Mr. Collins and the quintet below. Stanley put his palms on the brick ledge of the windowsill and leaned out to add the support of his visible presence to Mr. Collins.

"*We ain't breakin' any law! Go to hell!*"

"I mean what I say!" shouted Mr. Collins. "I'm a working man!"

"*Go back to bed, grampa!*"

Then the redheaded man picked up a stone or a large cinder and made as if to throw it at Mr. Collins, whose voice shut off in the middle of a sentence. "*Shut up or we'll bust yuh windows!*" the redheaded man bellowed, then managed to catch the ball that was coming his way.

Another window went up, and Stanley was suddenly inspired to yell: "Isn't there another place to play ball around here? Can't you give us a break one Sunday?"

"Ah, the hell with 'em!" said one of the men.

The batted ball made a sick sound and spun up behind the batter, stopping in mid-air hardly four feet in front of Stanley's nose, before it started its descent. They were playing two-base baseball now with a stick bat and a soft ball.

The blond woman who lived on the floor above Stanley and to the left was having a sympathetic discussion with Mr. Collins: "Wouldn't you think that grown men—"

Mr. Collins, loudly: "Ah, they're worse than children! Hoodlums, that's what they are! Ought to get the police after them!"

"And the language they use! I've told my husband about 'em but he works Sundays and he just can't *realize!*"

"So her husband ain't home, huh?" said the redheaded man, and the others guffawed.

Stanley looked down on the bent, freckled back of the redheaded man who had removed his shirt now and whose hands were braced on his knees. It was a revolting sight—the white back mottled with brown freckles, rounded with fatty muscle and faintly shiny with sweat. I wish I had a BB gun, Stanley thought as he had often thought before. I'd shoot them, not enough to hurt them, just enough to annoy them. Annoy them the hell out of here!

A roar from five throats shocked him, shattered his thoughts and left him shaking.

He went into the bathroom and wet his face at the basin. Then he came back and closed his other window. The closed windows made very little difference in the sound. He bent toward his easel again, touching the brushtip to the partly drawn highlight on the nose. The tip of his brush had dried and stiffened. He moistened it in the turpentine cup.

"*Franky!*"

"*Run, boy run!*"

Stanley put the brush down. He had made a wide white mark on the nose. He wiped at it with a rag, trembling.

Now there was an uproar from below, as if all five were fighting. Stanley looked out. One of the pot-bellies and the redheaded man were wrestling for the ball by the hedges. With a wild, almost feminine laugh, the redhead toppled onto the hedges, yelping as the bushes scratched him.

Stanley flung the window up. "Would you please watch out for the hedge?" he shouted.

"*Ah, f'Chris'* sake!" yelled the redhead, getting up from one knee, at the same time yanking up a bush from the ground and hurling it in Stanley's direction.

The others laughed.

"You're not allowed to destroy public property!" Stanley retorted with a quick, bitter smile, as if he had them. His heart was racing.

"What d'yuh mean we're not allowed?" asked the blue jeans, crashing a foot into another bush.

"*Cut that out!*" Stanley yelled.

"Oh, pipe down!"

"I'm getting thirsty! Who's going for drinks?"

Now the redheaded man swung a foot and kicked another bush up into the air.

"Pick that hedge up again! Put it back!" Stanley shouted, clenching his fists.

"Pick up yer ass!"

Stanley crossed his room and yanked the door open, ran down the steps and out. Suddenly, he was standing in the middle of the lot in the bright sunshine. "You'd better put that hedge back!" Stanley yelled. "One of you'd better put all those bushes back!"

"Look who's here!"

"Oh, dry up! Come on, Joey!"

The ball hit Stanley on the shoulder, but he barely felt it, barely wondered if it had been directed at him. He was no match for any of the men physically, certainly not for all of them together, but this fact barely brushed the surface of his mind, either. He was mad enough to have attacked any or all of them, and it was only their scattered number that kept him from moving. He didn't know where to begin.

"Isn't any of you going to put those back?" he demanded.

"*No!*"

"Outa the way, Mac! You're gonna get hurt!"

While reaching for the ball near Stanley, the blue jeans put out an arm and shoved him. Stanley's neck made a snapping sound and he just managed to recover his balance without pitching on his face. No one was paying the least attention to him now. They were like a scattered, mobile army, confident of their ground. Stanley walked quickly toward the alley, oblivious of the ball that bounced off his head, oblivious of the laughter that followed.

The next thing he knew, he was in the cool, darkish hall of his building. His eye fell on the flat stone that was used now and then to prop the front door open. He picked it up and began to climb the stairs with it. He thought of hurling it out his window, down into the midst of them. The barbarians!

He rested the stone on his windowsill, still holding it between his hands. The man in the blue jeans was walking along by the brick wall, kicking at the remaining bushes. They had stopped playing for some reason.

"Got the stuff, fellows! Come 'n get it!" One of the pot-bellied men had arrived with his fists full of soft drink bottles.

Heads tipped back as they drank. There were animal murmurs and grunts of satisfaction. Stanley leaned farther out.

The redheaded man was sitting right below his window on a board propped up on a couple of rocks to make a bench. He couldn't miss if he dropped it, Stanley thought, and almost at the same time, he held the stone a few inches out from his sill and dropped it. Ducking back, Stanley heard a deep-pitched, lethal sounding crack, then a startled curse.

"Who did that?"

"Hey, Franky! *Franky!* Are you okay?"

Stanley heard a groan.

"We gotta get a doctor! Gimme a hand, somebody!"

"That bastard upstairs!" It came clearly.

Stanley jumped as something crashed through his other window, hit the shade and slid to the floor—a stone the size of a large egg.

Now he could hear their voices moving up the alley. Stanley expected them to come up the stairs for him. He clenched his fists and listened for feet on the stairs.

But nothing happened. Suddenly there was silence.

"Thank—*God*," Stanley heard the blond woman say, wearily.

The telephone would ring, he thought. That would be next. The police.

Stanley sat down in a chair, sat rigidly for several minutes. The rock had weighed eight or ten pounds, he thought. The very least that could have happened was that the man had suffered a concussion. But Stanley imagined the skull fractured, the brain partly crushed. Perhaps he had lived only a few moments after the impact.

He got up and went to his canvas. Boldly, he mixed a color for the entire nose, painted over the messy highlight, then attacked the background, making it a darker green. By the time he had finished the background, the nose was dry enough for him to put the highlight in, which he did quickly and surely. There was no sound anywhere except that of his rather accelerated breathing. He painted as if he had only five minutes more to paint, five minutes more to live before they came for him.

But by six o'clock, nobody had come. The telephone had not rung, and the picture was done. It was good, better than he had dared hope it would be. Stanley felt exhausted. He remembered that there was no coffee in the house. No milk, either. He'd have to have a little coffee. He'd have to go out.

Fear was sneaking up on him again. Were they waiting for him downstairs in front of the house? Or were they still at the hospital, watching their friend die? What if he were dead? You couldn't kill a man for playing ball below your window on Sunday—even though you might like to.

He tried to pull himself together, went into the bathroom and took a quick, cool shower, because he had been perspiring quite a bit. He put on a clean blue shirt and combed his hair. Then he pushed his wallet and keys into his pocket and went out. He saw no sign of the ballplayers on the sidewalk, or of anyone who seemed to be interested in him. He bought milk and coffee at the delicatessen around the corner, and on the way back he ran into the blond woman of about forty who lived on the floor above him.

"Wasn't that awful this afternoon!" she said to Stanley. "I saw you down there arguing with them. Good for you! You certainly scared them off." She shook her head despairingly. "But I suppose they'll be back next Sunday."

"Do they play Saturdays?" Stanley asked suddenly, and entirely out of nervousness, since he didn't care whether they played Saturdays or not.

"No," she said dubiously. "Well, they once did, but mostly it's Sundays. I swear to God I'm going to make Al stay home one Sunday so he can hear 'em. You must have it a little worse than me, being lower down." She shook her head again. She looked thin and tired, and there was a complicated meshwork of wrinkles under her lower lids. "Well, you've got my thanks for breakin' 'em up a little earlier today."

"Thank you," Stanley said, really saying it almost involuntarily to thank her for not mentioning, for not having seen what he had done.

They climbed the stairs together.

"Trust this super not to be around whenever somebody needs him," she said, loud enough to carry into the superintendent's second floor apartment, which they were then passing. "And to think we all give him big tips on Christmas!"

"It's pretty bad," Stanley said with a smile as he unlocked his door. "Well, let's hope next week's a little better."

"You said it. I hope it's pouring rain," she said, and went on up the stairs.

Stanley was in the habit of breakfasting at a small cafe between his house and the subway, and on Monday morning one of the ballplayers—the one who usually wore blue jeans—was in the cafe. He was having coffee and doughnuts when Stanley walked in, and he gave Stanley such an unpleasant look, continued for several minutes to give him such an unpleasant look, that a few other people in the cafe noticed it and began to watch them.

Stanley stammeringly ordered coffee. The redheaded man wasn't dead, he decided. He was probably hovering between life and death. If Franky were dead, or if he were perfectly all right now, the dark-haired man's expression would have been different. Stanley finished his coffee and passed the man on the way to pay his check. He expected the man to try to trip him, or at least to say something to him as he passed him, but he didn't.

That evening, when Stanley came home from work at a little after six, he saw two of the ballplayers—the dark-haired man again and one of the paunchy men who looked like a wrestler in his ordinary clothes—standing across the street. They stared at him as he went into his building. Upstairs in his apartment, Stanley pondered the possible significance of their standing across the street from where he lived. Had their friend just died, or was he nearer death? Had they just come from the funeral, perhaps? Both of them had been wearing dark suits, suits that might have been their best. Stanley listened for feet on the stairs. There was only the plodding tread of the old woman who lived with her dog on the top floor. She aired her dog at about this time every evening.

All at once Stanley noticed that his windows were shattered. Now he saw three or four stones and fragments of glass on his carpet. There was a stone on his bed, too. The window that had been broken Sunday had almost no glass in it now, and of the upper halves of the windows, which were paneled, only two or three panes remained, he saw when he raised the shades.

He set about methodically picking up the stones and the larger pieces of glass and putting them into a paper bag. Then he got his broom and swept. He was wondering when he would have the time to put the glass back—no use asking the super to do it—and he thought probably not before next weekend, unless he ordered the pieces during his lunch-hour tomorrow. He got his yardstick and measured the larger panes, which were of slightly different sizes because it was an old house, and then the little panes, and recorded the numbers on a paper which he put into his wallet. He'd have to buy putty, too.

He stiffened, hearing a faint click at his doorlock. "Who's there?" he called.

Silence.

He had an impulse to yank the door open, then realized he was afraid to. He listened for a few moments. There was no other sound, so he decided to forget the click. Maybe he had only imagined it.

When he came home the next evening, he couldn't get his door open. The key went in, but it wouldn't turn, not a fraction of an inch. Had they put something in it to jam it? Had that been the click he had heard last night? On the other hand, the lock had given him some trouble about six months ago, he remembered. For several days it had been difficult to open, and then it had got all right again. Or had that been the lock on his father's store door? He couldn't quite remember.

He leaned against the stair rail, staring at the key in the lock and wondering what to do.

The blond woman was coming up the stairs.

Stanley smiled and said, "Good evening."

"Hello, there. What happened? Forget your key?"

"No, I— The lock's a little stiff," he said.

"Oh. Always something wrong in this house, ain't there?" she said, moving on down the hall. "Did you ever see anything like it?"

"No," he agreed, smiling. But he looked after her anxiously. Usually, she stopped and chatted a little longer. Had she heard something about his dropping the rock? And she hadn't mentioned his broken windows, though she was home all day and had probably heard the noise.

Stanley turned and attacked the lock, turning the key with all his strength. The lock suddenly yielded. The door was open.

It took him until after midnight to get the panes in. And all the time he worked, he was conscious of the fact that the windows might be broken again when he got home tomorrow.

The following evening the same two men, the paunchy one and the dark-haired one who was in blue jeans and a shirt now, were standing across the street, and to Stanley's horror they crossed the street so as to meet him in front of his door. The paunchy one reached out and took a handful of Stanley's jacket and shirtfront.

"Listen, Mac," he said in Stanley's face, "you can go to jail for what you did Sunday. You know that, doncha?"

"I don't know what you're talking about!" Stanley said quickly.

"Oh, you *don't?*"

"No!" Stanley yelled.

The man let him go with a shove. Stanley straightened his jacket, and went on into his house. The lock was again difficult, but he flung himself against it with the energy of desperation. It yielded slowly, and when Stanley removed his key, a rubbery string came with it: they had stuffed his lock with chewing gum. Stanley wiped his key, with disgust, on the floor. He did not begin to shake until he had closed the door of his apartment. Then even as he shook, he thought: I've beaten them. They weren't coming after him. Broken windows, chewing gum? So what? They hadn't sought out the police. He had lied, of course, in saying he didn't know what they were talking about, but that had been the right reply, after all. He wouldn't have lied to a policeman, naturally, but they hadn't brought the police in yet.

Stanley began to feel better. Moreover, his windows were intact, he saw.

He decided that the redheaded man was probably going through a prolonged crisis. There was something subdued about the men's behavior, he thought. Or were they planning some worse attack? He wished he knew if the redheaded man were in a hospital or walking around. It was just possible, too, that the man had died, Stanley thought. Maybe the men weren't quite sure that it was he who had dropped the rock—Mr. Collins lived above Stanley and might have dropped it, for instance—and perhaps an investigation by the police was yet to come.

On Thursday evening, he passed Mr. Collins on the stairs as he was coming home. Mr. Collins was on his way to work. It struck Stanley that Mr. Collins' "Good evening" was cool. He wondered if Mr. Collins had heard about the rock and considered him a murderer, or at least some kind of psychopath, to have dropped a ten-pound rock on somebody's head?

Saturday came, and Stanley worked all day in his father's hardware store, went to a movie, and came home at about eleven. Two of the small panes in the upper part of one window were broken. Stanley thought them not important enough to fix until the weather grew cooler. He wouldn't have noticed it, if he hadn't deliberately checked the state of the windows.

He slept late Sunday morning, for he had been extremely tired the night before. It was nearly one o'clock when he set up his easel to paint. He had in mind to paint the aperture between two buildings, which contained a tree, that he could see straight out his window above the lot. He thought this Sunday might be a good Sunday to paint, because the ballplayers probably wouldn't come. Stanley pictured them dampened this Sunday, at least to the extent that they would find another vacant lot to play in.

He had not quite finished his sketch of the scene in charcoal on his canvas, when he heard them. For a moment, he thought he was imagining it, that he was having an auditory hallucination. But no. He heard them ever more clearly in the alley—their particular sullen bravado coming through the murmuring, a collective murmur as recognizable to Stanley as a single familiar voice. Stanley waited, a little way back from his window.

"Okay, boys, let's *go-o-o!*"

"*Yeeeeee-hoooooo!*" Sheer defiance, a challenge to any who might contest their right to play there.

Stanley went closer to the window, looking, wide-eyed, for the redheaded man. And there he was! A patch of bandage on the top of his head, but otherwise as brutishly energetic as ever. As Stanley watched, he hurled a catcher's mitt at a companion who was then bending over, hitting him in the buttocks.

Raucous, hooting laughter.

Then from above: "F'gosh sakes, why don't you guys grow up? Why don't you beat it? We've had enough of you around here!" It was the blond woman, and Stanley knew that Mr. Collins would not be far behind.

"*Ah, save yer throat!*"

"C'mon down 'n get in the game, sister!"

There was a new defiance in their voices today. They were louder. They were determined to win. They *had* won. They were back.

Stanley sat down on his bed, dazed, frustrated, and suddenly tired. He was glad the redheaded fellow wasn't dead. And yet with his relief something fighting and bitter rose up in him, something borne on a wave of unshed tears.

"Let's have it, Joey, let's *have* it!"

Thud!

"Hey, Franky! Franky, look! Ah-hah-*haaaaaa!*"

Stanley put his hands over his ears, lifted his feet onto the bed, and shut his eyes. He lay in a Z position, his legs drawn up, and tried to be perfectly calm and quiet. No use fighting, he thought. No use fighting, no use crying.

Then he thought of something and sat up abruptly. He wished he had put the hedge bushes back. Now it was too late, he supposed, because they had been lying out on the ground for a week. But how he wished he had! Just that gesture of defiance, just that bit of beauty launched again in their faces.

MARY LEARY

◊

Poor Is Poor, Broke Is Broke, and the Game Goes On

For the first time in two years, I played softball yesterday. Tired and disheartened from work and a heavy bout with the flu, I was lured by an impossible-to-refuse invitation. I used to play with a rag-tag East Village ensemble called the Dead Dogs, a unit that could be separated from virtually the entire tradition and remainder of baseball, softball, or anything related by our team's size (we often divided the eight to twelve people who showed up into two "teams") and appearance/substance: We were captained by two female poets, one of whom had a punk band and Crayola-colored hair; there was sometimes a nine-year-old boy in residence; there was a very large, fat poet who wanted to drink beer and drum up his literary-art 'zine more than play ball. The only man who showed consistently was about twenty-two and besides that, British, resulting in the frequent need to distinguish the game from cricket for him. More than a pick-up team, the Dawgs were a schlepp-up team, although that doesn't mean we didn't play well on occasion. We *were* baseball, we were everything, we were the world, we were its children. You could decide to pitch or play third base or do anything you wanted, and it was just fine because there were no men to boss or herd us around. And for throwing or running, we had only each other for comparison. Thus was built a "girl world" of baseball, a place to play a new game, in a new way, little of it completely intentional. Dead Dog softball boasted the freedom of picnic softball, little-kid softball, and throw-off-your-heels-and-play-beneath-the-stars softball.

Despite host Steve's reassurance that this was to be a pick-up game, not too serious, yesterday's Central Park outing was an entirely different sort of affair, one to strike fear into the heart of many a Dead Dawg. There was a dog there, to be sure—a waggish terrier pup, there were women, and there was beer. It was a gorgeous blue day, so nice that the slow, enormous snake of people awaiting Michelle Pfeiffer's appearance at Shakespeare in the Park seemed happy, comfortable. The air was deliciously cool, as it has been so uncharacteristically often this Manhattan summer, and as we strode across the Upper West Side I cherished fair-to-middling hopes of a good time. But I began to understand what softball can mean for some people when Steve, a writer of books and *New York Times* features, told us the players we were about to join had a permit for their field, and that once, when another group had wanted to play badly enough to offer Steve and the Gang money for it, they had declined. Actually, the conversation went like this:

Steve: " . . . blah, blah, blah, and we've had this field for seven years. We have a permit for it, and it's really hard to get a field here in Central Park."

Dave and me: "Oh, wow."

Steve: "Yeah. Once someone even offered us $2,000 to use the field for the afternoon."

Dave and me: "Did you take it?"

Steve (as if there could be no other answer, or we might be half-witted): "Of course not!"

We continued along in a state of mild shock. I mean, baseball is baseball—I love the game. But poor is poor, broke is broke, and Dave and I have once again been VERY broke, experiencing yet another of those epochs so anxious that if either of us had been offered work that Saturday, we'd have had no choice but to take it. Let's just say that on that fateful day I realized a new plateau of love—or fanaticism—for the sport, and began to feel small stirrings of trepidation as we marched relentlessly along, Herr Steve leading the way, bag of bats waving beside him, through groups of frisbee-throwers, tourists, and other innocent people.

Still, I was unprepared for the seriousness, the intensity that reigned upon our arrival. There were more men than have ever covered a playing field extended to me; piles of bats and mitts, and a real, clearly-marked triangle. This no-name group of people, big enough to form two actual teams, sported lots of women, but they seemed more deadly determined than the men—these sort of Celtic baseball warriors, willing to do battle to the death beside their mates. *Women who would never "throw like girls."* Although Dave and I knew no one other than Steve, there were but a few murmurs of introduction before the event was ON! Two sides formed with the efficiency

and speed of a life-sized cartoon. I ended up spending some time in retirement, the combination of being ordered to play the unfamiliar position of
catcher, being hit in the leg by the ball, encountering a number of surly
people, and being on medication overcoming any desire for play. I sat on
the bench, talked to a nice English teacher from New Brunswick, and at-
tempted to analyze this new crowd, this gang of kids who intimidated me.
Underlying everything was my attempt not to be prejudiced against this
lofty group despite its ability—and decision—to pay for a Central Park softball field. After all, isn't it easier to be in good shape, energetic, AND
efficient when one has a full-time, well-paid position and job security than
when one has struggled to get uptown from funky-down on the filthy subway, dog-tired from adjusting to an endless stream of temp and free-lance
situations, chronic money worries, and attempting to make one's name by
writing creative material that's born in the dark middles of sleepless nights,
that by its very nature doesn't "fit in"? Isn't it easier to be perfect, athletic,
and impatient when one always has a deep green playing field waiting for
one at the end of the week?

Things got better. The pitcher who had curve-balled my leg pitched no
more. A wonderful man, a sort of hero in khakis, showed up to pitch, shout
encouragement, and add a lot of warmth to the game. I watched Dave have
a wonderful time discovering something he'd never known—that he can
really play ball. He was tearing around the bases, at six-foot-six inspiring
cheers and comments like, "Who *is* that guy?", "He's like the *Natural*," and
"Slide, Dave, slide!" I got a vicarious thrill out of that. Later, Steve asked
me to be his runner, and the second time at bat he hit the ball hard enough
to send me to first and then second base, and then the end of the game
came, maybe an hour later, and the best part. The sun was setting, its rays
gilding the altocumulus patterns of clouds behind the Dakota castle. Most
players had left—about ten of us batted and fielded. And this is the beauty
that I love, the baseball that is mine—just a small group of people practicing
as the sky grows purple and pink, the air chillier. An old black man straightened up from collecting refundable bottles to shout, "Always catch the ball
on the first bounce!" at a right fielder. Running en masse to back the outfield whenever anything came their way, a group of Hispanic kids played
a football kind of softball. I'd developed a breath-stopping afternoon crush
on the Khaki Hero, an overgrown softball boy-man who looked perfect in
a baseball cap. It was a joy to watch him throw and catch with moves that
seemed to have been practiced for a good thirty years. Everyone leaving,
trailing away, alone, through the park, glove in hand, made me feel full and
weepy, full of wonder at baseball lovers and writers and feeling a strange,
lonely longing to know what each one thought about as he or she wandered

away into the dark. Must we separate after being touched by something so sweet, so sublime?

Women who could pitch and field, men of confidence and wit—I seem to have stumbled into a new softball echelon, and wonder if the difference between these players and the Dead Dogs stems from the fact that many of the Central Park players write nonfiction and other material that pays, as opposed to the poetic, punk-rockish, mostly-broke Dead Dogs. Could that (along with age, and the fact that most of yesterday's players had gone to good colleges) be the problem, part of what had intimidated me? For people with M.A.s and Ph.D.s do frighten me. Armed with my puny associate of arts degree, experience and chutzpah, I'm still coasting along at modest publishing gigs; my creative writing occasionally selected for small publications, with but a misty idea of whether I've attained what the world seems to call success. In any case I think a team with a permit and a $2,000 field is a good team, but a team with no name is another thing, and in that regard the Dawgs had their priorities straight.

HEATHER HENDERSON

◊

The Lefthander

He gave up five runs in one inning that day I met him for the first
time and his gray eyes were dark as the inside of a tornado in Hell.

What did you think of the poem I asked him. I was speaking of
Number Thirty Six which is one of several poems I wrote in honor of
Tyler Cranshaw the greatest player ever to wear the white and blue
and red New York Imperials uniform and I will argue the best
lefthanded pitcher in the history of baseball.

I could blow a better poem out of my ass he said.

Keen eyes to spot a batter's weakness or spy the quarry in the forest
they say he is a good shot and I know it is true. I have many lines of
defense and all were breached.

Mike Brown who was the Imperials public relations person became
nervous and I knew that he was thinking Tyler you cannot say such
things to this woman she is Hana Schulman the famous poet she has
won the Pulitzer Prize.

It was not a long silence but it felt like one. Then the hunter's gaze
wavered and to my everlasting surprise I saw regret but why? I was
unworthy prey perhaps.

Tyler shook his head and said I'm sorry. This is kind of a bad day for
me I didn't have my good control they were hitting the shit out of me
out there. Tyler Cranshaw squinting into the distance and scratching
the back of his neck and apologizing to me it was a splendid act for

him and what was most admirable was that he did it so quickly before the pieces of my heart fell to earth.

It is always like this with baseball especially Imperials baseball the heart shattered in ways large and small the despair always there along with the joy for which you would forgive all suffering.

Tell me what kind of poetry you like I said. Suddenly he was shy and said well on the farm during the winter it got dark real early and we'd spend a lot of time inside and sometimes Dad would make us turn off the TV and then he'd read aloud to us out of this big book of poems Longfellow Shakespeare all kinds of stuff Robert Service was his favorite.

I said if you grew up listening to Robert Service with the night winds of Minnesota whirling outside then you have an excellent poetical education and he stared at me alert for mockery but he saw there was none and then he almost smiled.

You'll laugh at this Tyler said. No I will not laugh I said. Well okay he said Dad made us learn some things by heart you know that one about the minutemen. By that rude bridge which arched the flood, their flag to April's breeze unfurled, here once the embattled farmers stood, and fired the shot heard round the world. There he stopped and I saw him redden.

Emerson I said. Spirit that made those heroes dare, to die and leave their children free.

Yeah that's a good one he said with a slow grin and then his guard was finally down and there was all America standing in front of me curious friendly confident a big southpaw strikeout artist hair wet from his shower.

I recited to him Souls above doubt, valor unbending, it will reward, they shall return, more than they were, and ever ascending.

I don't know that one he said. That is Emerson too I told him. Oh yeah really he said with honest interest. It made me want to laugh aloud I had expected to talk baseball and instead we were talking poetry it made me want to laugh but I had said I would not.

And how did you like Shakespeare I asked him. Tyler shrugged fine I guess. Very well I said I will write you a sonnet in iambic pentameter that will knock your socks off. Then we parted each of us smiling and afterwards I wrote Sonnet One followed by Two and Three departures from my usual style they have vexed the critics. Tyler told me he enjoyed the sonnets very much he liked it that they rhymed.

CAROL MASTERS

◇

Fly Ball

A fly ball
has nothing of flight about it
it's pushed out there
its trajectory absolute
as the slap of the bat

but no one has ever seen
a ball go into the glove
it's true
follow the arc
unblinking the slow climb up the last leg
of the mountain   the raising of a flag   salute
the sure sail home to the cup
of the mitt

suddenly the field breaks up
everyone running the same way
a terrible accident
Christ has landed
at International Airport
your presence is required

no it's just the game   over
you missed it
in that last inch
the ball disappears

in fact there's a moment when the ball never enters the
    glove
it decides to cock a wing
veer to the south
  so long folks   I'm off on a jet-
  stream the sweet south
  wind in my wingpits   we're all going
  all U.S. fly balls going to take off
  like popcorn roll down the coast
  and bloom like migratory monarchs
  on the trees of Argentina

no it's still coming
a single headlight   you below it
on the tracks
the ball ballooning
rides clear as an onion
breaking from its skin
that terrible moon

coming
damn thing never stops
blazing with possibilities
and it's yours   you claim it
whether you want it or not
it will come   what matters
is where you are

JUDY GOLDMAN

◇

Suicide

The newspaper lied.
They did not find you
on the floor. Instead
you spent the afternoon
pitching with your son,
your face catching the silence
of the yard
like a soft leather glove
lovingly broken in.
And the light, the remarkable light,
ran over you so carelessly
it looked like silver numbers on your shirt.
You threw the ball for hours
as if there were no chance
night would ever search the corners
like the crowd
finding places in the stands,
their eyes marking the hard mound of dirt
below. For hours.
As if there were nothing at all
left to explain.

VIOLA WEINBERG

◇

The Playoffs and Everything

O, to wake up again
and know nothing;
to neither waiver at a thought
nor stumble on a word,
but to bathe in the shimmering bliss
of unmeditated hopeful sensation,
innocent of the odds,
simply gluttonous
in the cove of desire,
fires burning
in the appetite
of that great and vacant
reservoir of possibilities—
the lights blazing
and the doors open.

Ah, to wake up again
and puzzle over the whole thing:
each ball of electricity
distinct from the other,
high blue plates of Autumn
clacking against
the changing wind,
the sky over the ballpark
snapping with
brisk white towels of clouds

on a high faint cloth of stars,
a cold, windy innocence
on the faraway diamond of earth
where we knew nothing
and knew it all.

HOLLY PRADO

◇

The Playoff Game

(October 13, 1981)

the rush
from home plate to first base is
always a chance you take the easy
out or
the next push to the next base to the next
wild pitch to the next story of a woman who says to me
"I fear both failure and success"

the way we think is so confusing the way we
complicate our motives
an easy out is an
easy out a single is a single

my hat doesn't keep the sun out of my eyes
I don't care
I watch one player throw the ball to another player
warming up
their arms strong from knowing the difference between
wins and losses I feel the heat
the simple heat of an October afternoon of wanting the Dodgers to
    win
as if the men with their good throwing arms good catching arms
good pitching arms good batting arms belong to me
at least I'm not confused
at least I can tell who's who in the difference between
Dodger uniforms and Expo uniforms
at least I can wear a blue shirt myself
and think "yes those are Dodger pennants"

as the souvenir vendor goes by with blue felt flags at least
I'm excited by ordinary being-on-somebody's-side

it's harder to live than we think
I know all our ideas of not being on anybody's side
of keeping our names off of mailing lists of
keeping our houses to ourselves
hoping to be neutral so that none of our smart friends will catch us
in a sentimental act catch us succeeding or failing

here's the green field green as childhood
the arena the stadium the space of the game
and the game doesn't go outside this green
if a ball is hit into the crowd it's gone
the game stays on the field
nobody worries about the ball itself
it would only be an existential question
a theoretical puzzle no one could answer while
Bill Russell and Steve Garvey and Ron Cey and
Burt Hooten and Davey Lopes would stand around
not using their good arms
wasting their time when they could be making double plays

simple winning and losing is ridiculous given what we really have to
    face
which is death
which is love
which is not losing our minds
which is family
which is decent work that doesn't destroy us
which is paying for everything
but even if I have to squint and get sunburned to see this game
I'm going to see who wins and loses
the Dodgers win
these guys do belong to me
I forget that nobody on any baseball team reads my poetry
I forget that I'm going to die
I remember my Aunt Mae who's eighty-four sitting in front of her T.V.
    set
eating a piece of pie watching the Dodgers play saying
"I don't think they get paid too much. after all
what can they do later?"

the good arms eventually fail but so what
so what if we have to pay for everything
so what if it's harder to be alive than we think
the sun is the sun making me squint
the green field has been the green field since before I was born
a fair ball is always a risk that goes one way or the other
it will always be an easy out or a foot on the base
aiming for the next base aiming for the next base aiming for
home plate

HOLLY PRADO

◊

The World Series Is About Writing Poems

For Eloise, who told me why baseball players' bodies
look the way they do

there's so much to remember
it's all in this pitch these legs that may
or may not
push to any base
someone wipes his mouth
there is so much spitting there is
wind you never count on
nothing's really a home game
is it

◊   ◊   ◊

how a ball
the most important player
becomes a souvenir
fast so fast

◊   ◊   ◊

no wonder there are so many italians and blacks
you have to have grown up in a tough neighborhood

◊   ◊   ◊

can't get it can't get it
it's gone the crowd
goes wild
at least half of them hate you

you're stuck with your glove
in all that sun

◊   ◊   ◊

pride
has nothing to do with it
one day you are suddenly obsessed with
velocity, failure, and being called
part of something larger than yourself
you will do anything to play
no matter how tired you are
all you want to do is connect all you want to do
is connect all
you want to do is connect

◊   ◊   ◊

nobody told me
how a bruise sticks to the knee for a long time
how even sliding into home can
crack a bone
or the whole skull

◊   ◊   ◊

the worst is that every play is shown
over and over
and you do watch it

ANN NEELON

◊

World Series

We are humbled by the vehemence of the earth,
which must finally have taken our sins to heart.
In this emergency, we begin to understand seismology, life and death
    colliding like tectonic plates.
Apocalypse is a radio broadcast: *I am standing outside a building in*
    which human beings are burning alive.
Last weekend, in the mountains, quaking aspens were a prefiguration.
It is still October, but we no longer whisper *beloved autumn flame.*

Nor are telephones immortal creatures.
In the first of thousands of aftershocks, we tremble into their ears:
"Mother, Father, Sister, Brother—I was true to my habits. I am
    therefore alive.
I was not driving on the freeway when it collapsed—a foolishness
of which you accused me because today is no different from any other
in only *one* respect: you insist on loving me to absurdity."

In the blackout, it is back to Genesis. Television undreamed of,
World Series eclipsed by earthquake, sacrifice upon the face of the
    deep.
"Let there be light, let there be light," cries out an old man
twenty years too fragile for the crowds at the ballpark, too senile to
    remember
that baseball was not invented until the seventh day
when God rested because the din of life, not death, gave Him a
    headache.

Somehow, in a nightmare's dictionary, baseball becomes a synonym for
 faith, hope, and charity.
Perhaps the catcher in his death mask strikes awe in us. Simple-minded
 in the aftermath,
perhaps we all grope toward the same analogy: the earth is to a
 baseball as the hand of God
is to *my* hand. Or perhaps, when the earth opened up to swallow us,
we wore a baseball diamond on one finger like a jewel from the bowels
 of the earth to help us pray:
Compel us, like black coal, to scintillation, in this twenty-second eon.

The dead begin to appear to us as baseball stars in pearl-gray uniforms.
The moon is a shadowy baseball we ask them to autograph.
The host on the radio talk show is unequivocal—*the World Series must
 be cancelled*—
but we do not defer to him. We rise for the National Anthem.
We sing sweetly, in spite of ourselves, like child prodigies shipwrecked
 on a desert island:
Oh say can you see, oh say can you see the world is not ending, the
 world is beginning again.

ALISON GORDON

◇

The Winter Game

The small plane banked sharply to the left, leaving the beaches and breakers of the Caribbean coastline behind, and headed toward the interior of Venezuela, across the coastal range.

It was a beautiful flight, the sunshine welcome just hours from the grey slush of Toronto. Bumping over the thermal currents rising from the landscape below is a nightmare to all but those who enjoy the sensation of really flying, and has filled many a manly ballplayer's heart with terror over the years.

My destination on that January afternoon in 1980 was Barquisimeto, an agricultural town of 600,000 in the state of Lara, home of Los Cardenales de Lara of the Liga Venezolana de Beisbol Professional.

When baseball is only a memory in the north, a rumour ringed on the calendar in red, it is thriving in the Caribbean. There are leagues in Venezuela, Puerto Rico, and the Dominican Republic that play a three-month season at approximately the Triple A level, meeting each February for the Caribbean World Series. Most teams in these leagues employ a handful of foreigners, American professionals from the high minors or low majors, "requested" by their parent organizations to spend the winter working.

They sign on for various reasons. Some young players get a leg up for the jump to the major leagues here. Pitchers can work on a new pitch, trying it out in game situations. Marginal veterans can try for an edge to keep them in the bigs for another season. Career minor-leaguers go there for the paycheque of $2,000 to $5,000 a month. Some, unknowns in North America, enjoy being stars far from home.

I had timed my trip to correspond with the end-of-season playoffs, and left for the ballpark as soon as I had checked in to the small hotel the Blue Jays had recommended, a cozy pensione in the heart of the town.

Barquisimeto is not Rio de Janeiro. It isn't even Caracas. Cut off from the tourist mainstream by the mountains all around it, it has very little to offer visitors, and non-Spanish-speaking guests like myself were rare. My Spanish phrase book and the friendliness of the hotel staff broke through the barriers, and I was soon on the way to Estadio Barquisimeto in a cab.

The streets were narrow, the sidewalks almost non-existent. The small stucco houses were painted in cheerful pastel colours, with windows shuttered to keep out the sun and rain, and ornately grilled to keep out uninvited guests. Political slogans were chalked on the walls, remnants of a recent election.

It is a rule of thumb that in any small town the best way to find the ballpark is to look for the light standards, and this was no exception. They were visible from the taxi window before the stadium came into sight, a small park surrounded by a forbidding wall, covered in stucco and studded with broken glass on the top to make sure only those who had bought tickets would come inside. The atmosphere, though, was warm and festive, and the fans were in the plaza outside hours before game time.

While waiting to get in, "los fanaticos" made themselves at home. Vendors strolled by selling food or tickets for that night's pool. For two bolivars (worth about a quarter each) you could guess which player from either team would score the first run. The payoff was ten to one. Families gathered around charcoal fires to cook up their *pinchos*, South American shishkebobs—a tailgate party, Venezuelan style. The air was full of fragrant smoke.

Inside the players were warming up as they do anywhere, the Cardenales and the visiting Tiburones (sharks) from LaGuaira, the Caracas seaport, playing pepper and fielding fungoes, bunting two in batting practice and shagging fly balls. Dozens of little ragged kids "helped," and the field was patrolled by corpulent, gun-toting policemen wearing mirrored sunglasses.

The scoreboard was being put through its paces, too, a dress rehearsal that only proved how international is the language of baseball. There were permanent spots to record "bolas," "strikes," and "outs" on the scoreboard. Commercial messages were flashed for Seguar de Lara, an insurance company, and Cervesa Polar, a beer with a bear on the label. Then came the game messages: *Flash* . . . NUEVO PITCHER . . . *Flash* . . . DOUBLE PLAY . . . *Flash* . . . JONRON . . . *Flash* . . . JON . . . *Flash* . . . RON . . . *Flash* . . . JONRON . . . *blink blink flash.*

No matter how you spell it, it's still out of the park.

Once the gates opened, the playoff tempo started to build. The locals shouted encouragement to their favourite players and heckled the Tiburones. Groups settled into their seats and ordered up cold Polars from the vendors, some of them tiny children, selling bottles out of buckets full of ice. Some had brought picnics, others hailed vendors selling *arepas*, corn meal buns stuffed with meat or tuna or cheese. *Tostones*, banana chips, were also popular.

José Jimenez was a local favourite. A very old man, he sold individually wrapped *pastelitos*, small cheese or meat tarts, tossing them dramatically and accurately rows away and making spectacular catches of coins thrown his way. He joked with the regulars, chiding the ones who wouldn't buy his wares that day. They insulted him back, to great laughter all around. I was told that Jimenez had seven daughters, no sons, and that he had sent each of them to university. They are now doctors, lawyers, and teachers thanks to their father and his *pastelitos*.

The stands were divided between the cheap seats and the expensive ones, each section served by a separate entrance outside the park. Prices ranged from sixteen bolivars for reserved seats behind home plate to three bolivars for the centrefield bleachers (students, half-price). Unlike common North American practice, there was no sneaking up from the cheap seats into the boxes. To discourage moving, there were ten-foot-high chain-link fences between sections, with four strands of barbed wire on the top.

The real elite didn't sit in the stands. For them there was a special box, a concrete bunker at field level, slightly to the left of home plate. Here, sealed behind glass in air-conditioned chill, sat the owners and their guests, mostly men, in two uncomfortable rows. They filled their big bellies with copious amounts of scotch, even during the Sunday games that began at 11:30 a.m. In the middle of the game, they could open the door and talk to the players or the manager on the bench. Wouldn't George Steinbrenner love that?

In the major leagues there is sometimes too much formality. In Venezuela there was hardly enough. Players complained that there were so many well-wishers in the dugout they couldn't find room to sit down. A cute little kid named Enrique used to hang around and generally behave like the team mascot. During a game he could often be found either sitting between manager Vern Benson and pitching coach Bob Humphries on the bench or on one of their laps.

I watched some of the games from the radio booth, a tiny plywood structure at the top of the stands, no more than four feet deep and a dozen feet wide. I shared the space at various times with six announcers, a technician, and, occasionally, a small black cat. It was chaos. Each function, except the technician's, was doubled. Two men alternated play-by-play; there were two commentators; and two announcers just to read commercials. No cartridges with pre-recorded jingles in this studio. And, most assuredly, no dead air.

Every time there was a brief pause in the action, when the batter stepped out of the box to check a sign, when the pitcher went to the resin bag, or when an umpire called for new balls, one of the two announcers would jump in with a message. There were thirty separate sponsors for each game, and 400 commercials to work in. The messages were written in a loose-leaf notebook, one to a page. The notebook was three inches thick.

As is true anywhere in the world, the announcers had deep velvety voices, their Rs rolling like thunder across the airwaves. When play resumed, the other broadcasters would take over. If a commentator had a bit of colour or analysis, he simply snapped his fingers for attention, then said his piece.

Here, as in the dugout, there was none of the North American feeling of sacred ground. The fans turned and shouted at the announcers if they didn't agree with them. There was no hermetic sealing or fancy protection for the equipment. There was hardly any equipment.

The technician appeared to do very little work. He didn't ride levels or fiddle with dials. He had just one job. When *El Himna Nacional* was played in the stadium he took a microphone and stuck it out a hole in the studio wall to pick up the music for the radio audience. Other than that, he cracked jokes.

The din was marvelous, and the game not that hard to follow even if I closed my eyes, what with references to "un bouncer rolling foul," or "el centrefielder." A double was a "tubeyes," or two-base hit.

During the first game I watched from the press box, Ruben Mijares, the genial commentator who eventually became my interpreter, driver, and host, turned suddenly with his microphone and interviewed me at length about the playoff. In Spanish, translating my replies. All that was expected of me was to speak with all the authority of a major league beat writer about the skills of two teams I had watched for a total of two innings. I still wonder what I said.

Sitting in the stands, when I could find a seat, was an even more splendid experience. There was as much to watch up and down the rows as there was on the field, which was obscured by another chain-link fence, fifteen feet high and angled in at the top to discourage climbing.

When a foul was popped up behind the plate, it rolled up the netting over the stands, a cue for the kids, who would race up the fence, fitting their sneakers into the holes in the mesh, and fight to grab the ball through the netting before it could roll back down. Then, to great cheers of encouragement, the successful one would work the ball gradually down the outside of the fence, moving it from hand to hand stuck through the links, until he found a hole big enough to pull it through.

When people found out who I was (I was welcomed on the scoreboard each game and my picture was in the local paper) they would come and chat. Many were English students or simply teen-agers with a great fascination for all things North American, wearing sweatshirts from U.S. colleges that sold for small fortunes downtown. My dictionary became dog-eared from searching for phrases in both languages. The friendliness was almost overwhelming.

The music in the stands between innings was *salsa* and the patrons danced on the benches. There was no seventh-inning stretch, but that inning, and the fifth, were considered lucky. It was explained to me that the fifth inning is lucky because in bullfighting, the fifth bull is never bad.

Fan reaction to play on the field was hysterical and characterized by ear-piercing whistles and vituperative shouts. In the game against the Tiburones, the underdog Cardenales took an early lead and were up 4–0 by the fourth inning. Each time the Tiburones came to bat, the fans chanted "Uno-dos-tres" as the Sharks went down one-two-three. They turned and faced the visiting radio booth and shouted the numbers, waving the appropriate number of fingers in the air, laughing and stamping their feet.

The object of this derision was the LaGuaira announcer, a smooth gentleman with grey hair and a David Niven moustache, called Musiu, a variation on Monsieur. He was the local equivalent of Harry Caray in Chicago, a colourful character who rooted mightily for his home team, and was as well known as any of the players. The Cardenales fans revelled in his discomfort, and he cheerfully waved back at them while pulling faces of dismay.

By the ninth inning, it was "uno-dos-tres" from the first pitch and when the last out was made, the crowd went nuts. With great whoops of joy, not one, not two, but dozens and dozens of fans threw full cups of beer into the air. It ran in cascades down the steps. As the happy crowd milled around celebrating and the announcers read their final commercials and wrapped up the game, the final word was flashed on the scoreboard: "Recoge tu sardena muerta, Musiu,"–pick up your dead sardines.

The exuberance of the fans turned into adulation on the streets of Venezuela's baseball towns, where followers of the teams have tremendous loyalty and long memories.

Benson, who first came as a player, told a story about one man he encountered during the 1979–80 season. "I was the shortstop on the 1953 champion Pastorias of Maracaibo," he recalled. "This year we were in there playing a game and I went out for a walk. Suddenly a man ran out of his house shouting 'Ben-son, Ben-son–Pastorias champion!' You can't tell me they don't have some fans here!"

Benson, who had come back to Venezuela year after year, had an obvious affection for the country and the fans, but most of his American players didn't share his attitude. For them, winter ball is simply a place to work on their skills and further their careers. The fact that they play for a team is almost irrelevant. Most of them can't wait to go home. The adulation wears thin, and the Americans are homesick for people and things they understand. They get tired of being followed by laughing, cheering children on every street in town. What was an appealing novelty at first wears badly. Many players left before the season was over, claiming illness in the family or heavy business commitments. This led to a great deal of distrust on the part of the owners. The year I was there, two American players had simply gone AWOL, refusing to return after the Christmas break.

The American players are not particularly sophisticated, and very few appreciated the opportunity of spending time in a different culture. There are exceptions, of course, but most players resent having to get through their day without a McDonald's takeout around every corner and a television with all the soaps. Frustrated by inefficiency and slowness all around them, by the foreigners who perversely refuse to speak English, the athletes are less than model ambassadors at times.

One night I was going out to dinner with several of the ballplayers: I walked into the bar at my hotel in time to hear one of them cussing out the waiter for bringing the wrong drink. The waiter spoke no English, but he couldn't mistake the tone of the abuse. Worse still, unbeknownst to the ballplayer, sitting at the next table were two American couples, consultants at a local bottling plant, who knew exactly what "Go fuck yourself" meant. The Americans were appalled, in part because the attitude of the players went so against what they were trying to do in the country. They had been through orientation sessions before they even left the United States, and worked very hard at being model guests, unofficial ambassadors for The American Way. The player's rudeness offended them personally.

The only orientation the Cardinales ballplayers got was a short lecture from Benson, suggesting that they would have to adapt to Venezuelan ways and try not to get into any trouble. But no one told them how to deal with loneliness, living in a compound run by the army, with motel-like accommodations and carefully screened access to visitors. The only telephone was in the compound office, where every homesick conversation could be overheard by the officer on duty. "I know they can't understand what I'm saying," one ballplayer told me, "but it still bothers me to have them listen."

Players complained that there were too many silly rules they had to conform to. One told me about an impromptu basketball game broken up by the army because it was against regulations to play in shorts and no shirts. This was with temperatures heading into the nineties.

I went to a big end-of-season party given for the players by the owners and supporters of the team. It was held in the courtyard of a fancy mansion, and invitations were issued only to the best-connected people in town. Guests were let in through a gate; outside dozens of people waited for a glimpse of the players, trying every con in the book to get in. There was a touch of Fellini to the scene. Inside the gates, three bands alternated to supply music for dancing. The players sat uneasily at three or four tables, joined by giggling young women in their early twenties. Whisky was the drink, but it wasn't free; players bent on offering hospitality paid 200 bolivars per bottle, about $50. The young women mixed the scotch with cola and shared it freely with friends at nearby tables.

I remember Garth Iorg in particular. The clean-living Mormon with a wife and children at home in California was a particular favourite with the fans, even if the pronunciation of his name ("Orge") was beyond them. At the ballpark, he was announced as "Gar Iiiorrrrg", with a hard "g." At the party, they settled for one name only.

"Iiiorrrg, tu gusto salsa?" asked one teen temptress.

"Si," Iorg nodded agreeably, "mi gusto mucho."

"You want dance with me, Iiiorrrg," she continued. Iorg assumed an expression of great sorrow as his tablemates wondered how he was going to wriggle out of this one. "No, gracias," he said. "Y no possible dance. My knee is malo, much malo."

Others didn't share his reluctance to mingle with the señoritas. Daniel Boone, a diminutive lefthander then with an Angels' minor team, had recently arrived and spoke a hilarious mixture of Spanish and English with no embarrassment at all. As he danced by he paused at the table.

"Look at this girl," he said. "She is so beautiful I'd like to take her home with me—her and about ten of her friends. But I bet she's got a father here somewhere, and I bet he's got a forty-five."

Yes, indeed, they were a long way from home.

The married players sent to Venezuela faced a quandary. Although they would prefer to have their families with them, they were worried about their children getting sick in a foreign country, or how their wives would react to the experience. One wife told me she hated Venezuela because people always wanted to touch her blonde hair. Her husband went back several seasons because it was important to his career, but she only went once.

Jesse Barfield was an exception. He and his wife Marla had their first child, Joshua, in Barquisimeto in January 1983. Other players and their wives thought they were nuts, but the Barfields, born-again Christians, put it all in God's hands. Barfield joked that all he had to do was look at Luis Leal, the Blue Jays' chubby righthander, who was a home-town player, to know they could deliver healthy babies in Barquisimeto.

Jim Gott also brought his wife when he went south. Clenice spoke fluent

Spanish and had spent her eighteen-month Mormon missionary assignment in Guatemala. The two spent every off-day seeing as much as they could of the country, and took advantage of all it had to offer. But they were rare.

Perhaps because my visit lasted just ten days, I loved Barquisimeto. The last day of the season, a sunny Sunday, was Fan Appreciation Day, Venezuelan style. After the game, a stage was built on the field and awards were handed out to worthy Cardenales while musicians set up their instruments all around them.

Oscar d'Leon, one of the country's most popular *salsa* stars, gave a post-game concert. The first thing he did was invite the fans from the centrefield bleachers to come onto the field, which they did, racing across the grass toward the stage. Quickly, a section of the fence over the home dugout by third base disappeared, and those fans swarmed onto the field as well. There was no sense of violence here, though. I have felt more nervous in Yankee Stadium in mid-season. The fans did not have vandalism or destruction in mind; they simply wanted to get closer to the music, closer to the fun. As the afternoon wore on, ice-cream carts appeared in the outfield, and the beer vendors moved through the dancing throngs. Little kids rolled around in the dust. The sun beat down.

In the middle of it all were the players, some still in uniform, some with small children on their shoulders. Some danced; some took pictures; others stood back and watched in amazement. They signed autographs on scraps of paper, fuzzy pictures torn out of the newspaper, plastic cushions, even an arm and leg or two.

After a few hours, d'Leon packed it in and told them all to go home. Quite cheerfully they left the field and danced out of the park. All in all, it had not been a bad January afternoon.

Contributor Notes

◇

Jean Hastings Ardell's work has appeared in the *Los Angeles Times*, *Orange Coast*, and *Elysian Fields Quarterly*. Her husband, Daniel Miers Ardell, had a cup of coffee with the California Angels in 1961.

Eve Babitz is a novelist and short story writer who hails from Los Angeles.

Ann Bauleke covers sports for several Minnesota publications.

Ellen Cooney is the author of two novels: *Small-Town Girl* and *All the Way Home*.

Annie Dillard received the Pulitzer Prize for *Pilgrim at Tinker's Creek*. Other books include *Living by Fiction*, *Holy the Firm*, *The Writing Life*, *An American Childhood*, *Encounters with Chinese Writers*, *Teaching a Stone to Talk*, and *Tickets for a Prayer Wheel*.

Edna Ferber (1887–1968) won the Pulitzer Prize for *So Big* in 1924. Other novels include *Show Boat*, *Giant*, and *Cimarron*. Among the plays she wrote with George S. Kaufman are *Stage Door* and *Dinner at Eight*.

Susan Firer won the Cleveland State University Poetry Center Prize for *Lives of the Saints and Everything*, published in 1993 by the CSU Poetry Series.

Linda Gebroe is a freelance writer and communications consultant in San Francisco. Her baseball articles have appeared in *The Sporting News*, the *San Francisco Chronicle*, and *Giants* magazine.

Veronica Geng is a former fiction editor for *The New Yorker*.

Victoria Gill is a poet and French scholar.

Lulu Glaser was a popular comic opera prima donna around the turn of the century.

Judy Goldman's *Holding Back Winter* won a North Carolina Poetry Council Award, and *Wanting to Know the End* won the 1993 Gerald Cable Poetry Chapbook Competition from Silverfish Review.

Doris Kearns Goodwin is a presidential biographer, author of *The Fitzgeralds and the Kennedys*.

Alison Gordon is the author of *Foul Ball! Five Years in the American League* and three mysteries.

Vanalyne Green is a video artist whose work has been screened at the Whitney Museum, San Francisco Museum of Modern Art, and the American Film Institute. Her video *A Spy in the House that Ruth Built* premiered at the Museum of Modern Art in 1990.

Barbara Grizzuti Harrison is a journalist and novelist and currently a columnist for *Mirabella*.

Lesley Hazleton is a Seattle-based journalist, author, and pilot, who drives fast cars and flies slow planes. She is also the automotive columnist for *Lear's*.

Eloise Klein Healy has published four books of poetry—*Building Some Changes, A Packet Beating Like a Heart, Ordinary Wisdom,* and *Artemis in Echo Park,* which was nominated for the Lambda Book Award.

Heather Henderson grew up worshipping the Mets and now has a certain affection for the Red Sox. She is writing a novel about Hana Schulman and Tyler Cranshaw.

Patricia Highsmith's works include *Strangers on a Train, Found on the Street,* and most recently *Ripley Under Water* (Knopf). She has received the O. Henry Memorial and Edgar Allan Poe awards.

Mabel Hite was an actress and wife of Mike Donlin, an outfielder for six major league teams from 1899 to 1914.

Ann Hood's novels are *Something Blue, Somewhere Off the Coast of Maine,* and *Places to Stay the Night.*

S. W. M. Humason wrote for women's magazines in the 1940s.

Roberta Israeloff has written two books and writes regularly for several magazines. She is a contributing editor at *Parents* magazine, and is working on a novel.

Shirley Jackson is best known for her story "The Lottery." Her books include *We Have Always Lived in the Castle, Life Among the Savages,* and *Raising Demons.*

Josephine Jacobsen, who served as Poetry Consultant to the Library of Congress for two terms, has published thirteen books of poetry, criticism, and short stories. She received the Lenore Marshall Award for the best book of American poetry published in 1987.

Judy Katz-Levine's collected poems were published as *When the Arms of Our Dreams Embrace* by Saru Press International in 1991. The recipient of a poetry fellowship from the Massachusetts Artists Foundation, she edits her own magazine, *Noctiluca.*

Lucy Kennedy's *The Sunlit Field* was published by Crown in 1950.

Linda Kittell teaches at Washington State University and has recently finished a poetry manuscript based on Andrew Wyeth's paintings of Helga Testorf.

Carolyn Kizer received the Pulitzer Prize for Poetry in 1985 for *Yin*. She founded *Poetry Northwest* and was the first director of the Literature Program at the National Endowment for the Arts, 1966–1970.

Mary Leary's poetry, reviews, and columns have been featured in many magazines and anthologies. With David Smyth she combines music, writing, and performance in the rock combo Your Own Backyard.

Jane Leavy bought her first baseball glove with her grandmother at Saks Fifth Avenue. A former sportswriter and journalist for the *Washington Post*, she is currently finishing her second novel, *Fugazi*, which has nothing whatsoever to do with baseball.

Nancy Lemann's books include *Lives of the Saints, The Ritz of the Bayou*, and *Sportsman's Paradise*. Her stories and articles have appeared in *Esquire, The Paris Review, Spy, Vogue*, and *Elle*.

Bette Bao Lord's adult books include *Eighth Moon* and *Spring Moon*. This selection is from *In the Year of the Boar and Jackie Robinson*, a children's book about a Chinese girl who emigrates to the United States.

Merrill Markoe has written for the *Village Voice* and many magazines. This piece is from her humor collection *What the Dogs Have Taught Me*.

Carol Masters is a poet and peace activist in Minneapolis. Her work has appeared in many anthologies, including *This Sporting Life* and *Hummers, Knucklers and Slow Curves*.

Bernadette Mayer is a feminist sports fan/player. She is author of *Memory, Midwinter Day, Poetry, The Formal Field of Kissing*, and *A Bernadette Mayer Reader*. This poem "is a big hit in the NY Times Sports Dept. where my boyfriend works! Poets be aware!"

Gail Mazur's collections include *Nightfire* and *The Pose of Happiness*. She is founder and director of Blacksmith House Poetry Center in Cambridge, Massachusetts.

Susan McCarthy is an artist, working mostly in oils. She is married to Bill James of *Bill James Baseball Abstract* fame.

Jeredith Merrin is the author of *An Enabling Humility: Marianne Moore, Elizabeth Bishop and the Uses of Tradition* and was recently nominated for a Pushcart Prize. This poem "was written on the occasion of my only daughter's departure for college. It seems to me that one thing baseball does do, here and elsewhere, is to evoke a peculiarly *American* setting; and the mother and daughter in this poem are almost comparable to Continental versus American forces—the new world needing to break away from, even as it is informed by, the old."

Linda Mizejewski teaches film and literature at Ohio State University, and is the author of *Divine Decadence*, a book about cinema, literary adaptations, feminism, and politics.

Marianne Moore (1887–1972) received the Pulitzer Prize, Bollingen Prize, and the National Book Award in 1951 for *Collected Poems.*

Lillian Morrison is a widely published poet and anthologizer of sports poems for young readers.

Eileen Myles is a poet who has lived in New York City since 1974. Her most recent collections of stories are *Not Me* (Semiotexte), which was nominated for a Lambda Literary Award in 1992, and *Chelsea Girls* (Black Sparrow).

Rochelle Nameroff currently teaches at the University of Scranton. She won an Iowa Arts Fellowship in 1991.

Elinor Nauen's books of poetry are *CARS and other poems* and *Now That I Know Where I'm Going.* She has published many baseball-related poems and articles.

Ann Neelon is currently an assistant professor of English at Murray State University in Kentucky. She has also taught at Stanford University and been published in many literary magazines.

Mariah Burton Nelson is the author of *Are We Winning Yet? How Women Are Changing Sports and Sports Are Changing Women,* which was named best sports book of 1992 by the Amateur Athletic Foundation. Her second book, *The Stronger Women Get, the More Men Love Football,* will be published this year by Harcourt Brace Jovanovich.

Alice Notley has published more than a dozen books of poetry, including *Margaret and Dusty, At Night the States,* and *How Spring Comes.* She currently lives in Paris.

Molly O'Neill writes for *The New York Times Magazine.*

Linda Pastan's poems have appeared in the *Atlantic Monthly, The New Yorker,* and *Paris Review.* She has published eight volumes of poetry and is Poet Laureate of Maryland.

Letty Cottin Pogrebin, founder and currently contributing editor of *Ms.* magazine, is the author of seven books, including *Growing Up Free* and *Deborah, Golda and Me: Being Jewish and Female in America.*

Holly Prado's work has appeared in *The Streets Inside: Ten Los Angeles Poets* and can be heard on *Innings and Quarters,* a recording of sports poetry.

Anna Quindlen received a Pulitzer Prize in 1992. She has published two collections of her *New York Times* columns—*Living Out Loud* and *Thinking Out Loud*—and a novel, *Object Lessons.*

Elisavietta Ritchie's award-winning books include *Flying Time: Stories & Half-Stories, Tightening the Circle Over Eel Country,* and *Raking the Snow.*

Lynn Rigney Schott teaches high-school English in Kettle Falls, Washington. Her poetry has appeared in *The New Yorker, Idaho English Journal,* and *The Fireside Book of Baseball.* Her father, Bill Rigney, was a major league infielder and manager.

Oona Short writes for television, theater, and magazines. A former sports commentator, she is at work on a novel, *Foy in Mudville.* She was 1990 rookie of the year for her Brooklyn (NY) women's softball team.

Rebecca Stowe, a Tigers fan, is the author of the novel *Not the End of the World* and a short story collection, *One Big Happy Family.* She is working on a new novel.

May Swenson (1927–1989) is the author of many books, including *Things Taking Place: New and Selected Poems.*

Carol Tavris, Ph.D., is a social psychologist, writer, and lecturer. Her books include *The Mismeasure of Woman* (Simon & Schuster, 1992), *Anger: The Misunderstood Emotion,* and *The Longest War: Sex Differences in Perspective.*

Sarah Van Arsdale began playing softball at age twenty-one, in right field. She later enjoyed one summer of stardom at third base before going on to write poetry and fiction.

The late **Sara Vogan's** novel *In Shelly's Leg,* from which this selection is drawn, was published in hardback by Knopf, and in paperback by Graywolf.

Viola Weinberg has published three books of poetry *Any Woman Could Have Written This Book, Scrambled Clams and Bananas,* and *The Sum Complexities of the Humble Field.* Her songs have been recorded by half a dozen bands.

Hilma Wolitzer is the author of such novels as *Ending, In the Palomar Arms, Silver,* and *Hearts.*

Ina Eloise Young was sporting editor of the *Chronicle-News* (Trinidad, Colorado). At the time (c. 1908), according to *Baseball* magazine, she "enjoy[ed] the distinction of being the only woman in the world engaged in such work."

Bibliography

◊

The following publications may be of interest to readers of this collection.

NOVELS

Nancy Willard's beautiful and mysterious *Things Invisible to See* proved impossible to pull apart for an excerpt.

The eponymous Rachel of Silvia Tennenbaum's funny, wry *Rachel, the Rabbi's Wife,* is a Mets fan who muses about love and life at a game.

Mary-Ann Tirone Smith has a former Black Sox player in her poignant *The Port of Missing Men.*

The wonderful *Sleeping Arrangements* by Laura Cunningham takes place in the shadow of Yankee Stadium. "Golden, softly rounded, the old stadium had a Biblical look. I assumed it had been standing on 161st Street since before Christ."

The main character, an artistic kid, in *Mrs. Cooper's Boardinghouse* by Joan Lindau is trying to raise money to go to the World Series. But there's not actually a lot about baseball in the book.

In Zora Neale Hurston's *Their Eyes Were Watching God,* instead of finding comfort in religion—"a conventional choice for unhappily married women," points out Alice Walker in her introduction—Janie Crawford Starks plays checkers, falls for a younger man, and goes to baseball games. Baseball only gets this mention, however.

In Anne Tyler's *Dinner at the Homesick Restaurant,* Ezra Tull takes his mother, Pearl, to a Baltimore Orioles game. "Baseball was the only sport that made sense, she said: clear as Parcheesi, clever as chess."

Barbara Gregorich's *She's on First* is about the first woman to play in the major leagues.

Zanboomer by R. R. Knudson is a young adult novel about a remarkable athlete.

MEMOIRS

I excluded these categorically from *Diamonds* because they're not so much *by* women writers on baseball as "with" a male sportswriter.

My Luke and I, by Eleanor Gehrig (with a male sportswriter) is about Yankees great Lou Gehrig.

Me and the Babe by Mrs. Babe Ruth (with Bill Slocum) is annoying—for instance, you don't find out until halfway through that she's the second Mrs. Babe, and even has a name of her own, Claire.

In *My Dad, the Babe,* Dorothy Ruth Pirone (with Chris Martens) gets back at stepmom Claire.

Day with the Giants is actress Laraine Day's account of life with Leo Durocher (edited by Kyle Crichton).

Despite being married to the late Hall of Fame broadcaster Red Barber for sixty years, Lylah Barber's autobiography *Lylah* contains very little about baseball.

Cyndy (Steve) Garvey, Sharon (Mike) Hargrove, Charlene (Bob) Gibson, Danielle Gagnon (Mike) Torrez, Bobbie (Jim) Bouton, and Nancy (Mike) Marshall have also written tell-alls.

You've Got to Have Balls to Make It in This League is Pam Postema's (with Gene Wojciechowski) foul-mouthed but absorbing account of her life as an umpire, including an unsuccessful run at becoming the first woman ump in the majors. She got to AAA, one step short.

We Won Today: My Season with the Mets, by Kathryn Parker, is a real gee-whiz booster, to say the least.

ETCETERA

The indefatigable Erma Bombeck has touched on everything anyone can think of to write about. See "Ralph Corlis, The Coach Who Played to Lose," in *The Grass Is Always Greener Over the Septic Tank.*

A wonderful new anthology, *Birth of a Fan,* edited by Ron Fimrite, has several terrific essays by women.

Baseball by the Books: A History and Complete Bibliography of Baseball Fiction, by Andy McCue, is indispensable. Among its listings: *The Yachtville Boys* by Caroline E. Kelly Davis, the "second oldest book I have found with strong baseball content"; the hero ends up a missionary in Hindoostan.

Hummers, Knucklers, and Slow Curves: Contemporary Baseball Poems, edited by Don Johnson, is a strong collection, with lots of women.

Diamonds Are a Dyke's Best Friend—Reflections, Reminiscences, and Reports from the Field on the Lesbian National Pastime, edited by Yvonne Zipter.

Barbara Gregorich's *Women at Play: The Story of Women in Baseball* appeared in 1993.

A Whole New Ballgame by Sue Macy is the most recent book on the subject of the All-American Girls Professional Baseball League.

Jessamyn West's "Public-Address System" is a disturbing take on small–town neighborliness.

Two magazines that often print women:

Elysian Fields Quarterly, edited by Steve Lehman, St. Paul, MN.

Fan, edited by Michael Schacht, New York, NY.

Acknowledgments

◊

Many people helped a lot or a little. Thanks: Roger Angell, Michael P. Berberich, Linda J. Borish, Gateman I. Brown, my agent Sarah Chalfant of Wylie, Aitken & Stone, Kalia Doner, Maggie Dubris, Audrey L. Estebo, Heather Henderson, Don Johnson, Cindy Kling, Carolyn Kovacs, Harvey Kubernik, Steve Lehman, Joel Lewis, Maria Mancini, Andy McCue, Harry Maxwell McPherson, Charles N. Nauen, Alexandra Neil, Ron Padgett, R. Paplinger, Danny Peary, Earl "Uncle" Phillips, Elisavietta Ritchie, Alison Rogers, Kate Rounds, Rick Ruffner, Mike Schacht, Harris Schiff, Debbie Shattuck, Annie Silverman, Ed Smith, Mary-Ann Tirone Smith, Tima Smith, Carole Srole, Johnny "Enjs" Stanton, Rebecca Stowe, the late Bernie Titowsky, Betsy Uhrig and Alison Weidenfeld Buckholtz at Faber and Faber, Chuck Wachtel.

In addition, grateful acknowledgment is made to the following for permission to reprint material copyrighted or controlled by them:

Jean Hastings Ardell for "A Miracle Year," © 1993 by Jean Hastings. By permission of the author.

Eve Babitz for "Dodger Stadium," from *Slow Days, Fast Company*, Knopf 1977, © 1977 by Eve Babitz, first published in *Cosmopolitan*, 1974. By permission of the author.

Ann Bauleke for "Heroes," from *City Pages*, © 9/9/92 by Ann Bauleke. By permission of the author.

Ellen Cooney from *All the Way Home*, G. P. Putnam's Sons, © 1984 by Ellen Cooney. By permission of the author.

HarperCollins, Publishers, Inc. for selection from *An American Childhood* by Annie Dillard, © 1987 by Annie Dillard. Reprinted by permission of HarperCollins, Publishers, Inc.

Susan Firer for "A Night Game in Menomonie Park," first published in *This Sporting Life*, Milkweed Editions. Also published in *Hummers, Knucklers and Slow Curves*, University of Illinois Press, 1992, and *The Underground Communion Rail*, by Susan Firer, West End Press, 1993. © 1987 by Susan Firer. By permission of the author.

Linda Gebroe for "No Particular Place to Go," © 1993 by Linda Gebroe. By permission of the author.

Veronica Geng for "What Happened," from *Love Trouble Is My Business* by Veronica Geng, © 1988 by Veronica Geng. First appeared in *The New Yorker*. By permission of the author.

Victoria M. Gill for "Hommage à George Brett," © 1993 by Victoria M. Gill. By permission of the author.